The Amazon of Letters

The Life and Loves of Natalie Barney

by George Wickes

W. H. Allen
London

A Howard and Wyndham Company 1977

Contents

Introduction 7

PART I   THE LIFE OF NATALIE BARNEY

1.   Origins 15
2.   Beginnings 25
3.   Liane de Pougy 34
4.   Literary Debut 43
5.   Renée Vivien 53
6.   Renée's Side of the Story 69
7.   Lucie Delarue-Mardrus 78
8.   Theatricals 88
9.   20 rue Jacob 100
10.   Epigrams 112
11.   Remy de Gourmont 119
12.   The Legend of Lorély 130
13.   Lily de Clermont-Tonnerre
      and Romaine Brooks 139
14.   The Patroness of Letters 152
15.   The Matron Saint of Lesbos 171
16.   Dolly Wilde 183
17.   Godless Nuns in Gardens Florentine 190
18.   The No-Man's-Land of Old Age 197
19.   The Last Lover 201

PART II EPILOGUE

Introduction 209

1971
Natalie Barney 211
Berthe 215

1972
Berthe 220
Janine Lahovary 223
Jean Chalon 224

1973
Berthe 228
Jean Chalon 230
François Chapon 232
Cheryl Hughes 233

PART III OTHER POINTS OF VIEW

Eyre de Lanux 240
Virgil Thomson 244
Bettina Bergery 251
Truman Capote 255
Janet Flanner 260

Acknowledgments 269
Bibliography 273
Index 279

Introduction

Natalie Clifford Barney, who was born in Dayton, Ohio, in 1876 and who died in Paris in 1972 at the age of ninety-five, was a legendary figure in France but almost unknown in her native land. She is the *Amazone* to whom Remy de Gourmont addressed his *Lettres à l'Amazone*, she appears as a character in half a dozen works of fiction, and her name turns up in scores of memoirs. For sixty years her house in Paris provided the setting for an international salon frequented by many of the leading writers, artists, and intellectuals of the century. Her own writings, chiefly in French, include verse, drama, fiction, and essays, spanning the period from 1900 to 1963. But her reputation is due even more to her emancipated ideas and to the boldness she demonstrated in living them. She was unquestionably the leading lesbian of her time.

Natalie Barney was born with every advantage: wealth, beauty, magnetism, intelligence, talent. In two generations her family had gone from an immigrant ship and a log cabin in the wilderness to luxury liners and a four-story summer "cottage" in Bar Harbor, where picnics were served by butlers wearing white gloves. One grandfather had been a patron of the arts, and her mother, who was also musically gifted, became one of the leading women painters of her time. Natalie inherited some of her mother's musical talent and had a natural aptitude for literature.

7

Born to great wealth, she grew up spoiled, headstrong, and extraordinarily sure of herself. Endowed with a great deal of intelligence, she was only haphazardly educated, like most young women of her class, and was never an avid reader. The classical scholar Salomon Reinach expressed his amazed and amused admiration for this charming barbarian: "She reads nothing, knows nothing, intuits everything, this wild girl from Cincinnati." Another learned friend, André Rouveyre, said something similar: "Everything is a game to her. And indeed I have noticed that her penetrating astuteness grasps many things, even though she knows no philosophy."

But there are other sorts of learning besides book learning, and in these she excelled. Most obviously she excelled in applied psychology, deploying her intuition, empathy, and charm in all personal relations, especially in her career as a female Don Juan. This aspect of her biography is so prominent that it can easily eclipse the feminist principles that also had a place in her life. Not only was her thinking ahead of the times, but a strong will and a bold mind made her something of a pioneer. Extremely independent in her ideas, she questioned the conventional attitudes of her day on the subject of woman's place in the world and reached her own conclusions. What is more, she proceeded to lead her life according to her principles, determined to be as independent as any man. Of course, wealth was a great advantage, but not until the death of her father was she entirely free to live as she chose, and even then, great daring and strength of character were required. Unfortunately, not much of her feminism found its way into print, for she was neither crusader nor propagandist and preferred living to writing.

As a latter-day Sappho, she became a legend even in her youth, long before Remy de Gourmont made her famous as his *Amazone*. Her lesbian love affairs became common knowledge when her first book of poems appeared in 1900, and the following year a popular novel made her even more notorious as the seductress of the most desirable woman in Paris, Liane de Pougy. At the same time a book of poems was addressed to her by Renée Vivien, a frail poetess who was doomed to die young, and rumor later said that Natalie Barney was her undoing. Renée Vivien's biographer, André Germain, summed up the drama of their love from the night it began: "Renée

Vivien belonged to Lorély for life. And Lorély never belonged to her entirely, not even for an hour.''

Lorély was only one of the many poetic names that rhymed with Natalie or celebrated her powers as a siren, and Renée Vivien was only one of the many women who gave herself completely, only to discover that she must share this seductress with others. The motivation behind Natalie Barney's many conquests is as inscrutable as the cause of her lesbianism; close friends could only accept it as a natural phenomenon or say that she was born that way. One thing is certain: she preferred the excitement of the chase to the humdrum of monogamy. And she exercised her powers of seduction on every attractive woman, it seemed, who came within her orbit. The list of liaisons and "demi-liaisons" that she once compiled includes some forty names and omits casual affairs without number.

Yet Natalie Barney valued friends more highly than lovers and demonstrated throughout life a genius for friendship. "I have sometimes lost friends," she remarked, "but friends have never lost me." The women she esteemed may have been her lovers once, but they became much more than that when passion turned to a deep and lasting blend of love and friendship, for which no adequate word exists. Women like Colette, Eva Palmer Sikelianos, Lucie Delarue-Mardrus, the duchess de Clermont-Tonnerre, Romaine Brooks, and Gertrude Stein—women of intelligence, character, and talent, her equals in every way—became her dear friends for life. "When it comes to friendship," she said, "I am very lazy; once I confer friendship, I never take it back." Actually she took great pains in cultivating these friendships, ingratiating, encouraging, appreciating, entertaining, humoring, and placating as the occasion demanded, courting friends as if they were lovers.

There were masculine friends, too, for Natalie Barney had no prejudice against men. The most famous was Remy de Gourmont, but he was only one in a series of intelligent and cultivated men with whom she established close friendships. For a time she even contemplated marriage as a means of liberating herself from her subservient position as a daughter, but she certainly would have imposed her own terms, demanding complete freedom of action and exemption from conjugal obligations. She never in her life had any physical relationship with a man, but she liked to exercise her seductive powers of mind and body over men as well as women. In fact, she always said that she preferred to converse with a man rather than a woman and wanted her epitaph to characterize her as "the friend of men and lover of women."

Apart from her sexual bias, she was like a character out of Henry James, an attractive American heiress who might have married into the European nobility, and she moved easily in the world of Proust. In her case this was not simply a matter of being born into that international society of wealth and aristocracy; more than almost any other American she was at home with the French language and temperament, and as the years passed she established her own special place on the Paris literary scene. Remy de Gourmont's English translator, Richard Aldington, remarked, "I suppose Miss Barney has at some time been in a café, but she is not the kind of person you would think of inviting to such a place. Her world was that meeting place of society and literature which is better understood and organised in Paris than anywhere." Her salon became an institution, a common ground where the French could meet English, American, and other foreign writers who came to Paris. The repertory of her literary acquaintance is impressive, including such names as Anatole France, Proust, Gide, Cocteau, Colette, Valéry, Rilke, D'Annunzio, Joyce, Eliot, Pound, Hemingway, Fitzgerald, and Gertrude Stein. Not all of these writers frequented her salon, but Natalie Barney's memoirs record encounters with all the leading French writers of her time and close friendships with quite a few.

As a writer herself she was facile but undisciplined. The fact is that she did not care enough about her own writing to make a vocation of it. Every ten years, she said, she emptied the contents of her drawers into a book, and often the letters or sayings of others occupied considerable space in her books. Much of her poetry, drama, and fiction is downright bad, interesting only for what it tells about her life. Her real talent was for epigram, which came to her in conversation, without the rigors of composition, and she published three volumes of these *pensées*. Most readable are the three volumes of memoirs that document her literary friendships, particularly *Aventures de l'esprit*, which chronicles her adventures as a literary lion hunter, and *Souvenirs indiscrets,* which tells something of her biography through more personal relations with writers.

The first of her literary adventures was an encounter with Oscar Wilde at a seaside resort. This was in 1882, when Wilde was on a tour of the United States, and she was five years old. In *Aventures de l'esprit* she remembers running through a hotel lobby to escape from a gang of children when a tall man with long hair, the only person there, picked her up, sat her on his knee and told her a fascinating story, until her mother came looking for her. Mrs. Barney became a friend of Wilde's, perhaps as a result of this chance encounter. Later, when Natalie was seventeen, she learned that Wilde had been sentenced to prison and wrote to him at Reading Gaol, hoping to comfort him as he had once comforted her, but never knew whether the letter reached him. When she was twenty-five, she was engaged for a few weeks to Lord Alfred Douglas, who had been Wilde's nemesis, and much later, in her fifties, she had a love affair with Dolly Wilde, who was the reincarnation of her uncle Oscar. Finally, in 1950, Natalie Barney was one of the few who joined in the celebration of the fiftieth anniversary of Wilde's death, when she organized a literary gathering in his honor.

In her old age she talked with Philippe Jullian, who was writing a biography of Wilde, and linked her destiny with Wilde's in several additional ways. As a child, she said, she "insisted on being painted by Carolus-Duran as the Happy Prince," choosing that role from Wilde's collection of fairy tales. She also stated, ". . . when at fifteen I read Oscar Wilde's short stories my artistic vocation was decided." Curiously enough, this statement appears nowhere in her writings, and her only mention of Wilde occurs in that very brief childhood reminiscence. Yet it is true that of all the writers she admired, Wilde is the one she resembles the most.

Like him she assumed a pose of indolence and frivolity and firmly believed in making her life a work of art instead of sacrificing herself to create works of art. She appears to have had no illusions about her talents and to have exercised them mainly to further personal ends. Her writings were by-products of her life: her poems, addressed to the women she loved; her theatricals, designed mainly to entertain friends; her memoirs, the record of her friendships; and her *pensées*, the impromptu utterances of a sociable wit. Especially in her epigrams she resembled Wilde, with a similar fondness for the flippant paradox that was calculated to outrage and amuse. Most of all she resembled Wilde in being a gifted dilettante rather than a dedicated writer. Not that her talent can be compared with his, but the famous statement he made to André Gide is even more pertinent and revealing when applied to her: "Would you like to know the great drama of my life? It's that I've put my genius into my life; I've put only my talent into my works."

PART I

THE LIFE OF NATALIE BARNEY

1
Origins

As a little girl Natalie Barney used to lie awake at night, anxiously waiting for her mother to come home, afraid that some accident might befall her mother whenever she went out in the evening. Before leaving, her mother would kiss her goodnight, looking more beautiful than any dream, but Natalie could not go to sleep until her mother returned. When she heard the swish of her mother's dress going past her door, she would get out of bed and follow; barefoot and shivering with cold and excitement, she would stand outside her mother's bedroom door until the light went out. Any child who has not experienced a great love for mother or father, she remarked in *Souvenirs indiscrets,* has been deprived of one of life's deepest emotions.

Her parents were young and handsome, her childhood extraordinary—like everyone's, she said, preferring not to dwell on it at any length. Nor did she reveal much about her adolescence, except to describe herself as a sad and gentle page boy whose studies could be summarized in a couplet:

> My only books
> Were women's looks.

The story of her life, she felt, should be composed of her many loves and her loyal friendships, for only through the heartbeats of

15

others had she sounded her own, experienced joy and suffering, plumbed the mysteries, exacting more of life than it had to yield. And all her travels and writings were prompted by love or by a loving friendship.

For all her liberated ideas, Natalie Barney was no rebel. Her father may have been strict and stuffy, and as she grew up her will often clashed with his, but she tried to be a dutiful daughter as long as she could stand it, even to the point of entertaining suitors and becoming engaged several times. Eventually "the wild girl from Cincinnati" broke loose, and her father had ample reason to be scandalized when she publicly courted the most famous courtesan of Paris. Still, she obeyed his orders to come home and behaved like the conventional daughter of a rich American family. And throughout life her manners were always perfectly proper, suggesting neither flaming passion nor irreverent wit. To some she even appeared "Victorian." Chronologically she was, of course, Victorian—born in 1876—though in her private life she was anything but. Her lifetime straddled two centuries, she joked, justifying her style of riding forth as an Amazon; this complex pun works better in French, for in that language the word has the genteel denotation of riding habit as well as its lesbian connotations, and the classical image of the fierce warrior woman on horseback becomes a symbol of all militant feminism.

Like a good Victorian child she honored her father and mother, as they had honored theirs. On both sides there was a strong sense of family pride, which was inherited by Natalie and her sister Laura. The Barneys were not nouveau riche; and though they had only been rich for one generation, they fancied themselves as descendants of men and women who had played their part in American history. Like many Americans they were given to tracing their pedigree back to all sorts of distinguished ancestors and deeds, some of them dubious and some of their claims to distinction absurd. Natalie took particular satisfaction in her French origins, but she was also proud of having Jewish blood and was amused to think of the Puritan forebears on her father's side. She claimed that the mixture of Celt and Latin, Anglo-Saxon and Jew, gave her a sense of equilibrium. And invariably she referred to her family with pride.

Nowhere is this more apparent than in the somewhat mythical genealogy that she copied out in her old age. This includes a family legend that on her mother's side they were descended from the royal house of Bourbon, another that the first Barneys came over on the *Mayflower*, in 1660, and that one of them was the first clergyman or the first Baptist clergyman in Salem, Massachusetts. The family claimed several Revolutionary heroes, among them General Putnam, who became a relative when his daughter married a Barney, and Commodore Joshua Barney, who was probably not related at all. Which General Putnam was not specified, nor which Barney his daughter married, and there was a question mark after the date of the arrival of the *Mayflower*. Natalie Barney may have had only the vaguest notion of American history, but she made up for it in family pride. Her usually keen sense of the ridiculous was in abeyance when she piously wrote down the incongruous story of her great-grandmother, who had fifteen children, wonderfully manicured fingernails, and died at the age of seventy-eight while eating a huckleberry pie. The genealogy lists other oddities of this sort, along with the catalogues of famous connections. Any claim to distinction was worth recording.

The story of her mother's family came from a great-aunt who was born in Louisiana in 1803, lived to be 103 and passed on what must have seemed eyewitness reports of such events as her grandfather's flight from the French Revolution, the negotiation of the Louisiana Purchase by her father, "Honest" Judge Miller, and Lafayette's visit to her father's house. Judge Miller had sent a message to his wife in ringing historical tones: "Lafayette is coming, be prepared." Mrs. Miller, taking this announcement as a warning of danger, fled in panic with her children, her slaves, and her silver, leaving an empty house to welcome the famous guest. This anecdote, recorded in Natalie Barney's *Aventures de l'esprit,* not only reflects her great-aunt Louisa's storytelling abilities but suggests that this spirited old woman had a greater influence on Natalie than all the Barneys who ever lived. Aunt Louisa was a lady of very independent character who lived most of her long life in Baltimore yet resolutely refused to speak English. She cared nothing about money but took her pleasures seriously, entertained in great style, loved the

theater, and engaged a series of French maids whom she invariably
called Madeleine and whose main duty was to read novels to her.
Natalie was a favorite great-niece because she spoke perfect French
and loved all things French. In this she was only reflecting Aunt
Louisa's influence, for the old lady's French temperament and
strong character had made an early impression on Natalie and thus
helped form Natalie's French outlook, her independent nature and
her refusal to confuse sin with pleasure.

Aunt Louisa's husband was named Este, and he was supposed to
be a descendant of the noble Italian house of that name, just as her
father's partner, named Fulton, was supposed to be related to the in-
ventor of the steamboat. By the same logic Commodore Joshua Barney was claimed as a kinsman, although no connection could be established. Natalie had her own reasons for wanting the commodore
in her family tree, for he was her predecessor in Franco-American
affairs. As a young naval officer during the Revolution he was sent
to Paris with official dispatches for Benjamin Franklin and, while
there, was presented at court, where Queen Marie Antoinette and
her ladies kissed this dashing representative of the New World. A
jealous British officer composed a ditty which Natalie was fond of
quoting, probably because the refrain applied equally to her: "Barney, leave the girls alone."

Joshua Barney was a glamorous and romantic hero who not only
distinguished himself as a sea captain during the Revolution but later fought in the French Navy and served on several official missions
to cement Franco-American relations. Natalie Barney was devoted
to the same cause throughout her life and made every effort, especially through her salon, to promote understanding between her two
countries.

She never had much to say about the most remarkable men in her
lineage, her grandfathers. Eliam Eliakim Barney was born in a log
cabin in western New York State in 1807, the eldest of eleven children. After graduating from Union College he moved to Ohio and
became the founder, principal and classics professor of the Dayton
Academy. Because of ill health he retired from teaching in 1839 and
went into business but somehow found the time and energy to establish another school in Dayton, the Cooper Female Seminary, and to

serve as its first principal. In 1850 he and a partner started the Dayton Car Works, which soon became the most important local industry. E. E. Barney spent the next thirty years manufacturing railroad cars—at a time when the railroads were spanning the country—and became a great tycoon. At the beginning of the Civil War he gave $100,000 to equip a Union regiment, and for the rest of his life he contributed a tenth of his income to education. He died when Natalie was four, leaving an enormous fortune, a small share of which kept her wealthy to the end of her days.

Equally remarkable was her maternal grandfather, whom she never knew, for he died before she was born. But Samuel Nathan Pike had made a name for himself in Cincinnati, where Natalie spent her childhood and where his opera house stood as a monument to his memory. Family legend had it that the ancestral Pike was a court chamberlain in Holland whose son married a Jewish woman. But the first Pikes to arrive in America were poor German Jewish immigrants. (The name was Hecht, soon translated into its English equivalent.) Samuel was probably born in Germany and brought over as a small boy. Whatever his origins, he was an enterprising individual who made his way in the classic American style. He left home at the age of sixteen or seventeen, and after wandering as far south as Florida and as far west as Saint Louis, trying his hand at various business ventures in various places, he landed in Cincinnati and began making his fortune in whiskey about the same time E. E. Barney was making his in railroad cars in nearby Dayton. Samuel Pike married into the respectable Miller family and soon became one of the leading citizens of his adopted city, well on his way to becoming one of the richest businessmen in America.

Like E. E. Barney, he also became a philanthropist. Pike may not have had the advantages of a classical education, but he wrote poetry, played the flute and was passionately fond of music. According to tradition it was the singing of Jenny Lind, "the Swedish Nightingale," which inspired him to build an auditorium worthy of her talent and of "the Queen City of the West." In 1859 Pike's Opera House, built entirely at his own expense, became the center of music and drama that made Cincinnati the cultural capital of the Middle West. When it burned down seven years later, Pike's losses amounted to approximately a million dollars, but without hesitation he set about building another opera house on the same site. And shortly after that he built a third opera house in New York City, where by that time he had moved his business headquarters and established his family in a mansion of Fifth Avenue. Though he died young, Samuel Pike bequeathed to his daughter and granddaughter a rich legacy of patronage of the arts.

Natalie's father, Albert Clifford Barney, apparently inherited nothing but money; he showed no sign of having any of his father's acumen or talents of any sort. After his father's death Albert sold his interests in the Barney Car Works to the Pullman Sleeping Car Corporation and retired for life; he was then about thirty. People in Cincinnati commented derisively as he moved up in the social world and gradually transformed his identity from just plain "Al" to A. Clifford Barney; they predicted that his snobbery would end in hyphenation. To one of Natalie's French lovers he appeared the very model of an Anglo-Saxon aristocrat, but another dismissed him as an idle clubman who spent his days doing nothing and his evenings drinking. Natalie herself described him as "lazily clever," an expression which she might also have applied to herself; otherwise father and daughter in no way resembled each other. He appears to have been exactly the wrong kind of father for a girl of her independent spirit, insisting on punctilious conformity to a rigid and narrow decorum. From childhood she remembered him as fatherly but strict, often stern and sometimes given to outbursts of temper. One of her childhood memories brings out this irrational side of his nature without explaining the reason. They were riding in a train one night when he woke up Natalie and her sister, saying that they must all three throw themselves under the wheels of the train. The circumstances suggest that his wife may have given him cause for jealousy on this occasion. Later it was Natalie who sent him into rages, as her lesbianism became notorious. He was only fifty-two when he died, all alone, at the Grand Hôtel in Monte Carlo. Natalie and one of her early lovers, Eva Palmer, accompanied his ashes across the Atlantic for burial.

Albert Barney left a fortune of $2,500,000 to each of his daughters. More important for Natalie, his death left them psychologically independent as well, free to live their lives as they wished. In Laura's case this meant living as her father would have wished, but Natalie had been struggling against his authoritarian rule ever since adolescence. One wonders how his wife put up with him, for there was nothing stodgy or repressive about this warm, outgoing woman whose motto was "Live and let live." One explanation is that they lived apart at least some of the time; when she studied in Paris, for instance, he preferred to stay in London—a choice which reflects something of their differences in temperament.

Alice Pike Barney could be said to have inherited her father's enterprising spirit; her life was operatic and theatrical in more ways than one. Obviously her circumstances were totally different from those of a poor immigrant boy. As a girl of seventeen she was presented at the English court, and while in London she met the African adventurer and discoverer of David Livingstone, Henry M. Stanley. She and Stanley fell in love, and for both it was to be their greatest romance. When Alice returned to New York, Stanley followed, and a few months after meeting they signed their betrothal in the following words: "We solemnly pledge ourselves to be married to one another on the return of Henry Morton Stanley from Africa. We call God to witness this pledge in writing." A week later she saw him off as he embarked for further adventures; he expected to be gone for two years but in fact did not return for three. In Africa Stanley christened his boat the *Lady Alice,* named a stretch of the Congo River the Lady Alice Rapids, and wrote her long, fervent letters. But Alice was young and beautiful and lively and courted by many beaux; and two years was a long time. Before the period of their pledge had expired she married Albert Barney, and not quite nine months later, about the time Stanley should have been getting back, a baby, Natalie, was born. Though Stanley later married, Alice remained the love of his life, and losing her was a major cause of his melancholy, according to his most recent biographer. Alice never forgot Stanley either, and after his death she painted a portrait of him from memory.

Natalie was born in Dayton, Ohio, but her childhood memories are of Cincinnati, where the family lived until she was about ten. They then moved to Washington, D. C., as did many Midwestern-

ers who fancied the fashionable life during that period. They built a
house on Rhode Island Avenue in 1887 and another in the open
fields on the outskirts of town in 1895. The first house was razed a
few years ago; the second, 2223 R Street, is now the residence of
the Burmese embassy. The family lived in neither of these houses
the year round but migrated with the seasons, summering in Maine,
where they had a large house overlooking the ocean, sometimes
wintering in Florida, and spending the spring in France, invariably
returning to Washington for the fall months and Christmas, with occasional visits to Ohio in between.

Alice, who shared her father's love of the arts, took up painting a
few years after her marriage, studied in Paris with Carolus-Duran,
Henner, and Whistler, and became an accomplished portrait painter. Some of her work, such as the pastel portraits of Whistler, Shaw
and Chesterton, can be seen at the Smithsonian Institution and at
Barney Studio House, which her daughters gave to the Smithsonian
in her memory. Alice painted a number of portraits of Natalie and
provided four portraits of other women as illustrations for Natalie's
first book, a volume of unmistakably lesbian poems. She also had a
keen interest in the drama, wrote and produced a number of plays,
and followed her father's example in launching the Sylvan Theater
in Washington, which survives to this day. A generous patroness of
the arts and leader in civic affairs, she played a major role in the artistic life of Washington, as her scrapbooks testify, with their many
clippings about all manner of social, philanthropic, and theatrical
enterprises that received her support.

Studio House, built two years after her husband's death, expresses Alice's flamboyant personality and wealthily bohemian style
in her later years. Located only half a block from the family residence, Studio House was not a place to live but a setting for musical
and theatrical entertainments, with a balcony for musicians and a
stage for plays. The inscription on the mantel in the studio seems to
reflect a proper society lady of taste: THE HIGHEST PROBLEM OF ART
IS TO CAUSE BY APPEARANCE THE ILLUSION OF HIGHER REALITY.
Proper she was not. She had been flirtatious during her husband's
lifetime, and if he succeeded in making her behave during the
twenty-six years of their marriage, his death emancipated her for

twenty-nine more years of merry widowhood. In her later photographs she appears increasingly youthful and curvaceous, rivaling Mae West and Lillian Russell. As she grew older she developed a weakness for young male models, even going so far as to marry one who was less than half her age, an artist named Christian Hemmick. The marriage left Natalie and Laura richer than ever; Hemmick did not want it thought that he was marrying an older woman for her money, so at his suggestion Alice transferred the entire fortune that she had inherited from her husband—three million dollars—to her daughters. As it turned out, Hemmick was more interested in boys, and the marriage did not last; he later sued for divorce on grounds of desertion. According to a family friend, however, the marriage was a success, for Alice liked to have an attractive man to look at across the breakfast table, and Hemmick liked to have someone entertaining to listen to.

Though at home in the highest circles of Washington society, Alice did not share Albert Barney's fondness for social life. "What is Capital life, after all?" one Washington newspaper quoted her as saying. "Small talk and lots to eat, an infinite series of teas and dinners. Art? There is none!" Alice never worried much about social conformity. At one point, when her theatricals seemed too bold, a gossip columnist clucked: "It is said that Mrs. Alice Clifford Barney stands upon the verge of social ostracism. She is a woman of undoubted cleverness, but has at last o'erleaped herself." This was during Albert's lifetime, when he was a restraining influence. In her old age Laura remembered that family life had changed radically after her father's death. Before, all was very correct, conventional and decorous; after, their way of life became openly bohemian. When Laura did a recumbent nude in concrete, Alice placed it on her lawn, and the press falsely rumored that this was a sculpture of Natalie, creating such a scandal that the police were summoned and gave orders that the sculpture be veiled with a tarpaulin.

Alice had a restless spirit and could not stand the same surroundings very long. She designed five successive houses but soon found them old-fashioned. In 1908 she rented the White House in Chelsea, which had once belonged to Whistler. In 1911, when she married Christian Hemmick, she was living in Paris. In 1924 she moved out to Hollywood, where she spent her last seven years, painting and writing plays and actively taking part in everything that was going on. Appropriately she died during a concert that she had sponsored, so peacefully that people sitting near her thought she had gone to sleep. As Natalie put it, her mother "died as harmoniously and simply as she had lived."

Natalie not only had a childhood passion for her mother but remained devoted to her throughout life and clearly took after her in many ways. Like her mother, she was tolerant, easygoing and generous in her impulses, loving people and loving life. Though less evidently flamboyant, Natalie was at least as liberated in her private life, far bolder and more adventurous in her love affairs. Her style of life—her salon, her stage setting, her decor—was a more restrained, classical version of her mother's at Studio House. Natalie's life centered more on people than on the arts, and there were other differences between them, but it is easy to see why she always sympathized with her mother's side of the family and always remembered the earliest love of all, that beautiful apparition by her bedside which caused her so many sleepless anxieties in childhood.

2
Beginnings

Natalie's childhood memories were of an idyllic world full of pets and playmates. She and her sister grew up in a big house in the country, overlooking the Ohio River. She also had memories of walking in the streets of Cincinnati with her father, trying to keep up with his pace while gazing with fascination at the cigar-store Indians. The beloved pets included a bulldog, a toy spaniel, a goat, two parrots, a few baby alligators, which they had acquired in Florida, and, most important of all, a Shetland pony named Tricksy, on which Natalie learned to ride. For many years riding was to be her favorite sport, the one that would suggest the nickname of ''Amazon.'' She also drove the pony cart and took her little sister along as passenger. Natalie was not only older but more assertive and daring, as she was always to be, just as Laura was to be more conservative. The contrast between the two sisters was later summed up by Natalie, who called Laura the angel, herself the devil. Natalie was the intelligent sister, Laura said, and the leader in their childhood games, while Laura represented caution and rectitude. When their mother did paintings of the girls, Laura was a good model, but Natalie wiggled. The rivalry between them persisted until their final years, but they also maintained a healthy respect for each other and a strong underlying sense of kinship.

Their earliest education was provided by a French governess who was too fat and too easily winded to keep up with their games, so she sat under a big tree in the garden and read to them when they got tired of playing. Though obviously spoiled and undisciplined, the two little girls learned French by listening to their governess read from the works of Jules Verne and other children's books, and Natalie for the rest of her life preferred to have someone read to her instead of doing her own reading. This apparently was the extent of their education until their father decided to take them to Europe for more formal schooling. Their mother had also decided to go to Europe, to study painting, and was to spend more than two years there, between 1886 and 1889, while their father returned to America for at least part of the time.

Natalie was about ten at the time of this big adventure. At first she had mixed emotions about leaving home and fears that she would see less of her mother now that they were traveling. And indeed her mother spent more time in the company of a seventeen-year-old niece who was traveling with them. But Natalie found that even on shipboard and in hotels family life continued, and she was soon absorbed in the many new impressions along the way. She was a very observant child with a good deal of curiosity. Already she had a well-developed, naughty sense of humor and would start her sister giggling by making jokes about unfamiliar household objects like the bidet, which Natalie dubbed "the French bathtub." Their mother contributed her share of irreverent humor with sketches of people they met in their travels; she had the caricaturist's knack of fixing the mannerisms and gestures of everyone who caught her eye.

In Europe the Barneys traveled around a bit before settling down. Natalie remembered being taken to the zoo in Belgium, which made her homesick for her pets. She also remembered being terrified by the paintings in the museums and becoming indignant at the sight of a woman and a dog pulling a milk cart while a man walked calmly alongside puffing on his pipe. From that moment on, Natalie said, she and Laura became ardent feminists.

In Paris Mrs. Barney had the girls' portraits painted by Carolus-Doran, with whom she then studied painting. So that Natalie's portrait would never appear dated, Mrs. Barney dressed her as a Renaissance page. In *Souvenirs indiscrets* Natalie reflects that this choice of costume may have been unwise, suggesting to her the role that she was to play in courting women. Not that Natalie objected to the costume or the role; later she and her friends delighted in all sorts of transvestite costumes, exchanging male and female roles as readily as the heroines in Shakespeare's comedies and with similar effect.

At the age of ten Natalie already felt the stirrings of sexual attraction for women. No longer able to keep her vigil by her mother's bedroom door, she began to turn her attention to her cousin, a dazzling blonde with whom she sometimes shared a bed when they were traveling. At night Natalie watched with fascination as her cousin took out a photograph of a young man, which she had hidden in her suitcase, and covered it with kisses before getting into bed and snuggling up against Natalie. The sight aroused strong emotions—a mixture of passion, jealousy and solicitude for her cousin who might marry this man.

After a time Mr. and Mrs. Barney left their daughters at a boarding school in Fontainebleau called Les Ruches. The school was frequented by girls from foreign countries who went there to learn French along with the polite arts of drawing, singing, dancing, riding, penmanship and deportment. There Natalie achieved her complete mastery of French as she studied composition and memorized the poetry of La Fontaine, Racine, Chénier and Hugo. She became totally bilingual, as hardly anyone ever does, and later, when she began writing poetry, preferred French to English as the language which expressed her best. French people who knew her said that she spoke perfect eighteenth-century French. This may sound like a left-handed compliment, but it was not intended ironically, for the eighteenth century represented the classic standard to which the Académie Française aspired. Considering how much importance the French attach to their language, making it the keystone of their education, Natalie Barney must be said to have been very well educated at Les Ruches. She may not have read widely or deeply, but she developed a ready wit, a quick ear, and the ability to put what she learned to good use.

At Les Ruches she learned more than French literature. The school and its turbulent passions were described many years later in a memoir entitled *Olivia*, published anonymously by Dorothy Bussy. Dorothy Strachey, as she was then (the sister of Lytton Strachey), had attended Les Ruches some years before the Barney sisters, and the mistresses who had created such an atmosphere of ardor and jealousy had since departed. Under the new management, Natalie remarks in *Souvenirs indiscrets,* the girls played croquet instead of playing at love. Still, as in all boarding schools, there were overheated emotions, and Natalie said that it was there that she learned to love her own sex. She had a crush on one of the older girls, who jokingly called her "my little husband." The relationship was innocent, Natalie commented in retrospect, presumably meaning that it went no further than playacting; but it was certainly a presage of things to come. So also were her earliest attempts at versifying, inspired by the Grecian beauty of this schoolgirl. To Natalie poetry was always to be the language of love.

In later years Natalie said that she could not remember a time when she did not know the facts of life, and she discovered that she was a lesbian at an early age. This discovery was probably made at Les Ruches, where she spent a year and a half in cloistered feminine society. At the age of ten or twelve she was already extremely interested in all manifestations and varieties of sex. During her stay two minor scandals set the school agog, one a straightforward flirtation between two of the older American girls and two French cavalry officers, the other a much more mysterious occurrence suggestive of strange fetishes and nocturnal visitations: one night, for no apparent reason, the hair of one of the little girls was cut off. This incident suggests that something remained of the atmosphere of *Olivia*, as does Natalie's language in describing those long strands of chestnut hair lying on the girl's bed at night, like a sleeping serpent lying at her side.

The mystery was not explained until much later. When the time came to leave Les Ruches and return to America, Natalie and Laura begged their parents to engage their favorite schoolmistress. This German teacher was only too willing to accompany them in order to rejoin her dearest friend, who was also a governess in Washington—in fact, the governess of the five daughters of the Barneys' neighbor on Scott Circle, the Vice-President of the United States.

Shortly after their return, Natalie and Laura awoke one night to see their teacher walking downstairs in her nightgown, holding in her hand a pair of scissors with which she proceeded to cut into pieces the straw hats belonging to Mr. Barney and a friend of the family. Needless to say, the sleepwalker had to go; but before she could be sent home, there were further sleepwalking episodes, until finally a dog collar was strapped to her ankle and chained to the foot of the bed.

Her successor was a wholesome Austrian girl who secretly nursed a broken heart. Natalie soon became her confidante, listening sympathetically to the tearful story of true love forbidden by the young man's noble family. When the girl wept for sorrow, Natalie whispered sweet nothings in her ear, leaning her head on the girl's shoulder and talking to her as though she were the lost lover who missed his sweetheart and loved her through Natalie. These words seemed to comfort the girl, who pressed Natalie to her bosom. By playing the lover's role Natalie healed the broken heart; gradually the Austrian girl recovered her spirits and her beautiful smile. Natalie was always to have an uncanny intuitive gift for establishing intimacy and an abiding interest in all affairs of the heart.

During adolescence she discovered that she possessed other powers as well. In her mother's studio she often watched while her mother painted the portraits of the most beautiful women of Washington society. One day one of the models, who had been out dancing the night before and was still so agitated that she could not hold a pose, asked Natalie to calm her nerves by caressing her palms. Natalie succeeded so well that the young woman lapsed into a somnolent state from which she could only be aroused to pose when Natalie stroked her ankles, almost hypnotically controlling the model's posture. Thus Natalie learned the art of touching, which she used thereafter to cure her mother's headaches or to calm her schoolmates' nerves during examination periods. But she found that her soothing influence could only be transmitted to her chosen friends.

Life in Washington offered many attractions. The city itself was enchanting, with parks and squares overflowing with magnolias, a woodland city with lush semitropical vegetation struggling against the restraint of civilization. In the vacant lots between the new mansions of the rich there were Negro squatters' shacks and Negro children playing. Occasionally an Italian organ-grinder would come by with his monkey, his music attracting black and white children alike.

From the first days of good weather Natalie often went riding with one of the Vice-President's daughters. Proud of their horses and riding habits, exhilarated to be at liberty in the balmy spring air, they rode through the burgeoning woods on the outskirts of the city. One day while out riding they came upon a marvelous sight: the greatest beauty of Washington society driving in a carriage drawn by a prize team, with her escort, an attaché of the British embassy, riding at her side. This lovely apparition was Victoria Leiter, who was to marry Lord Curzon, the future Vice-Regent of India. When Natalie and her friend came galloping up, the team bolted; and Miss Leiter, after she managed to bring her horses under control, scolded the girls instead of admiring their equestrian skill, as they had hoped. Looking even more beautiful in anger, she finally softened to the girls' flattering compliments and favored them with a smile.

This episode from Natalie's adolescence strangely prefigures a scene in the Bois de Boulogne a few years later, when Natalie was to fall in love at the sight of another famous beauty out riding in her carriage. In the earlier instance it was her friend who was smitten by the beautiful creature. The two girls then had the delicious pleasure of exchanging confidences, Natalie confessing that she had a crush on a girl with whom she spent her summers and maintained a fervent correspondence during the rest of the year.

No doubt this was Evalina Palmer, better known as Eva, who was Natalie's first love and who, according to one source, initiated Natalie into the rites of Lesbos. This strange girl looked like a medieval virgin with her sea-green eyes, pale complexion and masses of red hair that seemed too heavy for her fragile neck. Once, when Natalie was watching her comb that wealth of hair, which reached down to her ankles, Eva seized a pair of scissors, cut off a handful of hair and gave it to Natalie, saying that her hair was her rival and this was her revenge. Natalie kept that strand of hair in a tortoiseshell case until her old age. For a period of twelve or fifteen years she and Eva were intimates, spending summers together in Maine, attending the same school in New York and later living together in Paris, where they continued to play prominent roles in each other's lives.

Natalie completed her formal education at Miss Ely's School for Girls at the age of seventeen and spent the following year in Europe, traveling and taking music lessons. While traveling, she kept a diary-scrapbook, which tells tantalizingly little. On June 9, 1894, she sailed for Europe in the company of two sisters, Grace and Carol Lee, under the chaperonage of Miss Ely. They were to spend the summer sightseeing in northern Europe. At that time Germany was particularly attractive to American tourists, especially those with an interest in music, and for some years Natalie had been studying the violin. Many entries in her diary reveal a genuine and well-developed taste for music, as she visits Wagner's house, attends the Bayreuth festival and hears concerts elsewhere. Otherwise her jottings about museums, palaces and churches merely reflect the dutiful tourist.

A sense of humor appears occasionally, along with her astute observation of people. On board ship she itemizes her fellow passengers: a mysterious blonde who is usually seasick, a maiden with rosy cheeks and a doleful expression, a contingent of boarding school girls from Baltimore. With a mixture of curiosity and irony she observes their behavior, such as the outrageous flirting of one of the boarding school girls with an unappealing gentleman on his way to Germany to meet a fiancée who proves to be even more unappetizing. One fellow passenger evidently attracted Natalie more than all the others, for the diary mentions her repeatedly and preserves her address and autograph—"Yours lovingly, Leonora Howland"—the only one Natalie took the trouble to save. After Mrs. Howland left the ship at Southampton, Natalie found the voyage very dull. Presumably Mr. Howland, who accompanied his wife, disembarked at Southampton, too, but his departure is not noted in the diary. Nor is he mentioned later, in Paris, when Mrs. Howland appears frequently. These scraps of evidence suggest that Natalie had a shipboard romance of sorts, probably a young girl's infatuation with a slightly older woman of the world.

Miss Ely and her charges sailed on to Bremerhaven and proceeded thence toward Moscow. At the Russian border their baggage disappeared, and the young ladies were almost denied entrance because the passport only mentioned Miss Ely. They were rescued from this predicament by a gallant American named Mr. Oswald Cancel, who offered to be of assistance, found their baggage, served as their interpreter and escorted them across the border. Mr. Cancel was obviously captivated by the fair Miss Barney. Her scrapbook contains a letter that he wrote some two months later, quite properly addressed to Miss Ely, requesting photographs of all the ladies and, with due apologies, singling out the beautiful "Lorelei," Miss Barney, whose blue eyes were the loveliest he had ever seen. Those pale blue eyes were to have a devastating effect on a number of men as well as women during the coming years.

The diary tells little about Natalie's brief visit to Czarist Russia, and in later years she retained few impressions of that vanished world. Evidently she was more interested in Mrs. Howland, whom she met again in Paris later in the summer and with whom she lunched or dined or drove in the Bois or went to the theater almost every day. In the midst of these activities came a cable from Natalie's Papa with the message that she was to remain with Grace Lee, the traveling companion she preferred, or be enrolled in a strict school in Paris. Was this intended as a form of discipline? Had Natalie misbehaved? Or was Mr. Barney simply sending further instructions to Miss Ely as the summer tour came to an end? The message is cryptic, and too little is known of the circumstances to say. If Natalie had been anyone else, there would be no reason to speculate.

In any event the instructions were not carried out; instead Natalie went back to Germany for the balance of her year abroad. Probably this was an alternate plan that her parents had considered, and quite possibly there was no need for a strict school. Of course, Natalie was to be chaperoned, like any respectable young lady in those days. She spent the month of September in the home of Frau Lepman, in Jena, in the company of other American or English girls, whom she scrutinized in her usual fashion, finding the bright, sarcastic one interesting and the sad, starving one probably lovesick; she also described herself as "very bored and tired of life." No doubt the company of her contemporaries and the study of German in a small provincial city was a decided letdown after the brilliant life of Paris in the company of Mrs. Howland.

Toward the end of the month that Natalie spent in Jena, Herr Kapellmeister Rösel came to visit and tried out her violin, producing music such as she had never heard from it before. Evidently Natalie made another conquest on this occasion, for Herr Rösel later returned to play for her the opera he had just completed. Flattered to be the first person ever to hear this new composition, she offered appreciative and knowledgeable criticism. Natalie spent the next six months in Dresden, studying German (which she never mastered) and taking violin lessons with Herr Konzertmeister Petri, who had been recommended by Herr Rösel. Her other activities in Dresden included fencing and dancing. In other words, this sojourn abroad represented the proper finishing of a proper young lady's education.

3
Liane de Pougy

"How often in the blurred reflection of a carriage window have I seen the masterpiece Whistler could have painted!" In her first book of epigrams Natalie allowed this rare autobiographical note to intrude, commemorating a decisive choice she made once between art and love. The event took place, or rather did not take place, when she was staying in a *pension* in Montparnasse, next door to Whistler's academy. This could have been either in 1896–97 or 1898–99, when Alice Barney took her daughters to Paris while she studied painting. Whistler's personality must have appealed to Alice as much as his art, and the bohemian life must have been a welcome change from Washington society, not to mention an escape from a stuffy husband. Her facility as a painter seems to have impressed Whistler, who cautioned her, "Do not let cleverness run away with you, Mrs. Barney." He also appreciated her company and made a practice of coming to tea every week after class.

Natalie later regretted that she had never met the artist, whose caustic wit would have appealed to her. She could have seen him by simply opening the door that separated them. But during his visits she was too engrossed in the passionate letters she was writing to emerge from her room. Before leaving Paris, Alice commissioned Whistler to paint a portrait of Natalie and left behind the sum she had agreed to pay. Nothing ever came of this plan because Natalie was too preoccupied with affairs of the heart and never went to the painter's studio to pose. Instead she spent all the money her mother had left on flowers and presents for the women she was courting. This episode, which occurred when she was twenty or twenty-two, characterizes Natalie's reckless indifference to all considerations but love, not only in her early years but all through her life.

The first sojourn in Paris can be dated from a Washington society column noting that the Barneys were sailing for Europe on July 11, 1896. Their party included Natalie's fiancé, Mr. William Morrow. Toward the end of March, 1897, the Washington papers announced that Mrs. Barney and her daughters were soon returning from a winter in Europe. Mr. Barney, who never seemed to stay in Paris long, had come home before this. No further mention is made of Mr. Morrow, but he may have played a supporting role in Natalie's love life two years later.

There are no newspaper clippings in Alice's scrapbook to report the date of her return, but Natalie stayed on in Paris until the month of May and was supposed to take part in an event that filled the Paris papers with real news. This was the charity bazaar, held on May 4, at which a fire broke out and a great many society women perished amid horrible scenes. Natalie was to have been in charge of a booth—perhaps another pretext for staying on in Paris—and her parents were desperate with anxiety when they heard the news of the disaster. As it happened, Natalie had not gone to the charity bazaar at all but had taken the opportunity to spend the day with a Spanish woman with whom she was having a love affair. As she was leaving the woman's house, she saw the reflection of the fire in the sky and declared that it was glowing to celebrate their love.

After this escapade Natalie was required to return to America and behave herself. For the next year she led the life of the debutante, with the usual round of dances and parties. In Bar Harbor that summer she performed in a theatrical entertainment which was probably staged by her mother. In the fall she made her debut in Washington and was described—one might almost say advertised—in the press as follows:

No young woman of the gay set at the capital is more admired than Miss Nathalie Barney, daughter of Mr. and Mrs. A. Clifford Barney of Rhode Island avenue. Miss Barney is very fair, with quantities of golden hair dressed always in the latest Parisian style. Her features are pretty, her figure dainty. She is a girl who appears in fluff and frills, jewels, floating draperies, and who is picturesque in every costume she wears. Miss Barney speaks several languages, having been educated abroad. She plays the violin and mandolin, having studied the former with one of the great European instructors. She rides and drives admirably, dances gracefully and is a witty conversationalist. Her histrionic ability is remarkable, and her appearance in an "Egyptian Vaudeville," presented at Kebo Club, Bar Harbor, last summer created a furore among the society of that place.

It was some months later, probably in the spring of 1898, that a gossip columnist smugly rejoiced that Mrs. Barney had "at last o'erleaped herself" and stood "on the verge of social ostracism."

Her much advertised theatricals of last week—given to call attention to young Miss Barney—caused a great stir in Washington. Miss Barney's performance in Sardou's risky play, "L'Etrangère," has caused many of the more careful and reserved matrons to draw back from Mrs. Barney and her set. At the Kettledrum, early in the Winter, Miss Barney recited a monologue about the virgin Mary and Mary Magdalene which the Catholics considered blasphemous, and the Barneys are likely to find themselves *tabu* among the more exclusive women.

These performances could just as well have been Natalie's idea as her mother's. Sardou's *Americans Abroad* had enjoyed a run on Broadway about the time Natalie attended Miss Ely's School in New York, and the situation was one that would appeal to her. So would a monologue about a fallen woman. Natalie did not mind shocking society, but she could not have been aware of any blasphemy, for she was a religious illiterate. The few references to religion in her life all prove that this was a subject to which she was totally indifferent and of which she was remarkably ignorant. Thus she was capable of writing a poem about Judas, canonizing him as the only one of the disciples who died for Christ.

In the summer of 1898 the Barney family returned to France for an entire year. Once again Albert went back to America while Alice studied painting. It was during the course of this year, in 1898, that Alice painted her striking portrait of Whistler. It was also during this year, in the spring of 1899, that Natalie's first famous romantic exploit occurred. She was then twenty-two.

The scene opens in the Bois de Boulogne in the days of open carriages, which, as Natalie explains in *Souvenirs indiscrets,* "gave one the leisure to exchange long looks and half-smiles in passing." One day Natalie was out riding with a suitor when they came upon a procession of open carriages in which a number of ravishing beauties displayed their charms. Natalie, who had never seen such a sight, was dazzled, particularly by one whose slender, androgynous elegance outshone all the rest. Her escort, thinking to disabuse her, explained that this was not a great lady but the famous courtesan Liane de Pougy. Because she had led a sheltered life, Natalie did not understand the ways of the demimonde and supposed that this beautiful young woman was the victim of predatory males. Therefore, she made up her mind to rescue the poor creature from the life she was leading and to provide her with a decent home—if necessary, by marrying the rich young man who was courting her. It did not take her long to find out how mistaken she was.

Far from being a miserable bird in a gilded cage, Liane de Pougy was in full control of her lot as one of the most brilliant courtesans of *la belle époque,* a period when the grand horizontals enjoyed a privileged position in elegant society. The courtesans were not mere prostitutes; the rich and powerful men of the world who kept them appreciated their wit, charm and intelligence as well as their physical beauty. Liane de Pougy, whose real name was Anne-Marie Chassaigne, had come from a respectable family in the provinces and had deliberately chosen the life she led in the metropolis. Like others in her profession, she assumed an aristocratic name; unlike most, she ended up marrying a real prince, becoming, as Princess Ghika, a perfectly acceptable member of society. After her husband's death she retired to a convent, changing her name, for the last time, to Sister Mary Magdalene of Repentance.

In the late 1890s Liane de Pougy was at the height of her glory.

Natalie, once she understood the courtesan's status, was not the
least bit daunted; on the contrary, she began sending flowers and
importunate letters asking for a rendezvous. Although such a propo-
sition was unheard of, Liane was amused and decided to play a joke
on this brash American girl by concealing herself behind a screen
and watching while a friend took her place on the chaise lounge in
her darkened boudoir. At night all cats are gray, says a French prov-
erb, but the friend belonged to another era and could hardly have
passed for a reigning beauty, even in the dark. (Her greatest moment had come many years before and was now immortalized in a
stained-glass window allegorically depicting the visit to her estab-
lishment of Napoleon III. Such was the art and artifice of the demimonde.)

At the appointed hour Natalie arrived in a fever of excitement,
dressed in the costume of a page, which she had bought for the occasion, and armed with a bouquet of flowers. Just as she was kneel-
ing before the reclining form, she heard a snicker and realized that
she had been tricked. Her disappointment was only momentary,
however, as Liane emerged from behind the screen and presented
herself all the more dramatically. To the infatuated Natalie she
looked like an angel from a painting by Fra Angelico, her heavenly
head covered with short curls, her slender figure dressed all in
white, appearing almost transparent. But this was no pure spirit.
Her hand, when she put it on Natalie's shoulder, felt as heavy as
marble.

Something about this American girl took her fancy, so she invited
Natalie to go out riding with her in the Bois de Boulogne. But first
she had to prepare her appearance, and, as Natalie watched spell-
bound, Liane performed the rites of the boudoir, brightening the red
of her lips, darkening her eyes, perfuming herself, changing from a
monastic robe to a stylish dress, arming herself with pearls and other accoutrements. The ritual was like the arming of a champion going forth to meet the adversary. And Natalie was the attendant page
sitting at her feet in the carriage, invisible to bystanders. As they set
off for the Bois behind two fat white horses, Liane declared that she
liked Natalie, liked her spirit, her wit and her long blond hair.

Discreetly Natalie drew the veil at this point in her *Souvenirs in-*

discrets, probably because there was no need for her to be more explicit. The story of the ensuing love affair had been published for all the world to read in a novel by Liane de Pougy, *Idylle saphique,* which created quite a sensation when it appeared in 1901. Contemporaries had no trouble identifying the principal characters; the heroine, for instance, is a transparent self-portrait, a famous courtesan who at the age of twenty-three is bored with the sophisticated pleasures of Paris. And though the novel fictionalizes certain events, such as melodramatic deaths, the character portrayals are essentially accurate.

The story begins very much as it did in real life. The courtesan, Annhine de Lys, is visited by a pretty, very blond American girl dressed as a Florentine page. Her name, Emily Florence Temple Bradfford, echoes that of Natalie Clifford Barney, with Florence thrown in for good measure to provide one of the nicknames, Flossie, by which the character is addressed in the novel and Natalie was addressed by Liane in real life. The other nickname was Moon-Beam, which may sound ridiculous in English but which was evidently meant to suggest nocturnal magic, mystery and luminosity; and, of course, the moon was the goddess of women. Both nicknames were subsequently taken up by others, notably by Colette, who modeled a character in one of her novels after Natalie and called her Miss Flossie. Presumably Natalie liked these and other names that were conferred upon her, in fiction and in real life. The elements of masquerade and playacting were to figure prominently in her early love affairs.

In the novel Flossie falls in love with Annhine when she sees her in the audience at the Folies Bergère. (In real life Liane had appeared on stage at the Folies Bergère.) Dressed as a page, Flossie comes to pay her respects and offers to serve her beloved. Although several years younger—only twenty—she is an experienced seductress, whereas Annhine is reluctant from start to finish. The morning after their first meeting, Flossie again calls on Annhine and is ushered into her bedroom, where she finds the courtesan reclining on a unique replica of a famous bed that belonged to the mistress of Louis XV. They proceed to the bathroom, which is decorated in the purest Louis XV style, a sanctuary described in lovingly lavish detail.

When Annhine removes her lacy nightgown, Flossie flings herself at her feet, fervently embracing and kissing her ankles, her knees, her legs, her thighs, losing herself in a delirium. Annhine escapes by leaping into her perfumed bath, but soon invites Moon-Beam to join her if she will promise to behave. After the bath, they massage each other and indulge in erotic play but stop short of actual lovemaking. As a novelist, Liane de Pougy relies on a simple formula: the plot consists of a series of seduction scenes which invariably come to naught.

That evening, at the theater, Flossie reclines at Annhine's feet on the floor of her box. The play is *Hamlet,* with Sarah Bernhardt playing the lead. (This production, which opened in Paris on May 20, 1899, dates the love affair.) During intermission Flossie and Annhine launch into philosophical discourse, Flossie identifying the plight of women with Hamlet's impotent rage against tyranny: "For what is there for women who feel the passion for action when pitiless Destiny hold them in chains? Destiny made us women at a time when the law of men is the only law that is recognized."

Flossie has a faithful, docile millionaire fiancé named Will, whom she proposes to marry in order to make Annhine rich and independent. Flossie is very willful, obviously accustomed to having her way and pushing people around. She is also a butterfly, going from one to another, usually stopping only once. Her last affair, with a married woman named Jane, is the only liaison that has lasted more than a matter of days. When Jane hears of Flossie's new love and meets Annhine at a masked ball, she stabs herself and dies at Annhine's feet. The courtesan leaves Paris in horror, traveling to Italy, Spain and Portugal, where she has affairs with various men but is always disappointed. Returning to Paris, she is again courted by Flossie, but becomes consumptive and dies, attended by Flossie, disguised as a nun.

Toward the end of the novel Annhine asks Flossie about her past, and Flossie explains that she has always preferred what is pretty, tender, delicate and fragile, and hence has always liked women, those exquisite flowers with souls. She was initiated into her first joys by a girl named Eva, with red hair like a living flame, who was now either dead or married, which amounted to the same thing. But much earlier, at the age of eight, she felt vague desires for an older cousin when she watched her praying at her bedside or kissing a man's picture.

Some of these details, such as the little girl's feelings for her older cousin, are taken directly from Natalie's life. At times Liane de Pougy did not even bother to invent names. Jane cannot be identified, but Eva is clearly a portrait, or rather a reproduction, of Eva Palmer, who was a striking beauty with spectacular long red hair. Even the fiancé named Will may very well be based on a real person by the same name, Mr. William Morrow. In the novel Will is the son of a railroad builder and is worth five or six million dollars in his own right. This could be a fictional reflection of the source of Albert Barney's wealth, but it would not be at all surprising if the Barneys had been friendly with the families of other railroad magnates.

With such materials Liane de Pougy scarcely needed to tax her powers of invention. In portraying the character of Flossie she did not find it necessary to fictionalize at all. The same can be said of other novelists who wrote about Natalie Barney. In transferring her character and episodes from her life to the pages of fiction, they generally did not bother to improve on the original. Hence the novels written about her early loves are a source of information and insight that cannot be found anywhere else. *Idylle saphique,* the first of these novels, is probably quite accurate in depicting Natalie as a bold, experienced and promiscuous seductress of women. If so, by the age of twenty-two she was already well launched in her career as a female Don Juan.

At the same time Natalie had a number of male suitors, partly to please her father but also to please herself. There is plenty of evidence that she was not only attractive to men but quite willing to be courted by them. Her diary of 1894 documents the effect she had on a passing acquaintance, Mr. Oswald Cancel; at seventeen she was already the irresistible siren Lorelei, with her pale blue eyes and long blond hair. Though rather short and not conventionally beautiful, she had great natural presence and created a striking effect upon the beholder without any effort on her part. There was something about her, some kind of magnetism, that dazzled men and women alike when they first met her and impressed those who were not dazzled. Extremely intelligent and perceptive, she grew into a self-possessed young woman, very sure of herself, fully aware of her powers and quite prepared to exercise them. And though she always enjoyed the company of men and did not mind flirting with them, she never had any doubt about her predilection for women.

Liane de Pougy was her first famous conquest, but *Idylle saphique* indicates that there had been many other conquests before this. Her seduction of Liane was remarkable in many ways, not the least of which was the fact that Liane succumbed. Lesbianism may have enjoyed a certain vogue among the Decadents of the 1890s—as illustrated by art nouveau—but Liane was certainly not a lesbian. Yet she could not have been entirely reluctant, or she would have repelled Natalie's advances; instead she encouraged them and became a willing partner in the love affair. Two years later she made a public avowal of the affair when she published her thinly disguised narrative of that Sapphic idyll. Meanwhile she wrote love letters to Natalie and went on writing them long after their romance had ended. Natalie was to publish one of these in *Souvenirs indiscrets.*

The love affair ended abruptly when Natalie's father caught her reading a love letter from Liane. He immediately packed her off to America, and there she was forced to resume the role of the marriageable young lady. Her father was anxious to get her properly married, and she is reputed to have been engaged no less than three times, once to Lord Alfred Douglas when he was fortune-hunting in America. But Albert Barney, who had already been sufficiently alarmed by Natalie's behavior, was appalled at the possibility of having his family linked with the Oscar Wilde scandal and broke off the engagement. That may have been Natalie's mischievous intention, for she had surely made up her mind against marriage. Washington social life was too formal for her taste, but she put up with it and managed to behave discreetly, though she continued to send flowers and love letters and poems to women she fancied.

4
Literary Debut

The love poems that Natalie wrote at this time were clumsy bits of free verse. To improve her style she began to study French versification on the advice of an old and trusted friend, the French ambassador Jules Cambon. It seems extraordinary that Natalie would have shown her love poems to a man, but throughout life she was to have male confidants, and Cambon was only the first in a series. With women there were often emotional hazards and complications; with men she could be totally candid and express her most intimate ideas. Cambon was typical of the men Natalie preferred: an experienced man of the world who shared her interest in women, an ironic, somewhat philosophical, completely unsentimental spectator of the human comedy. If his wit smacked too much of the plays of Marivaux, that was only to be expected of one accustomed to the niceties of diplomatic expression; and Natalie may have learned something of the art of repartee in conversing with this charming companion.

The young men with whom Natalie danced and flirted may have been rich, handsome and noble, but they seemed fatuous in comparison with the older and wiser men who became her real friends—men like Remy de Gourmont, Philippe Berthelot, Salomon Reinach, Bernard Berenson and André Rouveyre. Scholars, statesmen, writers—all of them cultivated intellectuals—they provided her higher education in the most agreeable way possible, through witty conversation that ranged from the most serious topics to the most frivolous and always remained intelligent, intimate and easy.

Natalie soon had her fill of Washington society and was more than ready to return to Paris to resume her exploration of other worlds. She also wanted to pursue her literary studies, if only to further her pursuit of women. Luckily her mother again decided to spend the winter in Paris in order to devote herself entirely to painting. This time Alice Barney worked at the Académie Jullian and rented a large house with a studio on the Avenue Victor Hugo, in a fashionable residential area near the Bois de Boulogne, far removed from the bohemian haunts of Whistler on the Left Bank. In this neighborhood Natalie was to spend most of the next ten years.

From this point on Paris gradually became her principal place of residence. At the family's urging she continued to spend a summer in Bar Harbor or a winter in Washington, but her homing instincts always brought her back; and after her father's death, in 1902, Paris became her permanent home. Though she was more independent by then, the move represented no break with the past—after all, the Barneys had often stayed in Paris in the course of their travels—and Natalie did not decide to live there in defiance of her father's wishes. Quite probably she did not make a deliberate decision at all but simply found herself more at home there and gradually settled in. Obviously Paris was much more to her liking than Washington because she was much freer in Paris, free from the restraints of American society and less inhibited by conventional French society, with which she had little to do.

"Paris has always seemed to me the only city," she said, "where you can live and express yourself as you please." France, with its Napoleonic Code, was the only country whose laws tolerated homosexuality at that time. And the Parisians, tolerant of all kinds of behavior, left people alone. In contrast, the Anglo-Saxons, with their blue-nosed puritanism, were forever imposing prohibitions. Then, too, Paris was a city for women. London, with its masculine club life, was a man's city, while in Paris men took second place. That explained why Natalie's father frequently stayed in London when her mother stayed in Paris, why Natalie herself went to London as infrequently and briefly as possible and why she never ceased making fun of English men with their frozen emotions and starched manners. "In England," she joked, "nothing is designed for women, not even the men." But above all it was freedom that Paris allowed, and for Natalie that meant freedom to love as she pleased, love being the only thing in life that seemed essential.

In 1899, when she and her mother settled in for the winter, they kept away from the social life of the American colony in order to concentrate on their studies in the arts. While Alice worked at her painting, Natalie studied poetry and worked at her writing. Through Jules Cambon she met Professor Charles Brun, a classical scholar who instructed her in French prosody. At the same time she probably read a good deal of French poetry and formed her taste for the Romantics: Lamartine, Vigny, Gautier and Baudelaire. In English, too, she preferred the Romantic poets, particularly Byron and Keats, along with the inevitable Shakespeare. There was nothing remarkable about her tastes, which were those of her time; nor was there anything remarkable about the poetry she wrote—that is, nothing remarkable about its style. The content was scandalous.

Natalie's first book appeared in 1900, a slim volume of verse entitled *Quelques Portraits-Sonnets de femmes*. This is, frankly, apprentice work, and unfinished at that, with footnotes indicating alternate readings and several fragments of poems that were never completed. The author's apologetic preface presents her as an American who has been struggling to master the strict rules of French rhyme and meter in order to please a pedantic schoolmaster. The poems themselves, mostly sonnets, reveal that the author was an apt pupil whose schoolmaster had curbed every effort to experiment with versification and had probably stifled every attempt at original expression. The style, the imagery and the language of love are all familiar to anyone who has browsed through conventional nineteenth-century French verse. The most daring departures from the commonplace occur in a dedication to the memory of Mallarmé and in a poem echoing Baudelaire, describing kisses as "flowers of evil." But in 1900 it was not too shockingly modern to admire Mallarmé and Baudelaire, both safely dead. The style of Natalie's poetry was never to progress beyond this point. Though she had obvi-

ously made a great effort to master French verse, she was never to
strive for much more than competence.

The result is a strange discrepancy between the banality of style
and the daring candor of the subject matter. Almost all of the poems
are love poems, and the book is unquestionably lesbian, frankly
passionate and promiscuous. Most of the women who inspired the
poems are identified only by initials, if at all. Two are named: Sarah
Bernhardt and Princess Troubetzkoy. The divine Sarah, whom Natalie had seen in the role of Hamlet the year before, is now praised
for taking another masculine role in Rostand's *L'Aiglon*; in both
roles the sexual ambiguity must have appealed to Natalie. The poem
addressed to Princess Troubetzkoy could be read as a conventional
sonneteer's "portrait of my lady," the only difference being that in
this case the courtly poet is herself a lady; however, this poem is
less explicit than some of the others and can be construed as mere
flattery rather than a declaration of love. Princess Troubetzkoy was
an American who wrote under her maiden name, Amélie Rives. She
and her husband, a painter, were friends of the Barneys and had
been their summer guests in Bar Harbor. One newspaper critic
hailed the publication of Natalie's book by calling her "the new
Amélie Rives." Another, more specific, announced, "Sappho
Sings in Washington." There can be no doubt about the lesbian
character of the collection and of the loves that the author sings. The
women addressed in most of these poems are undoubtedly Natalie's
intimates and early lovers. Two of them can be identified: "L"
must be Liane, especially when one of the two poems dedicated to
her expresses love for the goddess Diane; and "P.M.T." stands for
Pauline M. Tarn, of whom more will be said. Though it is tempting
to speculate about others, none of them can be identified with any
degree of certainty, nor is there information about the love affairs
that inspired these poems. There are thirty-four poems in all, addressed to some two dozen different women, a slender output for a
poet but a remarkable record for a lover in her early twenties.

The book was illustrated with four portraits of women by Alice
Barney and the Carolus-Duran portrait of Natalie as frontispiece, as
if to state that the youthful role of page prefaced the author's later
loves. Presumably Alice's portraits were of women Natalie loved;

but, if so, Alice did not know this when they posed for her, any more than she knew what purpose the portraits would serve as illustrations for the book. Evidently Natalie's parents were not too well informed on her private life at this time—a year before the publication of *Idylle saphique*. But as soon as her father read the poems, he understood all too well what his daughter had been up to. Outraged, he went to the publisher and bought up all the copies of the book in order to destroy them, along with the plates. However, Natalie had already distributed a number of copies and probably concealed others, so that a few survive. At her death she still had a copy with revisions penciled in the text, as though she had once thought of publishing the poems again.

In the preface to the book the author explained why she chose to write in French. That language, she said, was the only one that made her think poetically. "I have lived too much of my everyday life in English to preserve any feeling for that language. Writing French verse comes naturally to me." These songs, she commented, were as spontaneous as the nightingale's; but she found French prosody tyrannical and rebelled against its restraints. There is a fundamental contradiction here that always characterized Natalie's style of living as well as her syle of expression, confining spontaneous impulses within strict forms. Her life was American in its unplanned casualness; her speech, French in its controlled precision. She wrote mostly in French because that language expressed her essentially classical temperament. No matter how tempestuous her love affairs, she remained incurably rational, regarding the emotions with a detachment and irony that many took for cold cynicism. Ultimately she found the form that expressed her best in the epigram, the witty spur of the moment fixed with classical economy and form.

By the time the book appeared Natalie had become acquainted with two other writers, one of whom was to play a major role in her life for a time, the other to influence her writing. The first of these was Pauline Tarn, an English girl slightly younger than Natalie who wrote in French under the pseudonym Renée Vivien. The second was Pierre Louÿs, a young French poet who had already made a name for himself as one of the new voices of the 1890s.

"Would Renée Vivien have found her way without me?" Natalie asked in the preface to *Souvenirs indiscrets*, intending by this rhetorical question to establish one of her two major claims to literary fame, the other being that she brought Remy de Gourmont back to life. Renée Vivien found her way when Natalie introduced her to Sappho and to Sapphic love. Their love will be the subject of the next two chapters; more to the point here is the consequence that Renée Vivien started writing love poems to Natalie and at Natalie's suggestion published her first volume of poems, *Études et préludes* (1901). She also studied Greek with Natalie's tutor, Charles Brun, in order to translate Sappho into French verse. Renée Vivien was clearly a talented poet and one who took her writing seriously, as Natalie discovered with surprise; for Natalie's own ambition was to make her life a work of art, and life came ahead of poetry in her scale of values. "My life is my work," she said, "my writings are but the result."

In addition to her poems Natalie was writing a novel which was never to be published. Evidently this was not fiction at all but simply an autobiographical narrative; in *Aventures de l'esprit* she calls it a *roman vécu*—a novel that has been lived. Probably it was an epistolary novel, as its title suggests, *Lettres à une Connue*—letters to a woman she had known. Or perhaps the narrative was interspersed with letters, as are her later volumes of memoirs. One thing is certain: the woman was Liane de Pougy. In other words, Natalie wrote her account of their Sapphic idyll in 1899, two years before Liane's book appeared in print. Since Natalie's was never published, it is tempting to speculate that perhaps the manuscript served as a draft for Liane's book or that Natalie, having failed to publish hers, urged Liane to write their love story. Of course, Liane, who published several other novels, was perfectly capable of writing *Idylle saphique* on her own.

Not surprisingly, the courtesan-novelist understood the taste of her time and knew how to titillate her audience without exceeding the limits of public decency. Natalie, who believed in facing facts squarely, lacked both the courtesan's delicate touch and the novelist's power of invention. The story, as she told it, was too literally based in fact. The publisher who had accepted her poems was shocked by her novel and refused to consider it. Whereupon Natalie made up her mind to turn elsewhere for assistance and wrote a letter to a writer who might be sympathetic.

Pierre Louÿs was only thirty at the time, but he already had quite a reputation, both in literary circles, where he was highly regarded, and with the general public. His novel *Aphrodite* had created a sensation a few years before with its detailed description of the courtesan's life in ancient Alexandria. Though banned in the United States, an illustrated copy turned up in the possession of a friend of the Barneys, and Natalie read it one summer beside a swimming pool in Bar Harbor. She was still a child at the time, she says in *Aventures de l'esprit*, but as a matter of fact she was twenty when the novel appeared, so her childish innocence must have been relative. Presumably this was before her affair with Liane de Pougy.

Later, in France, she read another book by Pierre Louÿs which impressed her even more. *Les Chansons de Bilitis* is a volume of erotic prose poems supposedly written by a poetess contemporary with Sappho and translated from the ancient Greek by Louÿs. Bilitis is merely a woman's name that occurs in several Greek poems, but the learned author endowed her with a biography and gave his book the scholarly trappings of a bibliography and textual notes. This was one of the most successful literary hoaxes of the nineteenth century, and even when the hoax was uncovered, the author was admired for his erudite Hellenism and his purity of style in writing lascivious love poems. Recently the name Bilitis has been adopted by a lesbian organization, the Daughters of Bilitis, not only because many of Louÿs' poems celebrate lesbian love but also in recognition of the author's dedication: "This little book of ancient love is respectfully dedicated to the young women of the future society."

Natalie had reason to take this dedication personally and later responded in kind by dedicating her next book "to Monsieur Pierre Louÿs by a young woman of the future society." In the meantime she had become acquainted with him. When she wrote that her publisher refused to consider her novel, he replied that he would get it published no matter how shocking it might be. Accompanied by Renée Vivien, Natalie paid a call on Louÿs and delivered her manuscript. The notorious author proved to be a mild-mannered gentleman who shunned publicity, but he received them graciously, presenting each of them with his *Chansons de Bilitis* in a deluxe edition. Renée's copy he inscribed with a line from Keats' "Ode on a Grecian Urn," which he divided tellingly into two:

> Forever wilt thou love,
> And she be fair!

His inscription in Natalie's copy addressed her as a "young woman of the future society." But there was nothing he could do to get her novel published; despite all his efforts, no publisher would take it. The characters were too literally based on real people, and the writing left much to be desired.

In *Aventures de l'esprit* Natalie published the letters Louÿs wrote to her, several of which offer criticism and advice. One of these explains what was wrong with her novel. Some of the letters in the novel, he commented, were written in an idiom that was slightly outmoded, expressing sentiments in a style that had been discredited through overuse by second-rate writers. This failing was to characterize much of Natalie's writing. Because she was not truly dedicated to literature, she never took the pains to express herself as well as she might but fell back on the ready-made phrase, content to produce work that was facile but derivative. She was an indifferent writer, both in the sense of not caring and in the sense that her work was undistinguished.

Yet she had talent. Louÿs found some passages in the novel "admirable," advised her to rewrite it in a different form and offered to give specific guidance. He was confident that she could make something of the novel and even willing to provide a preface if she would rewrite it. Urging her to go on writing, he prophesied, "You will be famous, I am sure of it." In another letter Louÿs commented on the book of poetry Natalie had sent him and on some poems by Renée Vivien. He found Renée's poems beautiful but preferred Natalie's; and after reading their love poems he advised her to write the story of their relationship as the first chapter of her novel. Once again he urged her to rewrite the novel, praising its merits and offering to outline the book as it should be revised. But Natalie had no literary ambitions and never took the trouble to follow his advice.

Louÿs became her friend and remained a friend for the rest of his life. This was the first of those literary friendships that she wrote about in *Aventures de l'esprit* and cultivated throughout her life. She liked him personally—that was the basis of the friendship—but she also admired his art and aesthetics. In fact, she found his work so much to her liking that she imitated it in her second book, published in 1902. *Cinq Petits Dialogues grecs* is written in very much the same vein as Louÿs' books about pagan love, employing the same kind of poetic prose and expressing the same attitudes toward the same subjects.

The first of these five little dialogues is set in the time of Sappho, like his *Chansons de Bilitis*, and sings of Sapphic love. The second, a debate on the merits of the old Greek hedonism versus the new Christian religion, uses arguments that Louÿs set forth in his preface to *Aphrodite*, defending the life of the senses, as it was accepted in ancient Greece, against the denial of the body by Christianity. The other three dialogues are conducted by experienced courtesans and deal with situations somewhat reminiscent of those in *Aphrodite*. In one, for instance, the courtesan rails against a man who tries to force himself upon her; in another, a young girl envies the beauty and jewels of a courtesan, but the courtesan advises her to remain a virgin. Natalie acknowledged Louÿs not only in her dedication but in publishing the book under the pseudonym Tryphé, which she probably took from the preface to *Aphrodite*.

Cinq Petits Dialogues grecs shows that Natalie was very much in sympathy with the cult of Hellenism celebrated by Pierre Louÿs and others. Of course, she had reasons of her own for harking back to the spirit of ancient Greece, not all of them related to the love of classical learning. These reasons are best expressed in the first dialogue, the only one which is explicitly lesbian, when one of the characters sings the praises of Sappho. Like all women who have followed their natures, like all those who have dared to live, like destiny itself, Sappho is irresistible. Her love will outlive the ages. Her passions are fleeting, but they make one dream of the infinite.

She is more faithful in her inconstancy than others in their fidelity. She is an elemental force, like fire; a flame which destroys and glorifies. She is like a goddess of whom even Aphrodite is jealous, but at the same time she is a mortal woman, subject to all the torments of love.

This long and eloquent apostrophe to Sappho is the most striking passage in the entire book. Here, for once, the author seems to be speaking in her own voice, expressing something deeply and intimately felt—nothing less than the conviction that she is the reincarnation of Sappho. Natalie usually regarded herself with detachment, but in this speech she seems to be dedicating herself to reliving the life of the ancient Greek poetess, of whom she writes: "Her poetry and her music are but the accompaniment of her loves. . . . When she speaks, she seems to exist only for art; when she loves, one knows that she lives only for love."

5
Renée Vivien

There is not a single feature of her youthful face that I do not viv-idly recall. Everything in it bespoke childishness, roguishness, and the propensity to laughter. Impossible to find anywhere in that face, from the fair hair to the sweet dimple of the weak little chin, any line that was not a line of laughter, any sign of the hidden tragic melan-choly that throbs in the poetry of Renée Vivien.

—Colette, *Le Pur et l'impur*

Colette would never have predicted that Renée Vivien would at-tempt suicide, would in effect commit suicide by wasting away to an early death. Colette was a neighbor of Renée, saw her frequently and received many letters from her, but was not privy to her inner-most thoughts. Thus she saw only the laughing childlike exterior and could not fathom the underlying melancholy and longing for death. Nevertheless Colette was an astute observer and, unlike most of those who wrote about Renée Vivien, was not emotionally in-volved. Her full-length portrait in *Le Pur et l'impur* may have dissatisfied Natalie, but it is more reliable than anything Natalie ever wrote about Renée. Colette watched her neighbor's behavior with detachment and curiosity, baffled by the apparent contradictions: the coarseness of speech that contrasted strangely with the poetry, the

despair concealed beneath the childishness that she affected in her
letters, the deceptive appearance.

> The charming face of Renée Vivien reflected only a part of that child-
> like quality, in the rounded cheek, soft and downy, in the innocent
> short upper lip, so typically English, curled up and revealing four lit-
> tle front teeth. A bright smile constantly lit up her eyes, a chestnut-
> brown which became greenish in the sunlight. She wore her long,
> beautiful ash-blond hair, which was fine and straight, massed at the
> top of her head, from which stray locks came down now and then like
> wisps of fine straw.

It was easy to be deceived by this exterior, but Natalie said that
from the first day they met she was struck by Renée's preoccupation
with death. Therefore, she saw it as her mission to bring sunshine
and warmth into Renée's life, just as earlier she had undertaken the
quixotic task of rescuing Liane from an unworthy existence. In neither case was she disinterested, and if she devoted herself over a period of ten years to the cause of saving Renée, it was obviously because she was deeply involved. Renée was Natalie's first great love.
Compared with this, Natalie's affair with Liane was but a passing
fancy. And for Renée, Natalie was the love of her life. For two
years they were deeply in love with each other, lived together and
shared in an intimacy such as neither had known before. After that
they were separated for a time, and their relationship was never the
same again. Still drawn to each other, they succeeded once or twice
in reliving those moments of ardor that had originally brought them
together; but their love was frustrated in its later stages, complicated
by jealousies and characterized more by recriminations than by
affection or understanding.

In many ways Natalie and Renée appeared well-matched. Born
into the same moneyed class and endowed with intelligence and talent, they had much in common to begin with. Renée was the product
of an international marriage such as Henry James might have
arranged between the English gentry and American wealth; but
otherwise her family background and upbringing were similar to
Natalie's. Her childhood was somewhat unsettled by her parents'

travels, and she was educated in boarding schools on the Continent. In Paris, at the age of thirteen, she formed a deep attachment to an American girl named Violet Shilleto, with whom she lived happily for three years until her parents brought her back to England. There she made her debut and was presented at court, like any marriageable daughter of good family. But beneath this exterior lurked a desperate character. Her reaction to the debutante's social round was like Natalie's, only much more vehement; instead of boredom she felt panic, revulsion at the thought of marriage, rebellion and the need to escape. Renée was always to be more emotional and uncompromising than Natalie, who was generally more amenable, even willing to go along with her father's intentions to marry her off. Natalie was also gregarious, whereas Renée, passionately committed to individuals, was basically antisocial. Thus, although they had much in common, temperamentally they were totally different and ultimately destined to go their separate ways.

During the five years that she spent in England, Renée felt stifled by conventional society and longed to return to Paris as soon as she could make her escape. Finally, in 1898, when she came of age, she prevailed upon her parents and was allowed to live in Paris, with a chaperone. She had been in correspondence with Violet Shilleto during their years of separation, pouring out her heart to the only friend who could understand; and now she found lodgings in a *pension* near the Avenue du Bois de Boulogne, where Violet lived with her parents, in the same neighborhood where Natalie and her mother were to live soon after. Now it happened that the Shilletos had been neighbors of the Barneys in Cincinnati, and the four little girls— Natalie and Laura, Violet and her sister Mary—had been playmates and had learned French together. They had not seen each other for years, and Natalie was overjoyed to meet Violet and Mary by chance one day in the Bois de Boulogne. The sisters had grown up, but their characters were still the same; and Natalie rediscovered the brown eyes and gentle gravity of Violet, who had always attracted her. As soon as they heard that Natalie wrote poetry, the sisters decided that she must meet their friend Renée and proposed that they all go to the theater together.

Just as they were setting out for the theater, Natalie received a letter from Liane de Pougy and became so flustered that she paid no attention when Renée was introduced, except to note that she was rather pretty but otherwise unimpressive. At the theater, unable to follow either the play or her friends' conversation, she finally withdrew to read Liane's long, mood-drenched letter from Portugal, which reminisced sadly about their lost love. After the play, her friends proposed a ride in the Bois, and as they drove along in their carriage on that frosty evening, Violet asked Renée to recite one of her poems. As soon as she heard the opening lines, Natalie forgot all about Liane. Moved by the poetry and overcome by its sadness, Natalie made up her mind to rescue this talented girl by giving her a desire for life.

The poem voiced a yearning for sleep, darkness and death, which Renée's appearance also expressed. Though her eyes often sparkled gaily, there was also melancholy in her look. And everything about her seemed pathetic; the somber colors and ill-fitting clothes that she wore, the weak chin and dull complexion, the awkward gestures and trembling hands, the demoralized set of her shoulders. Yet she had a childlike sense of fun that sometimes made her seem ten years old, and her color glowed when she grew animated. Natalie saw in Renée the same contradictions observed by Colette. But the real mystery was how this rather mediocre young woman came to be possessed of poetic genius.

Shortly after this first encounter, the Shilletos departed for Nice, where they had a villa, leaving Natalie and Renée to become better acquainted. After seeing them off, Renée invited Natalie to the Ice Palace so that she could demonstrate how well she skated. There is something of the ingenue about Renée in this scene as described in *Souvenirs indiscrets*—the slender figure flying gracefully over the ice while in the background Natalie espied several professional beauties whom she had last seen in the company of Liane. And generally there was an air of virginal innocence about Renée, whose love for Violet had been intense but not physical. Yet she seems to have welcomed the love that Natalie was to bring into her life. It was she who set the stage one night by inviting Natalie to her room, which she had filled with white lilies—the flowers she had dedicated to Natalie—dazzling and asphyxiating the senses, transforming the room into a chapel of love in which the two devotees knelt before each other. Natalie left at daybreak, her footprints in the frost marking the path from Renée's door to her own. The circumstances of this wintry courtship were poetic enough in Natalie's fairly matter-of-fact account; Renée was to transmute them into a Symbolist novel.

Looking back, Natalie found their love ill-matched from the start, her own based on desire while Renée seemed hardly aroused physically. Natalie's love was fired by her senses; Renée's, inflamed by her imagination. After each tryst Renée would send flowers and poems, expressing her adoration in extravagant terms. Even more extravagantly, when they began living together, she covered Natalie with jewelry, forcing her to wear all kinds of Lalique rings, necklaces, bracelets on her arms and ankles, and a strange comb shaped like a golden dragon spewing forth opals in her hair, until Natalie felt like an idol on a pedestal. Though embarrassed, Natalie recognized the need Renée felt to worship somebody or something and suspected that a Christian soul lurked beneath her paganism. Not everyone who wished could be a pagan, Natalie remarked, not even one whose writing was inspired by Sappho. But at least Renée's poetry was turning from death to love, and "Vivien," the pseudonym she chose when she began publishing her poems, signified that she had been reborn to life. Throughout their love affair, Natalie's avowed purpose was to give Renée the will to live.

But all was not solemnity and gloom in their relationship. Renée had a lively sense of humor, and she and Natalie often laughed together. When Renée's first book of poems was published under the name R. Vivien, some readers assumed that the author was a man addressing his mistress, "Lorély." Where a self-satisfied young critic who made a career of discovering new talent gave a lecture based on this assumption, Renée and Natalie sat in the audience, convulsed with laughter. Later, when it became known that Renée was a woman and admirers sought her out, she had her chaperone pose as Renée Vivien. The chaperone was an ample woman, with a beaked nose crowned by a large wart, whose unpoetic aspect was enough to disillusion the most ardent poetry-lovers. This moral guardian, to the great delight of Renée and Natalie, fell in love with their classics professor. He, too, was something of a caricature—a tall, thin, bony, ink-stained individual who wore a dusty frock coat and whose pince-nez were forever falling off his nose. This grotesque couple, Natalie remarked, were hardly designed to convert the two young women to normal love.

Their entertainments also reflected Natalie's fondness for masquerade and make-believe. She liked to be photographed in various costumes with her lovers, each taking turns posing as page or mistress, shepherd or nymph. Natalie also posed as Hamlet, probably inspired by Sarah Bernhardt and by a sonnet Renée addressed to Natalie, discovering in her the attributes of both Hamlet and Ophelia:

> Your royal youth has the melancholy
> Of the North, where mists blot out all color:
> Pale as Ophelia, grave as Hamlet,
> You mingle desire and discord with tears.
>
> You pass in a blaze of fine madness,
> Like her, lavishing flowers and songs,
> Like him, concealing pain with pride,
> Forgetting nothing in your fixed gaze.
>
> Smile, blonde love; dream, dark lover;
> Your double self attracts a double love,
> And your flesh burns cold like a candle.
>
> My heart is disconcerted when I see in you
> The forehead of a pensive prince, the blue eyes of a maid,
> Now one, now the other, now both at once.

In other poems Renée addressed Natalie as "Atthis," giving her the name of one of Sappho's favorite loves. And Natalie, who had introduced Renée to Sappho, proposed that they band together with other poetesses in a group like that which Sappho had gathered around her on Lesbos. This idea occurred to her when she came across a book of poems by a young English writer, Olive Custance. When Natalie wrote to Olive proposing that they form a Sapphic circle and sent Renée's book of poems together with her own, Olive replied that nothing would please her better,

For I would dance to make you smile and sing
Of those who with some sweet mad sin have played,
And how Love walks with delicate feet afraid
Twixt maid and maid.

This and other schemes to revive the golden age of Sappho have been held up to ridicule, but it is hard to say how serious Natalie was or just what she had in mind. Given her ironic sense of humor, it appears unlikely that she could have taken the idea too literally, though she was genuinely impressed by Sappho as a kindred spirit, and in this she was not flattering herself. At twenty-three or twenty-four, Natalie had an incredibly clear-eyed view of herself and of Sappho, this at a time when Victoria still reigned and Sappho in translation sounded like Swinburne or Christina Rossetti. Nowadays Sappho is no longer bowdlerized, but she continues to be sentimentalized and sensationalized. Natalie, though she had little poetic talent and less Greek, nevertheless saw through the translations and perceived the essential woman. This was the kind of woman she wanted to be—a lover of beauty and the life of the senses, frankly sensual in her love of women and free to love as she chose. In this she was like the ancient Greeks who celebrated the life of the body and regarded love as an aesthetic pleasure, not a moral issue. Genuinely pagan—pre-Christian, non-Hebraic and anti-Romantic—she was free of the trammels that have controlled the behavior of most lovers of this millennium. It is important to understand this if Natalie is not to appear utterly cynical in her love affairs. This outlook Renée was quite incapable of appreciating, for all her love of Sappho's poetry and for all the paganism in her early poems and stories.

Olive Custance came to Paris in the spring of 1901. When Natalie kissed this fresh young creature blossoming with color and vibrant with poetry, she felt as if she were embracing the English countryside. Renée sulked, protesting that she disliked the company of her compatriots, finding Olive too cheerful and unworthy of her poetry. Citing chapter and verse from Sappho, Natalie reminded Renée that Sappho had welcomed all who came from afar to join her circle, even those of whom she was jealous. She also pointed out that it was possible to be at once fickle and faithful in love, as Atthis and Sappho had been when they had fallen in love with other women and still remained true to each other. By this she meant that no one could come between them; but, ironically, that very night a message came from Violet Shilleto, who was wasting away with a mysterious ailment and wanted Renée at her bedside. Renée left immediately for Nice, leaving Natalie suddenly bereft and lonely.

But Natalie was not one to languish. The next day she accepted Olive's invitation to tea with her mother and a handsome young Englishman called Freddy, who was the son and heir of the Viscount of Canterbury. That afternoon Natalie invited Olive to visit her again; and Freddy, as he escorted Natalie to her carriage, shyly asked to be invited, too. Supposing that he was jealous, she explained that they were only going to discuss poetry and suggested that he call for Olive afterward. But she soon learned that Freddy had fallen in love with her. When Olive reported this unexpected development, Natalie said, "Tell him I'm in love with you." Freddy did not care; he was not to be dissuaded, but he was not a demanding suitor, either; all he asked was to see Natalie once in a while. So from time to time they went out together with Olive and her mother, Freddy gazing at Natalie and saying clever things with his charming stammer until Natalie finally found him annoying.

Needless to say, she was much more attracted to Olive, especially after an evening they spent bathed in moonlight and poetry. One evening was not enough, however; Natalie wanted to be alone with Olive for a longer time. So when Mrs. Custance and Freddy returned to England, Olive and Natalie went off to Venice, accompanied by the inevitable chaperone, the ugly one whose Aztec profile somewhat spoiled the romance of riding in a gondola. And what was to have been a romantic escapade ended in misery when both young women came down with malaria.

While they lay shivering in their beds, the chaperone was the one to have a romantic adventure—with a sea captain. So Natalie remained faithful in her fashion, and Olive hung the photograph of her lover over her bed. This was none other than Lord Alfred Douglas, who was also deeply in love with Olive, the more so because both families opposed the marriage. The obvious solution was reminiscent of the scheme Natalie had hatched to rescue Liane with the help of her millionaire suitor Will: this time she would rescue Olive by marrying Douglas, and the three of them would live happily ever after in a *ménage à trois*. With these plans the young women ended their chaste Venetian romance, Olive returning to England and Natalie to Paris.

Soon after this, in June, 1901, Natalie learned of the death of Violet Shilleto, and Renée returned to Paris overwhelmed by grief. Rejecting Natalie's sympathy, she locked herself in her room, sometimes sobbing all night long or keening in an ecstasy of sorrow. Once again she was drawn toward death, this time more obsessively than before. When Natalie investigated what Renée was writing, she found poem after poem dedicated to death, even one in which she, Natalie, was being mourned as a beloved corpse. But Renée stubbornly refused to confide in her, perhaps blaming Natalie for having come between herself and Violet. Most of the time Renée went about in a trance, ignoring Natalie's presence; then, one day, Natalie began packing for a trip to America, and Renée suddenly announced that she was going, too.

Hoping to bring Renée back into the sunlight, Natalie took her along for a summer in Bar Harbor, arriving on a boat called the *Sappho*. There she found the intimate companion of her adolescence, Eva Palmer, with whom Renée spent the evenings quietly studying Greek while Natalie, in accordance with her parents' wishes, participated in the social life of Bar Harbor. Often, when Natalie came home after dancing into the early hours of the morning, the three of them would go swimming together in pools of clear spring water, sometimes taking a camera along to record their gambols. The photograph of Natalie as a wood nymph arrayed in the great outdoors probably dates from one of these outings. At one time there were many such photographs in Natalie's collection, chaste examples of Pre-Raphaelite nudity with lilies and irises as props; but after Natalie's death, all the others were burned in a regrettable suttee.

After the summer at Bar Harbor, Eva, Renée, and Natalie spent the fall in Bryn Mawr, Pennsylvania, where Eva had gone to college. Natalie found the atmosphere of the college stimulating, attended the literature classes of Miss Gwynn and literally sat at her feet, reading a poem she had written in her honor. There was something self-conscious about Natalie seated on her stool at the feet of this intellectual feminist, something reminiscent of the photographs for which she posed: she seemed to be watching herself from outside and fancying herself in certain roles. While Natalie was absorbed in these heady encounters with Professor Mary Gwynn, Renée was off moping in a nearby graveyard, inconsolable as ever and haunted by death. The summer sunlight was forgotten, and the autumn weather had brought back her melancholy moods. Besides, she and Natalie were now to part: Natalie, to spend the winter in Washington with her family; Renée, to return to Paris and live in the apartment below the Shilletos', the better to brood on Violet's death. And although they were supposed to be reunited in Paris the following spring, both must have suspected that their life together was at an end.

Back in Paris, Renée began to lead the morbid life that was to characterize her remaining years. She no longer answered Natalie's letters and no longer visited Mary Shilleto, from whom Natalie heard that Renée was furnishing her apartment in a strange manner. There are several descriptions of that apartment—with its dim light, heavy hangings and Oriental decor—the most vivid by Romaine Brooks, who viewed the setting with a painter's eye:

> There comes before me the dark heavily curtained room, overreaching itself in lugubrious effects: grim life-sized Oriental figures sitting propped up on chairs, phosphorescent Buddhas glowing dimly in the folds of black draperies. The air is heavy with perfumed incense. A curtain draws aside and Renée Vivien stands before us attired in Louis XVI male costume. Her straight blond hair falls to her shoulders, her flower-like face is bent down; she does not lift it even to greet us. Though I know that she is a very gifted poetess it is difficult to detect other than a seemingly affected and childish personality. Besides it is the claptrap of her surroundings that holds perforce the attention. We lunch seated on the floor Oriental fashion and scant food is served on ancient Damascus ware, cracked and stained. During the meal Renée Vivien leaves us to bring in from the garden her pet frogs and a serpent which she twines round her wrist.

The poems that Renée wrote after her return to Paris were full of violets and death; all her passion had turned to grief and remorse.

When a later volume of poetry appeared, Natalie was to find references to herself in the past tense, notably in one poem recalling their moments together and ending with the refrain "I loved you, Atthis."

During the time Renée was writing such poems and no longer communicating by letter, Natalie was being the dutiful daughter in Washington, all the while seething with anxiety to know what was happening to Renée. Finally, in the spring of 1902, she returned to Paris and immediately rushed to Renée's apartment, only to be informed that Renée was out. Waiting in the courtyard outside, she saw Renée drive up and ran out to meet her, but Renée ordered her chauffeur to drive on. Natalie then went sadly upstairs to call on Mary Shilleto but learned nothing that would explain Renée's mysterious behavior until that evening, when Renée appeared in the garden below, walking with another woman with whom she was plainly on intimate terms. In *Souvenirs indiscrets* Natalie describes this woman as a fat, rich and domineering Valkyrie and wonders what magic spell she had cast. Others have also blamed this woman for her evil domination and identified her as a Dutch baroness, Hélène van Zuylen de Nievelt, née Rothschild. From this point on, Renée, who had dedicated her first volume to "N——," dedicated all her books to "H. L. C. B."; the last two initials may suggest Clifford Barney or Charles Brun, the classics professor who helped Renée with her translations; but all four initials belonged to Renée's new lover, whose given name was Helen Betty Louise Caroline. Together the two of them collaborated on several volumes of verse and prose published under the pseudonym Paule Riversdale.

Natalie jilted presents an unusual spectacle, trying to convince herself that her only concern was Renée's happiness and that Renée's later poems revealed a continuing love. Ignoring the indications that Renée no longer wished to see her, she preferred to believe that only her rival's watchful jealousy kept them apart. Baffled, yet ever the woman of action, she tried to win back Renée by addressing poems to her in Sapphic meters and riding her horse in front of Renée's house. When these tactics aroused no response, she enlisted the help of friends in several operatic maneuvers. Disguised as street singers, she and the opera star Emma Calvé serenaded Renée one night; that is Calvé sang the lament of Orpheus for his Eurydice, and when Renée opened her window, Natalie threw her a bouquet containing a sonnet in which she begged to see her. The poem and the flowers were promptly sent back with a curt note from Renée's chaperone asking Natalie to cease and desist. Next, Natalie asked Eva Palmer to intercede for her, and though Renée welcomed Eva, she refused to see Natalie. Instead she made advances to Eva and invited her to the opera, thus giving Natalie the opportunity she sought, for Natalie took Eva's place in Renée's box. For once the ruse worked, as Renée received her with open arms and they sat listening to Schumann's *Manfred,* clasped in an embrace. After the opera Renée drove Natalie home, promising to meet her again the next day. But Renée had a change of heart overnight and failed to appear for the rendezvous. When Natalie telephoned, Renée said that she could not relive the past; but upon hearing that Natalie's father was gravely ill, she offered her assistance. Sick at heart but unyielding in her pride, Natalie answered, "I need no one," and hung up.

Natalie had just received a telegram that her father was dying of heart failure in Monte Carlo. Before the train could get her there, he had died, after awaking from a happy dream that Natalie was marrying Freddy. Natalie, who had heard too much about death from Renée, beheld a corpse for the first time in her life. She was surprised to find how peaceful her father looked, as if he were saying, "Do not come too near, this is the only untroubled moment, the only quiet ever known. Keep the memory of it and do not mourn." Probably influenced by Renée's morbid outlook rather than the fear of death itself, Natalie had a lifelong aversion to funerals and mourning. But on this occasion, with none of her family in Europe, she saw it as her duty to have him cremated in Paris and to escort his ashes back to America, accompanied by the ever-loyal Eva and Freddy. Then, after all the obsequies and legal formalities had been completed, Natalie, having inherited a share of her father's wealth and gained her independence, returned to Paris and settled with Eva in Freddy's apartment, almost directly across the street from Renée's, determined to pursue her obsession to regain Renée.

Some time seems to have elapsed, or else Natalie was not as single-minded in her pursuit of Renée as her memoirs would suggest; for her father died in December, 1902, and the next chapter in the romance occurred a year and a half later. And of course, Natalie had other love affairs in the meanwhile, though none that made her forget Renée. In the summer of 1904, learning that Renée had gone to the Wagner festival in Bayreuth, Natalie and Eva went there to seek her. From the balcony of the opera house they had no trouble finding her, nor did Renée try to escape when Eva told her that Natalie was there. Instead she readily traded seats with Eva and every night thereafter sat holding hands with Natalie, both of them transported by Wagner's music. This reunion provided Natalie with the opportunity to give Renée the sequence of prose poems she had been writing for some time, *Je me souviens,* commemorating their love and expressing her sense of loss. The last prose poem, written in Bayreuth as Renée's departure approached, asked her to come for a rendezvous in a sad and lonely garden in the middle of the city:

> A deserted palace is reflected in the lifeless water. Amid the faded leaves two similar but hostile swans come and go without leaving any wake. This place has no life of its own but the reflection of things past, no dreams but of memory.

Renée answered this appeal and went to the garden for a tearful farewell on the night of her departure. However, she promised to meet Natalie in Vienna and to go with her to Lesbos. Natalie would have been happy to have Renée to herself anywhere in the world, but Renée, still apprehensive, seemed willing only to accept Natalie on Sappho's island. Thrilled at this pilgrimage and full of poetic sentiments, she rose at dawn as their ship approached the harbor at Mytilene, only to have her romantic illusions shattered by the sound of a phonograph blaring out a vulgar French song. The women of the island and the debased language they spoke proved a further disappointment; the only good-looking Lesbians they saw were stevedores, fishermen, and shepherds. But the place had a charm to which they easily succumbed, and their poems sang of this enchanted island with its balmy seas, fragrance of jasmine and beautiful nights full of love. They rented two little villas in an orchard, where

Renée vowed she would stay, forever waiting for Natalie; and Natalie pointed out that she had no reason to go away. During this idyllic interlude Renée worked on her translation of Sappho, and Natalie once again proposed that they found a Sapphic school of poetry and love.

The dream was abruptly ended by a letter from Renée's baroness announcing that she was about to leave for Lesbos. In the face of this formidable and determined person of unlimited wealth and power, Renée gave way and decided that it was best for her to return in order to break the news that she intended to live with Natalie. That, at least, is Natalie's explanation in *Souvenirs indiscrets,* and the letters Renée wrote in the ensuing period confirm it. There was a strong element of fatalism in Renée's actions, and she may have been rationalizing her behavior out of weakness or soft-heartedness, hoping things would work out somehow and not wanting to hurt anybody's feelings. Of course, her proposal of returning to Lesbos with Natalie was bound to be rejected by the baroness, and she must have known it. Weak and passive as she was, Renée may even have chosen to subject her will to another's in order to escape from Natalie's all-consuming passion. Whatever the reason, she wrote loving letters to Natalie that gently, gradually, regretfully slipped into the retrospective tense, and before long she was writing to ask Natalie to give up the lease on her villa, as she was planning to return to Lesbos with the baroness. From her villa Renée wrote that Natalie's blond ghost still haunted the orchard; but the letter was unmistakably a farewell, as was another, which concluded, "Return to the sea, my Siren, since I the daughter of Earth have returned to the black depths." Persephone had gone back to the underworld.

For the last five years of Renée's life, she and Natalie continued to write letters and occasionally contrived to meet, always fleetingly and unsatisfactorily. In one of her letters Renée asks Natalie to come and see her any evening; in another she is heartbroken because she is unable to come that night; in others she vacillates between apprehension and desire. Several times Natalie attended soirees at Renée's apartment, finding old acquaintances there like their classics professor, Charles Brun, who had remained faithful to Renée. At one of these soirees Colette danced and the actress Marguerite Moreno recited poetry. Natalie brought her new love with her several times, an actress with golden eyes; and on one occasion she agreed to have dinner with Renée's lover, who was no longer jealous of Natalie but curious to meet her. Natalie describes that encounter in *Souvenirs indiscrets*. The baroness had bought a sumptuous evening dress for the occasion, and Natalie paid "that opulent person" an ironic compliment, comparing the sumptuous evening gown she had bought for the occasion to the blue Aegean, with its silver islands ringed with diamonds, while each of them remembered Lesbos in her own way. At the end of the evening the aggressive baroness offered to drive Natalie home and would have followed Natalie into her house if she had been allowed.

There are several descriptions of Renée as she appeared during her last years. Clearly she had lost all her will to live and was wasting away. "Her life was but a long suicide," Natalie said; and, as a matter of fact, Renée seems to have attempted suicide more than once. She also made desperate efforts to escape from her possessive lover and finally succeeded by joining some of her relatives on a voyage around the world. While she was gone, Natalie moved away from the neighborhood of the Bois de Boulogne, where she and Renée had lived so intensely, to the Rue Jacob, on the Left Bank, hoping that there she could welcome Renée in a place that had no unhappy memories. But Renée wrote that she no longer saw anyone and did not want to see Natalie, that their old love must be forgotten and buried. This brief note, written on Renée's stationery, with a garland of violets across the top, may be the last word Natalie received from Renée. Six months later, in November, 1909, she heard that Renée was gravely ill and promptly went to her apartment to ask for news, bringing a bunch of violets. At the door she was met by a butler she had never seen before, who announced in a matter-of-fact voice, "Mademoiselle has just died," in the same tone as he might have said, "Mademoiselle has just gone out." Thrusting the violets at him, Natalie staggered to the street and collapsed on a bench in a faint.

Three days before her death Renée had converted to Catholicism in order to be reunited in heaven with Violet Shilleto, who had also died a Catholic. According to one account, Renée's dying words were "This is the best moment of my life." According to another, she died breathing the name she had given to her blond siren: "Lorély." And her biographer, André Germain, claims that on her deathbed she said of Lorély, "She was my only love." Natalie was left grieving over Renée's souvenirs, but she had known ever since that brief interlude in Lesbos five years before that their love was doomed, just as she had known all along that she and Renée were as different as life and death. Though their love ended in defeat, Natalie consoled herself with the thought that it had also provided inspiration for Renée, whose miserable life had made her a great poet. She might also have observed that their love had inspired her own best poetry, that in *Je me souviens*.

The death of Renée evoked still more poetry, some of it seemingly dictated from beyond the grave, with Natalie merely serving as medium. The following year she announced a work in progress to be called *Le Tombeau de Renée Vivien*, but no such work was ever published. Four poems in memory of Renée appeared in Natalie's *Actes et entr'actes*, lamenting the death of the poet who was the "lover of autumn and of early death," celebrating her immortality in the company of other poets who died young—Keats and Chatterton, Villon and Marlowe—and offering the laments of sirens, watery spirits without body or heart, whose tears, like Renée's, were bitter as the sea.

At the death of Violet, Renée had lamented that this free spirit who loved the earth and sky should have been confined in a cold Christian funeral. Similarly, Natalie in one of her laments for Renée, noted the irony that this pagan who had repudiated Christ in her poetry should have died a Catholic and been given a Christian burial. Renée was buried in the little cemetery of Passy, in the section of Paris where she had spent most of her short, unhappy life. Natalie, who lived most of her long and happy life in another section of Paris, was buried in the same cemetery sixty-three years later, having somehow managed to obtain a plot there even though the cemetery was overcrowded. But she was not exactly reunited with Renée in death. Renée lies near the entrance to the cemetery, in a monumental family vault. Natalie is buried inconspicuously under a modest stone some distance away, side by side with her sister Laura.

6
Renée's Side of the Story

During the last eight years of her brief life Renée Vivien poured out a dozen volumes of poetry and three collections of short stories. She also wrote one so-called novel, *Une Femme m'apparut,* which tells the story of her love for Natalie. Like Natalie's book of prose-poems on the same subject, Renée's is closer to autobiography than to fiction, closer to poetry than to prose. This is not realistic narrative but a sequence of rhapsodies and exotic dream-visions. Still it provides some insight into the relationship that existed between Renée and Natalie and while presenting Renée's point of view, makes it possible to see both of them more clearly.

From the start the book gives off the feverish and sickly atmosphere in which Renée lived—a hectic overheated atmosphere, luxuriant with hothouse flowers, teeming with morbid dreams—the atmosphere of the late-nineteenth-century style of Decadence. Where Liane de Pougy narrated the story of a seduction in a series of objectively rendered scenes, Renée gives a highly subjective, expressionistic rendering of experiences that to her were mystical. This is a Symbolist love story, often interpreted in religious terms.

The story begins with the Angel of the Annunciation, a feminine spirit as enigmatic as Leonardo's John the Baptist. She says to the narrator (who is given no name but is clearly Renée), "I pity you because you have never suffered. . . . I pity your empty

heart. . . . I shall take you to Lorély. . . .'' This character, who
represents Natalie, is the priestess of a pagan cult that has just been
revived, the cult of Sapphic love.

Lorély is beautiful but cold, with eyes like ice, and is associated
with winter and moonlight. Her jewel is the moonstone, and when
she takes Renée out riding on a cold wintry night, she is like a Nor-
dic princess wrapped up in her white furs. In contemplating her,
Renée understands that insatiable love of woman that leads people
to seek her everywhere—in the fountains and the rivers, in the forest
and the sea. Lorély is like Undine and Viviane, an enchantress with
magical powers; she is all nymphs, goddesses and sirens; at times
she is even the incarnation of the Madonna.

But Lorély is suffering from ennui, she wants to fall in love, she
wants to be loved. Renée, who has never known anything but platonic love, succumbs. One evening, in a chapel, Lorély appears to
her in a mystical vision as the Virgin, standing on the moon with a
halo of stars. And in another religious scene Lorély unveils herself
by moonlight, the most perfect, immaculate flesh, transfigured for
mystic adoration. But there is nothing Christian about her. A pagan
exile from Lesbos, she asks, as Christmas approaches, ''What is
this Christmas? Does it commemorate the birth of Christ or the
death? I don't remember.'' Perhaps she never knew.

Though the priestess and goddess of love, Lorély remains unmoved by love. She loves many women without falling in love herself. She preaches against marriage to a girl of twenty, who aban-
dons her fiancé for Lorély, only to be abandoned herself a few
weeks later. Another woman, Doriane, suffers from unrequited love
for Lorély, who can only weep because she is incapable of love. Yet
she soon begins declaring her love for still another woman, Nedda,
and shortly thereafter announces that she was only playacting. Then
Renée, waiting for Lorély, wanders into her garden, where she
overhears Lorély exchanging declarations of love with a man! How
could she, my virginal priestess? The Spirit of Annunciation reap-
pears briefly to explain that Lorély likes to exercise her power over
men and that she finds torture amusing.

All of this is hard on poor Renée. To make things harder, her former love Ione is pining away. This chaste friend, with whom Renée
grew up, has been like a sister to her. Ione points out that Renée has

become a walking shadow since falling in love with Lorély, nothing but the reflection and echo of Lorély. Ione retires to a convent, where she finds peace and dies happy, mourned by Renée, who has now been deserted by Lorély. Ione's coffin is surrounded by white violets, for she liked violets best of all flowers and whiteness and daylight are associated with her, just as lilies and moonlight are associated with Lorély. Throughout the novel, flowers, jewels, seasons and times of day are symbolically expressive of different characters.

Doubly bereaved, Renée goes to Spain to forget her sorrows, only to see Ione resurrected in a dream and Lorély as an apparition of the Madonna of the Plague of Toledo. From this point on the narrative becomes less coherent, but it is evident that Renée is fated to return to her love for Lorély. Meanwhile, she is attracted to two other women, who are obviously introduced as foils to Lorély. Dagmar, with her necklace of opals, is a little fairy-tale princess, pretty as a piece of Saxe porcelain and ingenuous as a child, but, unfortunately, bisexual. Alas, one day her prince arrives. Then Eva appears, more like a vision than a real person, autumnal and compassionate. But Lorély returns, saying that she has come to take Renée back: "You belong to me because I am your first love and especially because I made you suffer. I am your destiny. You can flee me, but you can never forget me." At the end Renée must choose between Eva and Lorély, the archangels of destiny—one, of martyrdom and redemption; the other, of poison and perversity. Which shall it be? Instead of answering the question, the book ends inconclusively with *"Adieu et au revoir."*

An annotated copy of *Une Femme m'apparut* in the Bibliothèque Nationale identifies the characters as follows:

Lorély	NCB
Ione	*Violette S.*
Doriane	*Lucie Delarue-Mardrus*
Nedda	*Yvonne V.*
Dagmar	*S. P.*

The Bibliothèque Nationale copy came from Salomon Reinach, in a collection of about fifty related books. Reinach, a friend of Renée

and Natalie, was an archeologist with more than a classical interest
in Lesbos. In his scholarly way he conducted research into the
Renée-Natalie affair by assembling all the available documentation,
including the testimony of others. The marginal comments, though
written in his hand, are not necessarily his; they may have been copied from participants or witnesses of the Renée Vivien saga who
thus argue, in the margins of the book, about what actually happened.

The argument will never be settled, and the partisans of Renée
will continue to blame Natalie for sending Renée to an early grave.
But Salomon Reinach's detective work reveals that their grand passion lasted only two years, 1899–1901, and that Renée had other
love affairs in the years before her death in 1909. On the flyleaf of
another book by Renée, a collection of poems entitled *A l'Heure
des mains jointes,* Reinach cites names, dates, and addresses to establish the chronology beyond any doubt. But such evidence has
never explained what happened in a lovers' quarrel.

In writing a novel about the great love of her life, Renée was anything but dispassionate. Yet her narrative casts light on some of the
circumstances and some of the persons involved, and with the help
of Reinach's notes and other sources it is possible to reconstruct a
rough outline of the story or at least to recreate some sense of the
Sapphic society that centered around Natalie at the turn of the
century.

Ione was, of course, Violet Shilleto, who had been Renée's dearest friend since the age of thirteen. Violet brought Renée and Natalie together, but her death later caused them to part. Reinach's notes
on the sequence of events in 1901 suggest cause and effect: Violet
died in June, Renée broke off relations with Natalie, and Natalie left
for America. Actually Renée accompanied Natalie on that trip and
spent the summer in Bar Harbor, where she met Eva Palmer and
shared her love of solitude and Greek verse while Natalie went
dancing. Natalie had hoped that the summer would help Renée forget the death of Violet, but Renée remained inconsolable, full of remorse and in love with death. She returned to Europe in the fall and
avoided Natalie thereafter, except for the brief interlude in 1904,
when they went to Lesbos together. After that episode Renée wrote
Une femme m'apparut, which was published in 1904, and Natalie

wrote *Je me souviens,* dated August of the same year but not published until after Renée's death.

The parts played by two other characters in Renée's novel can be identified. Dagmar is Olive Custance, with whom Natalie went to Venice and with whom Renée had a liaison after her return from America. This would be shortly before or after Olive's marriage to her prince (as she addressed him in her love letters), Lord Alfred Douglas. And Doriane is Lucie Delarue-Mardrus, who was Natalie's love after Renée and about whom more will be said later.

The symbolism of flowers and jewels in the novel reflects the usage of this circle of friends. In the novel Dagmar wears a necklace of opals; in real life Olive Custance was called Opal and had published a volume of poetry entitled *Opals.* Similarly the Natalie Barney character, who is nicknamed Moon-Beam in *Idylle saphique,* wears moonstones in *Une Femme m'apparut.* And Renée adopted the violet as her emblem in memory of Violet Shilleto. Renée never ceased to mourn Violet and to write about violets and death in her poems. The religious symbolism in her novel could have been suggested by Violet's deathbed conversion to Catholicism. Renée brooded much over this death and the cold Anglican funeral service that followed in spite of Violet's wishes. But André Germain offers the more provocative suggestion that Renée's cult of the Virgin Mary expressed her yearning for a mother's love. If he is right, then Renée's mystical vision of Lorély as the Virgin in the novel must express a similar yearning. No wonder she was disappointed, if she turned to Natalie for motherly tenderness!

The pagan cult of Sapphic love may have been revived by Natalie, but Renée became its most ardent votary. In one of her poems she repudiated Christ, saying that his law had never been hers and she preferred to live as a pagan. In any event the cult was literary rather than religious. While Natalie was writing her *Cinq Petits Dialogues grecs,* Renée was learning Greek in order to translate Sappho into French. The idea of establishing a Sapphic utopia on Lesbos seems to have been taken more seriously by Renée; Natalie's account of their pilgrimage to Sappho's isle has its farcical elements. As a rule Natalie was fond of playacting, while Renée seems to have treated everything with intense seriousness.

One chapter of *Une Femme m'apparut,* translated below, makes

much of Lorély's wayward histrionic imagination—though some of
the imagining may be the author's. Still there is no doubt that Natalie Barney liked costumes and masquerades. In her early years she
staged theatrical performances and masked balls in her garden and
often posed for photographs in the costumes and roles that Renée
describes.

Like all nostalgic spirits, Lorély took pleasure in seeking out the
glamour of strange garments which transformed the mind as well as
the body and revived for an hour the grace of a vanished epoch.
    Sometimes she dressed as a Venetian page, wearing a moon-green
velvet suit that matched her hair. Her fingers wandered over a lute.
She had the feverish slenderness of a lovesick child, and her gestures
became wilful and supplicating at the same time.
    "I am a page in love with the Dogaresse," Lorély would say.
"She is so haughtily beautiful in her gondola with its prow encrusted
with gold and emeralds! . . . I carry her train, and from time to
time her careless glance falls on me. And I would die if she failed to
cast that careless glance on me. . . ."
    Sometimes she transformed herself into a little Greek shepherd.
Then an invisible music of pipes rose under her feet, and her eyes
laughed at the nakedness of the nymphs. Sometimes too she was a
sad, long-waisted chatelaine, whose dress hung stiffly in chaste folds.
In a pose that was weighted with grief she sat on a chair as straight as
a choir stall, and she murmured languishing words in a low voice, as
if she were speaking to her solitude.
    "I am bored. . . . I am so bored that sometimes to my surprise I
miss my husband. Would I cry if he fell in battle there in the Holy
Land? I don't believe so. But here I am bored to death. I am so weary
of contemplating the flight of clouds or the illuminations of my mis-
sal. I am weary of imagining innumerable sins in order to confess
them to the good monk whose innocent embarrassment entertains
me. My page is a simple-minded child with shiny red cheeks. I could
recite from beginning to end the stories that my four attendants have
told me too many times. . . . Besides, these ladies are very silly
and simple. Truly I am mortally bored. . . ."
    Lorély was by turns a Byzantine princess, a young English lord
whose dashing carriage and beautiful clothes François I had noticed
on the Field of the Cloth of Gold, a cruel sickly child, a wandering

minstrel with no wealth but his harp. . . . Sometimes she was an Egyptian dancer, sometimes a fairy dressed in iris petals and jeweled by the sparkling dew.

She became another person, without losing her own indefinable charm.

"I do the best to flee myself," she used to say, adjusting the finery of another age and a faraway land. "That's my poor consolation for not having succeeded in forgetting myself entirely or transforming myself by the magic of a genuine love. . . ."

Feverishly she chose and rejected fabrics and jewels.

"I am always like myself," she sighed.

And that long sigh was as tragic as a lamentation.

Instinctively Lorély worshipped the artificial. She liked to apply makeup to a complexion as pale as a white rose. Then the false red of her cheeks contrasted disconcertingly with the diminished glow of her hair.

"The true end of art," she used to say, "is to withdraw as far as possible from nature. He who strives to imitate nature in art is but a common copyist. . . . In painting I only like psychic landscapes, dream flowers and faces that no one will ever behold."

Like Aphrodite Lorély possessed a thousand souls and a thousand guises. And I loved her through all her metamorphoses.

Those who loved her suffered to see her inattentive—even in their arms—and always unsatiated. Some wept, others taxed her with reproaches, others remained bound to her by their very suffering. Still others understood that the heart of Lorély was heavy with a melancholy burden, with an intolerable need to love.

She would have given her youth, her beauty and her sophisticated intelligence to love like the most ordinary woman, to experience the unaffected sobs of a genuine passion. And this unquenched thirst sometimes made her impatient and fierce. One would have said that she harbored resentment against her lovers and against me for the love that we could not make her feel.

This passage sums up most of Renée's reproaches. She found Natalie fickle, cold, heartless, incapable of love, incapable of any feeling. Similar charges have been made frequently enough by others so that they cannot be lightly dismissed. But a profound difference in temperament kept Renée from ever understanding Natalie. Renée

was a Romantic who lost herself in emotional ecstasies. Natalie was
constitutionally incapable of losing her head. Her temper was classical, controlled, detached, skeptical. Though each was deeply in
love with the other, they were separated by the world of difference
between the heartthrob and the ironic smile.

If anyone was artificial, it was Renée, who transformed her life
into a work of art nouveau, her house into a funeral setting from Ed-
gar Allan Poe or an Oriental opium dream. No doubt Natalie did say
that the true end of art is to withdraw as far as possible from nature,
but Renée missed the flippancy behind this Wildean paradox.

In *Souvenirs indiscrets* Natalie protested indignantly against the
portrait Renée had drawn of her and criticized Renée for attributing
her own bad taste to Lorély while indulging in the worst excesses of
art nouveau with her orchids, snakes and fading black irises. Natalie
found the characters in the novel lifeless, and the mysticism, which
was meant to be magical, absurd. Above all she objected to being
cast in the role of the femme fatale incapable of love—she who had
never been capable of anything else! Certain passages, she allowed,
represented Renée's true feelings, and she quoted one in which Renée, on first meeting Lorély, realizes that she has met her destiny.
Souvenirs indiscrets, which appeared half a century after Renée's
death, is certainly the last word, but not the most objective.

One statement in that book sums up Renée quite accurately. In
her novel Renée had attributed to Natalie the morbid disease of
nineteenth-century Romanticism; Natalie properly retorted that if
anyone had made a career of neurotic melancholy it was Renée. Colette confirms this in *Le Pur et l'impur* when she describes Renée in
her declining days, deploring her childishness, her weakness, her
excesses and the atmosphere of gloom in which she lived. Colette's
account seems particularly reliable, not only because she was a
neighbor and eyewitness but also because she studied Renée's behavior with her extraordinary powers of observation. Her portrait is
remarkable for being at once compassionate and unsentimental. She
listened with sympathy to Renée's confessions, but her common
sense made her doubt much and disapprove more. She wondered
whether Renée's tyrannical lesbian lover ever existed, the "master"
whose summons came without warning and whose demands were

insatiable. This person's name was never mentioned, but she is commonly supposed to have been Baroness van Zuylen. Colette, who was no prude, was nonetheless shocked by Renée's uninhibited gossip about her sexual practices because it was like the talk of a child prostitute, at once crude and innocent. She watched this debauched child wasting away, living on alcohol, and diagnosed the cause of her death as "voluntary consumption."

7
Lucie Delarue-Mardrus

In 1902, when she returned to Paris and Renée refused to see her, Natalie was able to find comfort only in the company of new friends that she met at that time, Dr. J.-C. Mardrus and his wife, Lucie. A chapter in *Souvenirs indiscrets* describes these friends and the part they played in Natalie's life then and for many years afterward in a friendship that lasted until their deaths. The memoirs of Lucie Delarue-Mardrus tell something of the same story, while some of her poems and a novel reveal a more intimate acquaintance.

Lucie was twenty-two when she first met the three striking Sapphic beauties she portrays in her memoirs, Renée, Eva, and Natalie, and they were all a few years older. A beauty herself, she had already been married for two years to a remarkable man who had fallen in love when he heard her read her poetry, had proposed to her the very evening that he met her and married her two weeks later. Dr. Joseph-Charles-Victor Mardrus was a learned Orientalist already famous for his translation of the *Arabian Nights*. As his marriage suggests, he was also an irrepressible enthusiast who acted on impulse without worrying too much about the proper way of doing things. Exuberant, irascible and outspoken, he offended some with his uninhibited speech, but Natalie, who was unaffected herself, liked his bluntness and lack of affectation, did not mind being called Blondie or addressed in the familiar form. In fact he was the only man she ever addressed as *tu*. She referred to him as Dr. Jesus-Christ Mardrus, as did many people, some of whom honestly believed that was his proper name.

One of the Doctor's likable qualities was his willingness to put his wife's career ahead of his own. Lucie Delarue-Mardrus was in fact a very talented writer, soon to be discovered by the world when Count Robert de Montesquiou asked her to give a reading at his Pavilion of the Muses—partly with the malicious intent of offending a rival poet, Anna de Noailles. But Lucie was first discovered by Renée Vivien, who hailed her as "the greatest poetess of our time." Lucie had never heard of Renée until she received in the mail a volume of Renée's poetry with a very flattering inscription. This lesbian poetry struck a familiar chord, reminding Lucie of some poems she had written as a girl expressing her infatuation with another girl. When she wrote a letter of thanks, Renée replied that she would like to meet her and soon afterward came to call. While the Doctor looked forward to meeting one of his wife's admirers, Lucie awaited this visit in a state of agitation. Here is how Renée first appeared to them, as Lucie recalled in her memoirs.

> We saw a young blonde girl, with brown eyes, discouraged shoulders, dressed carelessly, very English in appearance. Still her faint voice betrayed no English accent.
>
> Her conversation seemed commonplace. She impressed us as being an ordinary girl from England, a marriageable daughter. However, one thing about her was unforgettable: her heavy, delicate eyelids with their long black eyelashes. One could say that her personality only appeared when she lowered her eyes.

Shortly after this first visit Renée invited the Mardrus to dinner. They were depressed by her large, gloomy apartment with its dim light, airless atmosphere, and heavy draperies that muffled all sound. They who loved to dine sumptuously, in the tradition of his native Egypt and her native Normandy, found themselves picking at a few little birds while Renée remarked, "I cannot stand meat." But the evening was not wasted; the funereal gloom and meager food were completely forgotten when another guest appeared.

After dinner we suddenly saw a surprising thin creature emerging
from the draperies, a veritable heroine out of Dante Gabriel Rossetti.
Her medieval dress of dark purple velvet outlined a rather angular,
archaic body. Two enormous braids of red hair encircled her head
like a laurel wreath. Her face was that of an Italian primitive with
blue eyes.

This apparition was, of course, Eva Palmer. Forgetting Renée,
Lucie now fixed all her attention upon Eva: "I didn't have eyes
enough to gaze at that girl from another age, beautiful as a poem."
Eva responded by inviting the Mardrus to come to the theater with
her the following day, and the Doctor, well aware of Lucie's eagerness, agreed. The following day proved even more fateful. At the
theater, as Lucie wrote in her memoirs, "I saw for the first time Natalie Barney, who was, is, and ever will be one of my dearest
friends." Lucie clearly recalls her first impressions of Natalie:

> She had none of the impressive style of Evelina Palmer. Her deli-
> cate complexion, her very feminine form, her fairy-tale blonde hair,
> her Parisian elegance concealed for a time the steely look of those
> eyes which saw everything and understood everything in a second.
> And what further increased the false impression that one got at first,
> she could—and still can to this day—blush like a shy novice.
> Several days after this introduction she invited us to dinner at her
> apartment in the Hôtel La Pérouse.
> I can see her again as she was when we arrived, dressed in pale
> blue chiffon, playing the violin while she waited for us.
> The remarks she made during that dinner, in a voice that she never
> raised (and which has always remained thus), her ironic smile, her
> ease of manner, her quiet and curious epigrams soon revealed that we
> were in the presence of a real person.

When Natalie was attracted to someone, she lost no time in establishing a friendship or intimacy. In this case she was attracted,
though in different ways, to both husband and wife. Three days later
she appeared at their surburban villa "with all her charms on display," and she came to visit again and again, sometimes delivered
there by her father as he went out for a drive. Lucie saw Albert Bar-

ney as "an elegant clubman from Washington," an "American aristocrat whose vigorous profile Natalie had inherited," but she could also see that he was baffled by his daughter and could not forgive her for having been the heroine of Liane de Pougy's widely read novel. Natalie recalled that her father was uneasy about leaving her at this strange, out-of-the-way place, in the company of these unconventional writers, and that he was particularly suspicious of this dark-eyed doctor with his foreign manners.

This may have been the last she saw of her father, who was to die at the end of that year, and she sympathized with his lot as a dutiful parent alone in Paris with a wayward daughter who gave him more worry than satisfaction. Yet this realization was not enough to make her behave. One evening, when her father had entrusted Natalie and Eva to an old family friend, the two young women expressed a longing for a little fresh air after being cooped up for hours at a boring classical drama. Hailing an open carriage, they drove up the Champs-Élysées to the Arc de Triomphe, where, on a mad impulse, Natalie got out of the carriage on one side and Eva got out on the other, leaving their chaperone sitting there helplessly. Natalie does not tell what adventure she found more tempting than sleep that night but instead tries to imagine her father's rage and frustration when the chaperone returned to the hotel alone.

Soon after this her father left, having accomplished his mission, he hoped, of launching Natalie in proper Paris society and having installed her in a little house with a wooded garden, in Neuilly. This house was on the banks of the Seine, overlooking the island of Puteaux, where there was an exclusive tennis club, the favorite resort of elegant Anglophiles at the turn of the century. Natalie loved tennis, but she did not take to the fashionable set, with its round of afternoon teas and dinner parties. Instead of joining in the social life of the club, she preferred the more stimulating company of the Mardrus in their villa outside the city, where the river banks were not paved, where there were few people and thousands of books. Their little rose garden was an enchanted spot with a tame gazelle wandering around free, and the house was full of Arabian souvenirs. The Doctor was Haroun al-Rashid incarnate, a mage, prophet and storyteller who might at any moment sail away on his magic carpet. In

Aventures de l'esprit Natalie paid him the supreme compliment—
that she had never known him to utter a cliché, much less write one.
And as evidence of his prophetic powers she cited his prediction that
Lord Carnarvon would die if he violated the tomb of the Pharaoh
Tutankhamen. Yet there was nothing solemn or pretentious about
the Doctor, who was a true innocent with a hearty sense of humor.

But it was not the exotic Doctor so much as his young and beautiful wife who drew Natalie to their house. As often as possible she
went there to see Lucie, and together they went walking or riding
along the Seine, Lucie dressed as a cowboy with a ten-gallon hat
while Natalie wore a conventional riding habit. On rainy days they
stayed indoors, and Lucie read poems that Natalie had inspired. In
the summertime Natalie visited the Mardrus at their summer home
in Normandy, lying in the hayfields and breathing the salt air with
the "Princess Amande," so named because her body was smooth
and pale as an almond. Sometimes Eva joined their "harem," as
Natalie called it, meaning by this that these were women's pre-
cincts, not that the women all belonged to the patriarch. Yet, incredibly enough, the Doctor once proposed to Natalie that she bear his
child in order to spare his wife for her literary efforts. This was a
matter-of-fact proposal made in the presence of his wife as a practical plan to distribute their labors equally. Natalie took it in the same
spirit, not the least offended, but declined the honor as being contrary to her nature. Even once in her life, and with the possibility of
such interesting results, she could not perform such an unnatural
act.

All this time Natalie was suffering from lovesickness for Renée,
and the disease proved contagious, as Lucie began writing desperate
love poems to Natalie. In her memoirs Lucie states that Natalie
initiated her to lesbian love; her love poems published posthumous-
ly in *Nos Secrètes Amours* reveal that this was the most devastating
experience of her life. Most of these are frankly sensual poems, in-
toxicated with desire and panting with passion. Several of them
reflect their quiet moments of lovemaking in their harem by the
Seine; others pulse with the rhythm of the sea and give off the tang
of salt air, like the rhythm and scent of their love. The poet had
dreamed of a siren who would come from the sea, and now such a

creature stood before her, with hair like the morning mist and eyes like drops of sea water; but she was a woman like herself, bringing horror, happiness and bafflement into the poet's life. These mixed emotions dominate the book, as joy turns to sorrow and suffering at the thought of all Natalie's former loves, and the hopeless desire for possession inevitably ends unsatisfied. Some poems rage against passion, resenting the tyranny of the flesh, longing to pound and scratch and strangle, only to succumb again to naked abandon. A poem entitled ''Portrait'' presents Natalie's contradictions, her perversity and her truthfulness, her infidelities and her faithful heart, concluding,

> My joy and my pain, my death and my life,
> My blonde bitch!

Lucie's stormy emotions may have inspired a play she wrote, *Sapho désesperée* (1906), in which Lucie herself appeared at least once. But though despairing of Natalie's love, she did not succumb to morbidity and defeat like Renée. Instead she sensibly said farewell, urging Natalie to return to her former love. Of course, sentiments expressed in a poem need not be taken as literal truth, especially when followed by another poem in which the lover returns the next morning. But the book ends with their love turning to friendship, and in life their love ended thus. Dr. Mardrus tolerated their love affair for two years, but having completed his sixteen-volume translation of the *Arabian Nights,* he began to grow restless and wanted to return to North Africa. In 1904 he embarked with his wife on a series of journeys which provided her with new subjects for her poetry. Before leaving, Lucie gave Natalie the manuscript of her love poems, which Natalie piously preserved and, many years later, after Lucie's death, published anonymously at her own expense.

In 1930 Lucie published a novel entitled *L'Ange et les Pervers,* a book which Natalie never mentions in the long chapter she devotes to the Mardrus. Lucie, in her memoirs, makes it clear that she is describing Natalie in that novel and the life to which Natalie had introduced her years before. The angel of the title is a hermaphrodite who should have been twins and who leads a double existence, alternating between Marion Hervin and Mario de Valdeclare. The perverse characters are frivolous, cynical Parisians belonging to several circles Marion/Mario alternately visits: theater people for whom he/she ghost-writes plays, homosexuals of both sexes—false hermaphrodites, he/she calls them, women acting like men and men acting like women. Marion attracts people of all sexes but, being neuter, is indifferent to their advances, aloof and critical of their way of life. He/she longs to withdraw from this heartless world by joining the Benedictine monks at Solesmes but lacks faith and eventually finds a better vocation.

Laurette Wells is the Natalie Barney character who figures in most of the action. Marion sees her faults all too clearly, but Laurette is the only person she likes, so she serves as an accomplice in Laurette's intrigues. Laurette wants to regain the affection of Aimée de Lagres, who has been taken over by a jealous and watchful countess, and proposes to serenade Aimée with her violin. The circumstances obviously resemble those of the Natalie–Renée–Baroness van Zuylen triangle, and these events take place in Neuilly, where all three lived until 1909, the year of Renée's death. Conceivably there could be some autobiographical elements in the character of Aimée, who was seduced from her husband by Laurette, then dropped four months later. Eventually Aimée returns to her husband, after having a baby by another man. Laurette, not so heartless after all, finds a foster home for the baby and keeps an eye on it for three years, after which Marion decides it is her vocation to be mother and father to this child and to give it the love she herself has neither had nor given.

Improbable as it sounds, the story is quite touching, reads well and makes its point effectively without seeming to preach. Most of the action centers around the activities initiated by Laurette, who is the most important character after the protagonist. The novel analyzes her thoroughly, showing her heartless way of playing cat and mouse with pretty ladies she does not even want, her desire to triumph and have her way, which Marion in a disillusioned moment sums up as the consequence of leisure, wealth and literature. Small wonder Natalie did not want to call attention to Lucie's novel. This is the most devastating exposé of Natalie ever written and no doubt the most accurate. It is evident the author studied her subject very carefully, observing every little detail, as in the following passage:

> Laurette's left eyebrow rose very slowly, a sign of astonishment or strong emotion for those who know her well. Her cold power was not apparent in her pink and white complexion or her spun glass hair but only in those heavy eyebrows, in the strong root of her slightly hooked nose and in the design of her sensual mouth with its beautiful healthy teeth. When she smiled, her mouth turned up at the corners and suddenly gave her entire face a sardonic expression.
>
> With the well-rounded lines of a very feminine body, hair like a fairy's, a faint voice, shy blushes, a delicate pastel coloring, she contrived—as if by deliberate artifice—the surprising effect of those eyes like a sword-blade, sparkling with intelligence, sarcasm and will, eyes that seemed to look at only one thing at a time and yet saw everything.

Marion asks Laurette why she has made a trip to Constantinople, then answers her own question.

> "No one will ever know, probably not even you yourself. When you travel you see nothing but the details of faces. In any event you said to me, 'Turkey? . . . a little woman entered my train compartment who made me forget why I had left home. How nicely her eyes were set in her head!' "
>
> Laurette began laughing with that laugh she has, almost as faint as her voice, but with a spontaneous gaiety as honest as a child's.

Marion chastises Laurette for her many faults, yet concludes with her virtues and particularly her loyalty. Laurette would stand by a friend who had committed a crime.

> "You are . . . perverse, dissolute, selfish, unjust, obstinate, sometimes avaricious, often play-acting, most of the time irritating . . . in sum, a monster. But you are a true rebel and always prepared to lead others in rebellion. And deep down inside you're a decent person."

Some of Laurette's faults can be attributed to her background and upbringing.

"For you are terribly American, for all your cosmopolitan airs. You make twenty-five rendezvous all over Paris for the same hour, not counting five minutes for the theater and a quarter of an hour for a concert. You have the restless disease which comes from being dragged around ocean liners, trains, and hotels while too young, like all little Yankees who are too rich."

Though educated in French boarding schools and speaking perfect French, Laurette remains fundamentally American in her optimism and self-confidence. She laughs like a girl of fourteen but acts like a businessman when it comes to organizing her love intrigues. This combination of girlishness and guile is most apparent when Marion reproaches Laurette for callously destroying a marriage.

"Your idle plots amuse me. You invent little situations, you play childish games with love. At bottom you are a bunch of schoolgirls— dangerous schoolgirls at that—for in the midst of all this there is a man who loved his wife and who has lost her, a woman who was leading a peaceful life and who is now launched on adventures that lead her astray."

Laurette's reply clearly represents Natalie's view on the subject: "It's *before* that she was astray."

In the character of Laurette Wells, Lucie presents the most revealing portrait of Natalie ever written and the most convincing. Not even in her memoirs did Lucie reproduce Natalie's character more exactly. Other writers tend to be emotional in describing Natalie, whether they criticize or romanticize her character. Lucie was both a better writer and a more objective observer than all the rest. By the time she wrote *L'Ange et les Pervers* she had been observing Natalie closely for almost thirty years, most of that time neither as lover nor enemy but as a friend who could not overlook certain failings. Her memoirs explain her feelings toward Natalie after the period represented in the novel, when they ceased being lovers:

Besides, after a little while Natalie became simply the bosom friend, the sister, the pure and faithful companion, whose pride, loyalty and nobility I have esteemed so highly for more than thirty years, despite her intolerable faults and vices, which would probably not exist but for the literary pose she adopts.

The relatively brief love affair between Lucie and Natalie was followed by a lifelong attachment for which the word friendship seems inadequate. This was to be the pattern that Natalie followed all her life with those she esteemed most, notably Romaine Brooks and the duchess de Clermont-Tonnerre, who remained her dearest friends for half a century. Passion was brief, but friendship endured, so Natalie wooed her friends even more assiduously than she did her lovers. Paradoxically, she was as constant in friendship as she was inconstant in love. This helps to explain why she was unable to establish a lasting relationship with Renée. No doubt the jealous Baroness van Zuylen did her best to keep them apart, but she probably would not have succeeded if Renée had been satisfied with less than eternal love from Natalie. Renée wanted passion to remain at a constant pitch of throbbing intensity. To Natalie such a state of affairs was as unthinkable and absurd as marriage.

8
Theatricals

From her mother's side Natalie acquired a taste for "theatricals," as they were called in the family circle, stage presentations that combined music, dance and mime. Grandfather Pike, to begin with, had been his own impresario, going to Europe to book singers and musicians for his opera house and engaging decorators and costume designers as well. Alice Pike Barney showed the same kind of initiative and the same fondness for music and spectacle. She wrote a ballet, *L'École à crinoline,* which she engaged Pavlova to produce, and she wrote many so-called plays that were really scenarios for theatrical spectacles. The verbal content may have been silly, for Alice's talents were not literary or dramatic; but she was musically gifted and had the painter's eye for visual effects, so the combination of music, rhythmic dancing, pageantry and tableau created the desired impression. After all, these were generally private entertainments performed by amateurs before an audience of friends. For Alice the arts were an essential part of social life.

Natalie collaborated with her mother in writing some of these theatricals and, as already noted, appeared as a performer in several stage productions, creating a furor in Bar Harbor with her performance in *An Egyptian Vaudeville* and shocking the matrons of Washington by appearing in Sardou's supposedly risqué play, *Americans Abroad.* In the latter case a gossip column noted that

Mrs. Barney's "much advertised theatricals" had been designed "to call attention to young Miss Barney," thereby indicating the social function of this production.

Following her mother's example, Natalie organized her own theatricals a few years later and integrated them into her social life. Not surprisingly, hers were more inclined to be literary and truly risqué, designed to appeal to a different kind of audience, one with entirely different tastes, but the underlying idea was the same. (Her sister Laura also used this form as a vehicle for her particular interests, publishing *God's Heroes,* a drama in five acts with episodes from the history of the Baha'i religion.)

Natalie's writings in dramatic form were published in two collections, *Cinq Petits Dialogues grecs* (1902) and *Actes et entr'actes* (1910). The earlier volume, dedicated to Pierre Louÿs and clearly written under his influence, reflects Natalie's preoccupation with Hellenism, which coincided with her love affair with Renée Vivien. Louÿs' influence determined not only the tone, the style and the form of the dialogues, but also the publisher, as this time he succeeded in finding one for her. Of course, he had created the aesthetics of erotic Hellenism and at the same time the demand that made Natalie's imitations publishable. But Natalie would not have submitted to his influence for purely literary reasons. His brand of Greek paganism obviously suited her, intellectually and otherwise. For her, life always took precedence over literature, and her writings were almost invariably the by-product of her other activities. Her dialogues reflect much of her thinking during the years they were written and possibly even some scenes from her life.

This is most apparent in the first dialogue, which is prefaced by a sonnet to Lesbos and written "to entertain L. and B." "L." could be Lucie Delarue-Mardrus and "B." another intimate with whom Natalie may have had an affair or at least gossiped about the love affairs of mutual friends. The dialogue, entitled "Douces Rivalités," describes a lesbian triangle such as they or their friends might have been involved in and prescribes gentleness instead of jealousy. The exemplary Eranna loves both Ione and Myrclis but magnanimously withdraws because they love each other. It is tempting to identify Ione as Violet Shilleto, the Ione of Renée Vivien's novel, especially when Eranna invites this Ione to walk among her violets. But, on the other hand, Eranna praises Ione's long red hair in terms that can only suggest Eva Palmer and remind us that Violet Shilleto was a brunette. The evidence is too contradictory to permit any identification, and in any case the identity of the characters matters less than the behavior they represent. What emerges above all is the good-natured spirit of this dialogue, written to entertain friends and to exemplify the golden mean in affairs of the heart.

Eranna's views on love in the first dialogue are plainly the author's. Her role in consoling and reconciling lovers is one that Natalie often played in life, and it is Eranna who apostrophizes Sappho in terms that describe Natalie's ideal. In the other dialogues, too, Natalie's ideas and opinions appear. At first glance some of the dialogues seem only literary in their origins, having little to do with her own experience. Three center on courtesans who might have been borrowed from the pages of Pierre Louÿs, but in each case the characters or their circumstances reflect Natalie's attitudes toward love. All three of these dialogues reject the possibility of finding satisfactory love with a man, and all three tend to be cynical rather than romantic on the subject of love. The remaining dialogue, debating the merits of Greek hedonism versus Christianity, unmistakably reflects her sympathies with the ancient Greek ways and her repudiation of a religion that denies the flesh.

Like Plato's dialogues, Natalie's employ a dramatic form mainly as a vehicle for ideas. There may be dramatic moments, notably in the final twists that end the two most cynical dialogues, scorning the idea of love as anything but physical. But on the whole the dialogues are bookish rather than dramatic and do not give the impression that they were written for the stage, though they may well have been performed in the presence of a small, intimate group. The dialogues of Pierre Louÿs are if anything less dramatic, yet one was produced by Natalie as part of a garden party. Colette's amusing account of this affair provides a glimpse of the social setting in which Natalie staged her early theatricals.

> One fine afternoon, on a lawn at Neuilly, in the gardens of Miss Nathalie Clifford-Barney, I played one of the two parts in Pierre Louÿs's *Dialogue au soleil couchant*. The name of the other impro-

vised actress was Miss Eva Palmer. She was an American and had
the most miraculous long red hair. Only on my elder half-sister have
I seen the wealth that poured from Eva's forehead to her feet. For the
Dialogue she bound its amazing abundance in ropes about her head
and put on a blue-green, more or less Greek tunic, while I felt I was
the perfect Daphnis in terra-cotta crêpe de Chine, cut very short, a
pair of Roman buskins, and a wreath in the Tahiti style.

Eva Palmer, white as a sheet, stammered out her words. I was so
stiff with stage fright that the rolling "r's" of my Burgundy accent
became positively Russian. Pierre Louÿs, author and guest, listened.
Or perhaps he did not listen, for we were undoubtedly pleasanter to
look at than to hear. But we believed that the whole of Paris under its
sunshades and its hats, which were immense that year, had its eyes
upon us. After the performance I plucked up the courage to ask
Louÿs if "it hadn't gone too badly."

He answered gravely: "I have experienced one of the greatest
emotions of my life."

"Oh! dear Louÿs!"

"I assure you! The unforgettable experience of hearing my work
spoken by Mark Twain and Tolstoy."

The climax of the afternoon's entertainment was yet to come.
What follows is more revealing of Natalie's flair as an impresario.
She liked to create a sensation, to startle and shock others, while she
herself stood by in her understated fashion and watched, as though
only a spectator. Her purpose was not to dramatize herself but to
create bold theatrical effects that would take others by surprise, possibly to share with them the childlike pleasure of being surprised,
possibly to enjoy the superior pleasure of being the puppeteer behind the scenes, pulling strings and at the same time watching the
effect on the audience. And after her father's death she ceased to
care about her reputation; if anything, she glorified in her notoriety.
Colette's narrative goes on after the congratulations of the audience.

But the next moment everyone had forgotten the Boston shepherdess
and the Moscow herdsman; from behind a screen of foliage a naked
woman had appeared, riding on a white horse, its strappings studded
with turquoises—a new dancer whose name was already known
among the studio and drawing-room cliques: Mata Hari.

She was a dancer who did not dance much, yet at Emma Calvé's, before the portable altar that she used as a backdrop, supported by a little group of colored attendants and musicians and framed in the pillars of a vast, white hall, she had been sufficiently snakelike and enigmatic to produce a good effect. The people who fell into such dithyrambic raptures and wrote so ecstatically of Mata Hari's person and talents must be wondering now what collective delusion possessed them. Her dancing and the naïve legends surrounding her were of no better quality than the ordinary claptrap of the current "Indian numbers" in the music hall. The only pleasant certainties on which her drawing-room audiences could count were a slender waist below breasts that she prudently kept hidden, a fine, supple moving back, muscular loins, long thighs, and slim knees. Her nose and mouth, which were both thick, and the rather oily brillance of her eyes did nothing to alter—on the contrary—our established notions of the Oriental. It should be said that the finale of her dance, the moment when Mata Hari, freed of her last girdle, fell forward modestly upon her belly, carried the male—and a good proportion of the female—spectators to the extreme limit of decent attention.

In the May sunshine, at Neuilly, despite the turquoises, the drooping black mane of hair, the tinsel diadem, and especially the long thigh against the white flanks of her Arab horse, the color of her skin was disconcerting, no longer brown and luscious as it had been by artificial light, but a dubious, uneven purple. Having finished her equestrian parade, she alighted and wrapped herself in a sari. She bowed, talked, was faintly disappointing.

Colette's disapproval of Mata Hari was not based on prudery, for when she met her again, at another of Natalie's garden parties, she found that she preferred Mata Hari naked to Mata Hari dressed and trying to act like a lady. Colette resented being addressed by this transparent fraud and had the satisfaction of overhearing a bystander say, quite audibly, "She, an Oriental? Don't be silly! Hamburg or Rotterdam, or possibly Berlin."

Mata Hari, who was born in Holland and had lived in Indonesia, made a profession of exotic dancing before beginning her more fabulous career as a German spy. No doubt Natalie saw through her as readily as Colette did, but Natalie liked to create a sensation, and Mata Hari served that purpose, whether naked or clothed. Natalie was also a collector of celebrities, and her collection included all kinds of people. After all, Colette was a rather dubious figure herself at this time, not the famous writer known to posterity but a music hall entertainer. There is this difference, however: Colette was a person with whom Natalie could be on equal terms, while she probably wasted no time in conversation with Mata Hari. Still, Mata Hari interested her enough as a celebrity so that years later, during the war, Natalie went to great lengths to find the French officer who had been in command of the firing squad that executed her for espionage, in order to get the exact details of her death rather than the more melodramatic account published in the popular press. And, oddly enough, Alice Pike Barney later wrote a play entitled *Mata Hari*—perhaps at Natalie's suggestion.

On at least one other occasion Natalie engaged Mata Hari as a performer, this time to do an erotic Javanese dance before a small audience composed exclusively of women. This performance and Mata Hari's appearance as Lady Godiva would give rise to many legends, including one in which she rode into the salon on an elephant. There would be similar tales about Colette, who a few years later played a role like Mata Hari's in a pantomime Natalie organized in memory of Renée Vivien. The following eyewitness report by André Germain appears in a chapter of his book on Proust, dealing with women of letters of the Proustian era, entitled "Amazones et Sirènes."

> Several years later I was to see Colette again, naked this time and imitating a faun. It was in a garden which belonged to a friend whose every wish I then obeyed, Nathalie Clifford Barney. (I admired her enormously but loved another more.) Nathalie had summoned me for a ceremony in honor of a poetess whom I had not known but pursued beyond the grave, Renée Vivien. The poems murmured and at the end sobbed by that unfortunate young woman struck me and charmed me, despite their pagan audacity. But I was touched and edified more by her repentance and Christian death than by the spectacle of her "lamentable life"—as she puts it. And so as not to frighten her shade, which was permanently reconciled with religion, I would have wished for her instead of theatrical displays simply Masses said for the repose of her soul.
>
> The imperious Nathalie decided otherwise. Three talented per-

formers gave her their assistance. One of them roused us to dream, so to speak, by the exquisitely modulated accents of the most expert flute playing. Then the feminine faun or rather the hamadryad who had fastened herself to a tree disengaged herself and came bounding toward us all with all the wayward grace of a wild cat. It was Colette. At the same time a harmonious voice recited beautiful lines that we heard poorly.

Later I went to see Nathalie alone to reproach her. But how could reticent Catholic poets influence those maddened beauties who, they say, once dismembered Orpheus? Nathalie silenced me by reciting again those beautiful lines which had been scarcely audible and by showing me a dedication: above the poem "To a Faun" were these two words, "For Colette. . . ."

As a Catholic André Germain naturally deplored the pagan ritual in memory of Renée Vivien, and as a sentimentalist he was a bit overwrought; but his account provides another glimpse of the kind of amateur theatricals Natalie staged in her garden during the prewar years and once again reveals the social function of the arts in her life. Music, poetry, mime and costume all played their part in these masques designed to appeal to the eye and ear without unduly taxing the mind.

In addition Natalie wrote full-fledged plays of a more literary sort, four of which were published, interspersed with poems, in *Actes et entr'actes*. These are formal verse dramas in a high Romantic vein, set in ancient Greece, fourteenth-century Avignon, and Renaissance Venice. Three of them seem more like literary exercises than anything having to do with Natalie's life or interests, although they do express her feminist views by presenting women of character in trying situations forced upon them by a masculine world. The fourth play, *Équivoque,* touches Natalie more closely, providing the fullest dramatization of the ideas in her earlier Greek dialogues. Based on a legend that Sappho committed suicide for love, this play is the ultimate expression of Natalie's Hellenism and demonstrates that Sappho had made her quite a serious student of Greek. The work is a scholarly tour de force, incorporating into the dialogue fragments from Sappho's writings and footnoting them in the original Greek. Yet for all her admiration of Sappho's poetry,

Natalie still valued life above art and took the occasion of Sappho's approaching death to voice one of her favorite ideas. When Sappho renounces poetry, one of her disciples says, "Your life is your most beautiful poem; you are your own immortal masterpiece." And when another disciple says that her songs are immortal, Sappho replies, "I sang for you, not for posterity. Fame for its own sake is vain, and what do I care for praise after death?"

No record survives of performances of the other plays in *Actes et entr'actes,* but it seems safe to assume that Natalie would have written them only with the prospect of performance and probably with particular performers in mind. In a sense they express the same impulse as the photographs in which she posed with her friends and lovers, gratifying the same fondness for fancy dress and striking poses. But beyond this the plays also express a highly organized social instinct. For Natalie was a social impresario who planned and stage-managed her entertainments with care. Another hostess might feel that she had done enough in offering tea and cookies to her guests, letting them entertain one another; but for Natalie the party must have a program. The text of *Équivoque* reveals that it was performed in Natalie's garden in June, 1906, and gives the names of the performers, all presumably friends of hers. Everything about the circumstances and the play itself reflects its social function, giving point to a gathering of friends with a common interest in the subject, the performers and each other. More than any other, this play fits into Natalie's life and demonstrates that her writing was not an end in itself but was prompted by love and friendship.

Among the performers in *Équivoque* were Mmes. Moreno, Palmer and Duncan; that is, the actress Marguerite Moreno, who played the role of Sappho; Eva Palmer, in the role of the young bride; and Penelope Sikelianos, the Greek wife of Raymond Duncan, playing the flute. At first this seems an incongruous mixture, like the odd conjunction of Eva Palmer and Colette, "the Boston shepherdess and the Moscow herdsman," in Pierre Louÿs' dialogue. But Natalie had a way of bringing unlikely people together, with unpredictable results. In this case fate seems to have taken a hand and launched Eva Palmer on a career of her own that went far beyond Natalie's modest efforts. Eva's role in the play was that of a girl who left Sappho in order to marry. Similarly, in real life, Eva left Natalie's circle that summer and was married the following year. Long enamored of Greece, Eva exchanged the love of Sappho which she had shared with Natalie and Renée for that of a living Greek poet. She spent that summer near Athens, in a roofless house that had been built by Isadora Duncan, and there she met Penelope Duncan's brother, Angelos Sikelianos. Like the Duncans she adopted ancient Greek dress, creating a sensation when she landed in New York the following year, on her way to Bar Harbor to be married. For the rest of their lives Eva and her husband devoted themselves to reviving the arts of ancient Greece, rediscovering the old methods of weaving, studying the relationships between music, dance, and drama, staging the classical dramas as authentically as possible, and trying to educate Greek peasants and American audiences alike. Their greatest accomplishment was the revival of the ancient dramatic festivals at Delphi, where at the end of her long life Eva chose to be buried.

Eva, who had been Natalie's intimate since adolescence and probably her first lover, was the first of many women in Natalie's life whose love was to turn into a friendship that transcended love. She exemplifies what Natalie had said to Renée about Sappho and Atthis remaining faithful to each other despite their other loves, what Natalie meant when she said that love was fleeting but true friendship eternal. In an unpublished note written after Eva's death Natalie recorded that she had carefully preserved the precious relic of Eva's love, the strand of flaming hair that Eva had cut off and given to her in a sudden dramatic gesture. She also noted that several years before her death Eva had written that she "owed her existence" to Natalie. What this probably meant was that Natalie had liberated her from the life into which she was born and introduced her to other ways of living, not only and not necessarily lesbianism but an emancipated feminism that left her free to follow her inclinations and make her life as she chose.

Like Natalie and Renée, Eva was a debutante who managed to break out of wealthy society into a far more creative life. Her brother, Courtlandt Palmer, was a composer, which was strange enough in New York society; but Eva was a woman, and if she had remained in that society, her talents would have been subordinated to her position as a society woman. Liberated from that milieu, she succeeded in exercising her very considerable gifts for composing, painting and writing, as well as drama. The parts she took in Natalie's theatricals were no measure of her talent as an actress, for she could have had a stage career; Sir Henry Irving once asked her to play Beatrice in his production of *Dante*. Eva may not have been more gifted than Natalie, but she accomplished more because she dedicated her talents in a single-minded commitment that was the very antithesis of Natalie's casual dalliance with the arts. Still, Natalie was the one who showed her the way at the start and, to this extent, launched Eva on her career. Eva was only one of the many accomplished women who became Natalie's friends, and obviously Natalie had such friends because she herself was a remarkable person.

Another of these friendships began when Colette appeared in Natalie's theatricals. In *Souvenirs indiscrets* Natalie remembers that she first saw Colette about 1900 and recognized her as a true original, out walking her pets in the Bois de Boulogne while courtesans and ladies of fashion went riding by in their carriages. At this time Colette was regarded merely as one of her husband's pets, an unsophisticated village girl who had unaccountably caught the fancy of a much older literary man-about-town, Henry Gauthier-Villars, better known by his pen name, Willy. No one then knew that he virtually chained her to the desk and forced her to write the "Claudine" novels, which he then published under his own name; but it was no secret that she was the original of Claudine, the heroine of the novels, for he paraded her around as part of his self-promotion. And though her true character was still submerged and her spirits miserably depressed by this bondage, she cut a striking figure that appealed to the artists of the time and created her celebrity as a saucy ingenue.

Such a celebrity may well have appealed to Natalie when she met Colette and Willy at the salon of a titled lady. Invited to their apartment, Natalie discovered with surprise that Colette had her own little gymnasium. The thought of deliberately doing exercises would never have occurred to Natalie, although she was very athletic herself and did a great deal of riding, swimming, rowing and tennis-playing. Evidently Colette and Natalie did not see much of each other at first because Willy, though unfaithful himself, was extremely jealous of any attachments his wife might form. He permitted Colette to appear in Pierre Louÿs' *Dialogue au soleil couchant,* possibly because it was good publicity, but he rudely refused to let her attend Mata Hari's Javanese dance-in-the-nude because he was angry at not being invited to this soiree for women only.

In 1903 Natalie made a brief fictional appearance as a character named Miss Flossie in Colette's novel, *Claudine s'en va.* Annie, the heroine of the novel, feels the magnetism of this American woman's smile but remembers that her husband, for some unknown reason, does not want her to associate with Miss Flossie. Neither does the thin redheaded girl who is with Miss Flossie and who regards Annie with inexplicable hatred. Colette's heroine is an ingenue; Colette herself understood jealousy thoroughly. But for some reason she did not develop the situation any further. Probably she did not know Natalie very well at the time she wrote this novel, though she knew her reputation well enough to borrow the nickname that Liane de Pougy had given her in *Idylle saphique.* The description of Miss Flossie is superficial, the character is viewed from a distance, and the title "Miss" suggests that Colette's acquaintance with Miss Barney was still on a formal footing.

Three years later, when Colette left Willy, she and Natalie came to know each other intimately. After her divorce Colette became a music hall entertainer in order to support herself. During this period she often visited Natalie, bringing some of her friends from the theater world, such as Marguerite Moreno and Sacha Guitry. Such friends helped put on the play that Natalie was then writing, *Équivoque,* while Colette watched from the audience. Natalie, who had a weakness for theater people, had a love affair with the actress Henriette Roggers and perhaps with other actresses as well; once, she pursued an actress all the way to Saint Petersburg, only to learn that a Russian colonel and a French diplomat had anticipated her.

Colette and Natalie were not really lovers. When Natalie drew up her list of liaisons and "demi-liaisons," Colette was among the latter. But Colette was one of those intimate friends who meant more to her than her lovers, and their friendship endured for life. Not without reservations, however. Natalie disapproved of Colette's willing submission to men, which she witnessed again when Colette's second husband, Henry de Jouvenel, coldly asserted his power over her in Natalie's presence. Natalie could not stand the thought of losing herself in daily intimacy with one person—that was why she disapproved of matrimony—and preferred the independence of the solitary life. But whatever their differences of opinion, both Colette and Natalie were able to rise above them, and each woman valued the other for her own sake.

Colette sometimes came to Natalie's salon and was a member of the "Académie des Femmes," of which more in another chapter. Colette's play *La Vagabonde* (1922) was premiered in Natalie's salon, with Colette and the designer Paul Poiret among the actors. And in the years before the second war Colette and Natalie saw a good deal of each other during their summers on the Riviera, where they had villas near each other. After the war, when Colette was bedridden, Natalie occasionally came to call. But far more eloquent testimony of their friendship is to be found in the many letters that they wrote to each other over a period of almost half a century, invariably expressing a deep and abiding affection.

9
2⁰ rue Jacob

During the first ten years of her residence in Paris Natalie lived on the right bank of the Seine, in the vicinity of the Bois de Boulogne. This was the fashionable, affluent, modern quarter where most of her friends lived and where she could have a house with a garden for her summertime entertainments. In 1909, however, she decided to move to an entirely different quarter, on the Left Bank, and found a house to her liking at the address she was to make famous, 20 rue Jacob. As if launching forth on a new life, she prepared for this move by consulting the astrologers. This act seems out of keeping with Natalie's skeptical turn of mind, but several people who were close to her, notably Berthe Cleyrergue, her faithful housekeeper of forty-five years, say that Natalie had an interest in numerology, and the fact is that she ordered not one but two horoscopes shortly before moving to the Rue Jacob. Here is the complete text of one of them:

October 31, 1876   9 A.M.

Tuesday   Ohio Lat. 40°

Appealing character and appearance. Great intelligence. Aptitude for science, the arts (music), teaching. Guarantee of success in this area or in the luxury trade—but more probably in the arts. Great ambition, self-confidence, business sense and understanding of life. Ingenious, inventive, daring and enterprising mind. Passions reasonable but lively and numerous.

Long and frequent voyages are auspicious and can lead to success and a reputation if you choose a career in the arts. However, one crossing will be dangerous for accident or sickness.

You have encountered many obstacles and difficulties in youth. A sudden change in curcumstances—the ruin or death of a parent—has thwarted your plans, but your prospects are excellent, and after several disappointments your position will be stable and very good. Your family is opposed—you will have disagreements and lawsuits from that quarter as well as struggles against false friends. Chance of profiting from lawsuits, but avoid rash acts: you are a bit reckless and often overconfident.

Very good social relations, powerful and useful friendships. A woman of high position is devoted to you. Chance of a legacy or gift coming from a woman.

Taste for independence which delays marriage. Several sorrows in love and several mysteries or impediments in your affections.

However, you will have a chance for a union bringing happiness and fortune, but before that you will have a serious disappointment.

Nervous or nervous-bilious temperament. Long life. Stone, turquoise. Days, Thursday, Friday. Flower, holly.

The year 1908–1909 is very good for travels, artistic success or successful enterprises, and for new relations which will be useful to you.

Danger of loss of money through friends, and enmities through affairs of the heart. Hidden enemies who will give you worries through servants and subordinates.

Chance of receiving money from family or from an unexpected source.

On the whole this seems a pretty shrewd assessment of Natalie's character and talents. Those who knew her were impressed by her intelligence, self-confidence and daring, and even her business sense. That her passions were ''reasonable but lively and numerous'' was no secret. ''Taste for independence which delays marriage'' can be interpreted as lesbianism, as can ''several mysteries and impediments in your affections.'' Evidently the astrologer was not aware of Natalie's wealth, and the usual dangerous voyages and hidden enemies may be dismissed as simply the conventions of astrology—or affairs of the heart. Natalie had certainly encountered obstacles in her youth, as the horoscope states, but the death of her father, far from thwarting her plans, put an end to family opposition and left her free to live as she chose. Properly interpreted, one prediction in the horoscope is very sound: ''The year 1908-1909 is very good for travels, artistic success or successful enterprises, and for new relations which will be useful to you.'' What the stars had in mind was not her trip to Saint Petersburg in pursuit of the actress, for that was an unsuccessful enterprise from which she returned empty-handed, save for a copy of Voltaire's *Candide*. No, clearly the travels in her destiny were only across Paris, and the successful enterprise was her salon, which would bring her new relations of an intellectual rather than amorous variety.

Whether she realized it or not, Natalie had at last discovered her vocation. The salon that she opened in October, 1909, was to continue for sixty years, during which her ''Fridays'' would become an institution. She may have been guided by her horoscope in choosing her ''day'' for the salon, and she must have taken into consideration that in French, Friday is Venus' day. Whatever the reason, every Friday from this time forth she was ''at home'' to friends and guests from five to eight P.M. whenever she was in Paris.

The setting she had chosen became an essential part of the atmosphere that was henceforth to be identified with her. First, however, she had to exercise her formidable will and powers of persuasion to establish her claim to the place, which someone else had rented before she appeared on the scene. But when she wanted something, whether in love or business, Natalie could be an irresistible force. Somehow she prevailed upon the landlord or the lessee or both and established herself in that house, from which not even a powerful minister of state was able to dislodge her until her death, at the age of ninety-five. She was all of thirty-two when she moved in, in the spring of 1909.

The Rue Jacob, which has not changed much over these sixty-odd years, is a quiet residential street lined with plain eighteenth-century façades interspersed with a few bookstores and antique shops. Located on the edge of the old Latin Quarter, around the corner from the Church of Saint-Germain-des-Prés, the street itself dates from the Middle Ages, but most of its historical associations are with the seventeenth and eighteenth centuries. Some of the great names in French literature of that period are associated with the street or its side streets: Racine, La Rochefoucauld, Saint-Simon, Voltaire. During that period it was the main artery of the Faubourg Saint-Germain, a favorite residence of the French nobility, who built palatial hôtels, private residences that were later to become the tourist hotels of a more democratic era. And to this day the Faubourg Saint-Germain is synonymous with the old, traditional upper crust of French society. In a sense it is a backwater, populated by an aristocracy that has little to do with the modern world, a society so old-fashioned and self-assured that a duchess can dress like a charwoman without appearing ridiculous.

Natalie must have seemed an anomaly at first—she would have been an anomaly anywhere, this striking blond, blue-eyed young American woman who came and went in a glass coach and who entertained a strange assortment of people—but during her long sojourn in the Faubourg Saint-Germain her style became as old-fashioned as that of any duchess. Not that Natalie consciously imitated her aristocratic neighbors—most of whom would not have received her in their houses—but she was as indifferent to fashion as they were. The interior of her house was notoriously dowdy, filled with miscellaneous bric-a-brac and furnished to a large extent with odd pieces given her by her mother because they were not worth transporting back to America. And for the rest of her life Natalie dressed simply, in a rather ageless style, wearing white tea gowns when she received guests and plain gray tailored suits when she went out to pay calls. Among her friends there are those who claim that her style was always outmoded, arrested in time, like the ancient aristocracy that still harked back to the days of Louis XIV. If Natalie was of a period, it was the turn of the century, not only in her style of dress and interior decoration but in her political and social views as well. One of the last meetings of her salon was held in May, 1968, while students were rioting in the immediate neighborhood.

Natalie acted as if nothing were going on. She was never one to pay attention to what was happening in the street.

Actually the house she lived in is off the street, in a world of its own. The building on the street at 20 rue Jacob is a four-storied affair divided into apartments, like most of its neighbors. A large gateway leads into a cobblestoned courtyard, and at the end of the court is the two-storied *pavillon,* a little house that stands by itself in the garden. The garden is quite spacious for this section of Paris and completely wild, with thin, weedy trees growing very tall, creating a shadowy atmosphere of subaqueous greenery. The untidy condition of the garden is surprising, for the French believe in pruning everything in neat geometric patterns, bringing order to nature's abandon. But in this, at least, Natalie betrayed her origins in American Romanticism, preferring to let things grow in their natural disorder.

The most distinctive feature of the property she rented is a small Doric temple tucked away in a corner of the garden. There are all sorts of legends about this temple, chiefly centering on the great actress Adrienne Lecouvreur, who was the idol of eighteenth-century Paris and the love of some of its greatest men, and who died young under mysterious circumstances, probably poisoned by a jealous rival. But contrary to legend, the temple was not a trysting place or a tomb of love, nor are its origins so ancient. The inscription on its pediment dedicates the temple *à l'amitié,* "to friendship," and official records show that it dates back only to the early nineteenth century. Some of Natalie's friends found it appropriate that she should become the vestal of friendship; others persisted in referring to the little outbuilding as the Temple of Love or the Temple of Venus.

During her early years at the Rue Jacob, Natalie continued to give garden parties as she had done in Neuilly, sometimes with a hundred or more guests attending. But her address became more famous for the smaller weekly gatherings of the salon, usually held indoors unless the weather was particularly good. The ground floor of Natalie's house included two drawing rooms, one of which looked out on the garden, and it was here that the habitués and invited guests gathered for tea and conversation. To Americans nowadays a literary salon may sound like a precious, periwigged ritual from another era, but in the Paris of Marcel Proust the salons still flourished. Proust himself made his way in society and gathered the materials for *Remembrance of Things Past* in the aristocratic salons, which were primarily social but which also appreciated intelligence, wit and learning, so that a young Jewish nobody could rub elbows with the ancient nobility. Some of the salons were political or musical or literary in their emphasis, reflecting the particular inclinations of the presiding hostess. Of the literary salons the most famous was that of Mme. Arman de Caillavet, with its tame lion, Anatole France, who was required to perform whether or not he felt up to the occasion. In his biography of Proust, George Painter gives a sketch of that salon which shows that the great conversationalist Anatole was sometimes less than brilliant and that salon wit could be strained.

> "On entering the drawing-room of Mme. Arman," wrote one of her guests, "one had the impression of being in a railway station, of which Anatole France was the stationmaster." Mme. Arman sat to the right of the fireplace, while France leaned against the mantelpiece, gesturing, stammering, hunting for the right word, but always holding forth. "His conversation was that of a superior but crashing bore," thought Henri de Regnier, who was, however, fond of talking himself; but to Fernand Gregh it seemed "literally enchanting with its mixture of irony and kindness, wit and grace, naturalness and erudition, fantasy and good sense." Towards Proust he adopted the paternal tone of Bergotte. "How do you manage to know so many things, Monsieur France?" asked Proust, and France replied: "It's quite simple, my dear Marcel. When I was your age I wasn't good-looking and popular like you. So instead of going into society I stayed at home and did nothing but read."

The idea of a salon was nothing new to Natalie. Even before she lived in Paris she had acquired from her background the idea of combining cultural interests with social occasions. Grandfather Pike had introduced European singers and musicians to Cincinnati society in his home, and Alice Pike Barney, impatient with the philistinism of Washington social life, had tried to give the arts a place in her soirees. A society column reported, "Mrs. Barney's dinners are always followed by music, recitations, or some artistic finale for the evening, to replace the usual bridge. . . ."

Though less interested in art, Natalie shared her mother's sentiments and had little patience with small talk. She believed in the art of intelligent conversation, which she practiced incisively herself, even as a very young woman. In Washington she had frequented diplomatic circles and learned the art of conversation from old professionals like Jules Cambon. In Paris, while she was still in her early twenties, she impressed far older people not only with her command of French, which was extraordinary enough, but with her ability to express original ideas with wit and authority. Never addicted to book learning, she was one of those who learn mostly from listening and who therefore rely largely on the conversation of intelligent and cultivated people for their own intellectual lives. In the highly articulate society of Paris, there was nothing unusual about this; the salons existed precisely for such an exchange of ideas.

During her early years in Paris, Natalie had an opportunity to observe how the salons functioned. Americans were not readily received in aristocratic society, and Natalie's notoriety made her *persona non grata* in certain circles. One of the leading literary women of the time, the poet Anna de Noailles, would have nothing to do with the likes of Natalie; when Natalie sent her the poems of Renée Vivien, the countess returned the book, scornfully remarking that she was not interested in the writings of such people. Another of the leading women writers, Princess Marthe Bibesco, knew Natalie but did not choose to be associated with her, except when she wanted an introduction to Remy de Gourmont. But there were others, equally aristocratic, if not equally talented, who gave Natalie entrée into certain salons. Count Robert de Montesquiou, the original of Proust's Baron de Charlus, had no fear of notoriety, being himself the most notorious homosexual in Paris. Montesquiou was a great dandy and aesthete who entertained on a lavish scale, organizing elaborate parties in his Pavilion of the Muses, presenting dancers from the Ballet Russe, the music of Debussy, or the poetry of Mallarmé and Verlaine read by the stars of the Comédie Française.

Though remembered chiefly for his faults, which were many, he should also be remembered for his good qualities. Daring, witty, eccentric, he showed more taste and originality than other members of his caste and was a discriminating patron of writers and artists. Some of the bluest blood in France flowed through his veins, and he knew everyone in the arts, so that when he took an interest in Natalie, he introduced her to the most brilliant society in Paris. Natalie remained loyal to Montesquiou in his later years, when most of his friends deserted him, and was one of the handful of mourners at his funeral—she, who hated funerals. He left her a Persian tapestry, which she hung on the wall of her drawing room, as if to make him a permanent member of her salon.

Two noble hostesses also became friends of Natalie. One of them was a wealthy American woman, Winnaretta Singer, an heiress to the sewing machine fortune, who had married the elegant but impoverished Prince Edmond de Polignac. This was frankly a marriage of convenience, in which both husband and wife tolerated each other's private lives; but they had one important thing in common, a great love of music, and together they founded one of the most enlightened and influential music salons. The princess collected attractive women as well as composers and needed no introduction to Natalie when they met at one of Montesquiou's gatherings.

Through the Mardrus, Natalie met another music lover, Elisabeth de Gramont, Duchess de Clermont-Tonnerre, who became one of her dearest friends. For a number of years they were lovers, but clearly they had more in common than passion; for their loving friendship lasted almost half a century, until the duchess' death. The duchess, who was a highly intelligent and talented woman, wrote four volumes of memoirs which make an excellent guidebook to Proust's Paris, giving an insider's view of the Faubourg Saint-Germain. Growing up in a great French household could mean a dreary social round followed by an unhappy marriage, she frankly complained, for this was a man's world. The first chapter of her memoirs explains how she began to recognize the limitations of her society. The scene opens with a visit to the salon of Mme. Arman de Caillavet, where the great Anatole France is holding forth. Though only ten minutes' walk from the Clermont-Tonnerre residence, this salon was totally unfamiliar territory and opened up a whole new world to her, an escape from the boredom of high society.

To a remarkable degree for a single woman of her reputation, Natalie became acquainted in French society. But she needed another kind of acquaintance to populate her salon. From the time she established her residence in Paris, she had been cultivating friendships with writers and intellectuals, and her circle of acquaintance had steadily widened. In addition to the women writers with whom she had love affairs, she made a point of seeking the company of men for serious conversation. Thus, in one household she had both kinds of friends—the poet Lucie Delarue-Mardrus and the great Orientalist Dr. J.-C. Mardrus. Through Pierre Louÿs she met other writers: André Gide, Marcel Schwob, Paul Valéry. From her classics professor, Charles Brun, she went on to establish a friendship with the great classical scholar Salomon Reinach. These friendships led in turn to others, and gradually she became acquainted with a considerable number of distinguished men.

It is clear that Natalie was esteemed by such men for her intelligence rather than her wealth and good looks. To say that they were attracted by her wit and charm makes her sound superficial and does justice neither to her nor to them. For her wit was the articulation of an original mind that quickly seized the complexity of an idea, and her charm was an intuitive response to people who interested her. Men of ideas—scholars, philosophers, statesmen, critics—found her remarkably easy to talk to and capable of establishing close rapport in short order. Men of ideas are human, too, and therefore all the more susceptible to an attractive woman who can put them at their ease, listen intelligently to what they have to say, and respond in kind.

Sometimes her relations with them were quite playful. Salomon Reinach, for all his scholarly eminence, often indulged in lighthearted banter; it was he who nicknamed her "the wild girl from Cincinnati." Pierre Louÿs and his friends sometimes played children's games with her. *Aventures de l'esprit* provides a glimpse of a lighthearted evening with such seemingly venerable figures as Louÿs, the poet-diplomat Paul Claudel, and the gray eminence of the French Foreign Office, Philippe Berthelot. The occasion was Natalie's thirty-first birthday, on October 31, 1907, and after dinner the company played games appropriate to Halloween. Claudel specialized in divination by apple peeling, throwing the peels over his shoulder to see what initial they would form. Berthelot, far from being fatigued by the cares of state, participated in the fun with more spirit than all the others. After the games the party turned to tests of memory, and Berthelot matched wits with Louÿs in correcting the text of a sonnet by Mallarmé. *Aventures de l'esprit* is dedicated to Berthelot, who was the kind of man Natalie liked best—a wise, witty and cultivated man of the world who, for all his absorption in politics, never lost his love for literature.

Such men were good company, able to converse with ease on a variety of subjects, especially literature, which was always the center of interest in Natalie's salon. And, of course, there were women of this stamp, too, as well as those who were invited for less intellectual reasons. Such friends became the habitués of the salon, those who had a standing invitation to come on Friday whenever they felt like it. In addition, Natalie usually invited people who might prove interesting and, occasionally, celebrities who served as special attractions. Her greatest coup was the appearance of the Bengali poet and Nobel Prize winner, Rabindranath Tagore, a strikingly handsome figure over six feet tall, dressed in flowing robes. Natalie wrote a poem describing this apparition from another world, rhythmically chanting his verses, transporting his audience to the Indies of their imagination.

Other celebrities included artists and composers like Auguste Rodin, Darius Milhaud and Florent Schmitt, but as a rule Natalie preferred writers. Among those to whom she devoted one or more chapters in her memoirs are Cocteau, Colette, D'Annunzio, Anatole France, Gide, Remy de Gourmont, Max Jacob, Proust, Gertrude Stein, Rilke and Valéry. Some of these were habitués, some came only a few times, and Proust never came to the salon at all, though he corresponded with Natalie and called on her once in the middle of the night. Some celebrities proved disappointing and their visits not worth mentioning in her memoirs. James Joyce, who did not enjoy being lionized, came to the salon only once or twice and embarrassed Natalie by criticizing Racine and Corneille until she cut him short.

As a rule, however, Natalie counted on her regulars to make the salon an attraction in itself. She tried to introduce a variety of people who might not otherwise meet and prided herself particularly on the international character of her salon. Thus, at different periods, Rilke, D'Annunzio and Gertrude Stein were much in evidence; during the twenties Natalie introduced a good many American and English writers to the French; and for many years the Lithuanian poet Milosz was a regular. Besides the writers there was always a sprinkling of learned intellectuals, with different specialties and professions. As a result the conversation could sometimes be quite heterogeneous, as in the following unique sample, preserved for posterity by Georges Cattaui:

> I remember one Friday afternoon the Arab magician Mardrus describing with charming emphasis a fabulous Moroccan palace. Next to him was the poet Milosz who had the expression and the profile of an eagle. How to describe the strange and bizarre dialogue between these two sorcerers, one from Egypt, the other from Lithuania, communing under the gaze of their American friend over the subtleties of gnossi and Kabbala? While this lyrical exhibition reached its climax, in another corner of the great salon . . . sneered two entirely different characters: Charles Rappoport, the socialist and Aulard, the historian. "All this," Aulard would say, "is enough to put one to sleep. I don't believe a word of it. Orientals are born liars and mythomaniacs. Alas, their fairy tales have become the beliefs of the West." I left these sceptics for the company of the mystical poet of *Mephiboseth.* "To be a really good Catholic, a complete Christian," Milosz would tell me, "one must also be, rather like you and I, a little Jewish. . . . Which is why so many of those who listen do not understand us."

It is hard to imagine Isadora Duncan conversing with an erudite professor like the historian Charles Seignobos, or even the painter Marie Laurencin finding much to say to the art historian Bernard Berenson. Natalie had a way of bringing together the most unlikely types, and that was one of the attractions of her salon. But she also relied on her club of regulars, who knew one another and had a good deal in common. During the early years of the salon, the regulars included scholars, like Mardrus, Reinach and Seignobos; political figures, like Berthelot and Paul Boncour; and an occasional artist, like the sculptor José de Charmoy. But mostly there were people from the literary world: editors, publishers, booksellers, and critics, as well as writers, including Edouard Champion, Bernard Grasset, André Germain, Edmond Jaloux, Francis de Miomandre and André Rouveyre, in addition to the more famous writers mentioned earlier, Max Jacob, Milosz, Rilke and Valéry.

Natalie was right at home in a salon. Naturally gregarious and quick to establish rapport with all manner of people, she was also endowed with the kind of conversational wit that enlivened such gatherings. Always the perfect hostess, she never dominated the conversation and never seemed to intervene, but unobtrusively saw to it that her guests felt at ease and met others who might interest them. She also fed them sumptuously, and her salon became famous for its delicious cakes and sandwiches. Some of these were literary delicacies, like the little cucumber sandwiches in imitation of those Oscar Wilde used to serve. In the early years of the salon Natalie only served tea, which may explain why she had the reputation of being a teetotaler; but later she served punch and champagne as well, and finally whiskey, though never cocktails. As a matter of fact, she appreciated good wines but deplored drunkenness and felt that strong waters had no place in a salon. Over the years the salon changed somewhat, but on the whole Natalie did not change much, and the ritual established in the early years persisted to the end.

10
Epigrams

The company of so many literary people in her salon may have given Natalie the idea of becoming a literary person herself. Before moving to the Rue Jacob she had published only two books: her volume of lesbian love poems, in 1900, and her Greek dialogues, published under a pseudonym in 1902. Another work, *The Woman Who Lives with Me,* had been privately printed in 1904, but that "short novel," shorter than most short stories, could hardly be counted as a book. Of course, she had gone on writing during the intervening years, but evidently she had felt no inclination to publish her work. Like the courtier-poets of the Renaissance, she was content to circulate her writing in manuscript, to have her love poems copied out by a calligrapher and presented to the ones who inspired them, or to have her work read in the presence of a small group of friends. "Fame," she remarked in one of her epigrams, "is to be known by those one would not wish to know."

Certainly it was not the desire for fame that moved her to publish now. Perhaps it was the urging of her literary friends or the desire to establish her credentials as a writer. Whatever her motive, she published three books during 1910, all of them containing work that had been written over the previous decade. *Je me souviens,* the sequence of prose poems tracing the story of her love for Renée Vivien, is dated 1904 at its close. *Actes et entr'actes,* which includes one play dated 1906, is introduced as a work of her youth and has all the look of a collected plays and poems written for various occasions during her years in Neuilly. And the third book, *Éparpillements,* also contains material that had accumulated over a period of years. This book is the one that reveals the most about Natalie's talents and habits as a writer.

Éparpillements means "scatterings," and the book contains the random jottings that she made in her journal. This is the closest thing to a writer's notebook, with all kinds of observations and remarks preserved for future reference and possible use. But the writer of this notebook refused to make a career of writing, preferring to remain an amateur instead of using the materials she had collected in writing novels, say, or essays. So she published merely a collection of bits and pieces, brief character sketches, scraps of dialogue, clever sayings. And, as a matter of fact, Natalie had here discovered the form of expression that suited her best: the art of fragments.

Éparpillements was the first of three volumes of *pensées* in which she distilled her wit and refined her observations on the human comedy. The word *pensées,* which means "thoughts," inevitably raises the ghost of Pascal and suggests philosophical thinking; but there are other *pensées* besides Pascal's, and the form as Natalie used it has a long and varied history going back to the classical epigram. In France it could just as readily be associated with Pascal's cynical contemporary La Rochefoucauld, but for the fact that he used the word *maximes.* La Rochefoucauld, with whom Natalie has frequently been compared, was a seventeenth-century nobleman who, after having lived a full life, frequented a salon which cultivated the kind of epigrammatic utterance in which he excelled. His published *Maximes* epitomize in elegant concision his disillusioned view of the human species. In English, too, the epigram has a long tradition, culminating in Natalie's lifetime with the aphorisms of Emerson and the witty paradoxes of Wilde. Needless to say, Natalie was more inclined to imitate the latter.

Some of her epigrams have a distinctly Wildean ring:

How many inner resources one needs to tolerate a life of leisure without fatigue.

The reverse works equally well:

How much power we need to yield to what we desire most.

Wilde specialized in reversing clichés or received ideas, giving a proverbial phrasing to the opposite of folk wisdom. So also, Natalie:

Fatalism is the lazy man's way of accepting the evitable.

Wilde always produced the unexpected, often by the simple device of turning the expected into a negative. So also Natalie:

Time engraves our faces with all the tears we have not shed.

Some of her remarks could have been spoken by one of those pretty heroines in Wilde's plays whose lines often leave the audience wondering whether she is shrewdly perceptive or simply absentminded.

I felt that he found me prettier than he had feared.

Another line quotes a mistress in praise of a lover:

He knew so well how not to kiss me.

And, of course, Natalie has several epigrams on the Wildean theme of being a poet in life instead of producing literature.

The epigrams are clearly a by-product of her own life, the wise and witty observations that struck her as memorable. Not all of them are her own, by any means, but she had the rare quality of being a good listener with a keen ear for what was said and how it was said, and she took the trouble to write things down. As might be expected, the greatest number of her remarks deal with love.

To have or not to have, which is worse?

Forever is too long.

Eros is the youngest of the gods. He is also the most tired.

Generally her view of love is unsentimental, not to say disillusioned: infidelity makes the heart grow fonder; habit dulls the lover's charm; courtship is its own reward; love is simply a series of enslavements; lovers bore each other; marriage means being neither alone nor together. These reflections need not be taken literally as Natalie's conclusions; they might be the expression of particular moods, for no one knew better than she how inconstant and inconsistent and contradictory love could be. Above all they should be read as an anthology of memorable sayings on the theme of love, generally skeptical but invariably reflecting a fascination with this all-too-human activity.

Not all the jottings are epigrammatic in form. Some present situations in miniature, overheard remarks, bits of dialogue.

> Lovers should also have their days off.

> "She's not worth the trouble."
> "My trouble's worth the trouble."

> Every night I dream that you are unfaithful to me, but last night I finally had a happy dream: you committed suicide for me.

> She called me "my love." This word became a habit, beginning sentences that would end otherwise. What a sad domesticated word, all that survives of a once-radiant feeling.

One exchange seems to sum up Natalie's whole attitude toward the subject.

> "What did you love the most?"
> "Love."
> "And if you had to make several choices?"
> "I would choose love several times."

A few feminist comments might also be taken as her own, favoring a life of creation rather than procreation.

> If maternity worked backwards, beginning with the pains of childbirth, there would still be mothers, but they would be willing heroines, not victims of a mistake or wretched martyrs of one of nature's

tricks. When will man be borne for the child's sake, not the child for the man's?

Needless to say, all of these *pensées* lose much in translation.

After love the subject that receives the greatest attention is society with all its pretense and affectation. Human behavior in general and manners in particular have always been the concern of the epigrammatist. In observing the comedy of manners Natalie had a deadly satirical eye. She would have been right at home in the eighteenth century, an age of satire which took a similar amused, detached view of the foibles and vanities of human behavior.

> On her walls she liked to see only portraits of herself, her mirrors.

> Twenty paces from me she was already preparing her face for a smile.

> He had the three badges of nonentity: a receding chin, the Legion of Honor and a wedding ring.

> In an artificial world she paraded the true gold of her hair.

In the artificial world of society most conversation is silly or banal, so it is easy to imagine Natalie's delight at overhearing such a gem as this:

> "Every man has his price," said an aristocrat (who must have been a millionaire), "but some have no commercial value, which is what saves them."

A good many of the *pensées* seem to have originated in her salon, where the conversation centered on literature and the other arts.

> The Romantics appropriated all the big words, leaving us only the little ones.

> I cannot understand those who spend hours in the theater watching scenes between people whom they would not listen to for five minutes in real life.

> How many painters have only seen color on the palettes of others.

To those who ask, "Have you read my book?" I reply, "I have not yet read Homer."

A number of brief characterizations seem to be based on types she observed in her salon. There are those who speak in order to hear themselves speak, others whose arrogant self-assurance makes her doubt the truth of what they say. She prefers those who speak indistinctly, fumbling for their words, and judges people by the ease with which she expresses herself in their company. Her own speech takes her by surprise:

Only after having said it do I think my thought.

This cannot be far from the truth. People who knew Natalie were struck by the swiftness of her repartee and the accuracy of her aim. She seemed to reply without taking thought, yet her offhand remarks had the same lucid, concise phrasing as her *pensées*. In other words, she spoke in epigrams. In writing them down she undoubtedly improved them, but so for that matter did the great master of the form, La Rochefoucauld, who rehearsed his sentences in collaboration with others and revised his *Maximes* through successive editions. Natalie never took such pains. She was satisfied to jot down her epigrams, but the original delight of the moment counted more.

In a section of *Éparpillements* devoted to critical comments, there is an extended reflection that begins as a character sketch and ends up reading like the author's defense of her art. Although buried in the latter pages, this passage, by far the longest in the entire book, would make an appropriate preface, not only to this book but to her complete works. This little manifesto begins by professing admiration for a writer who painstakingly files and labels his *pensées* like so many beautiful insects fixed on pins, making these specimens transcend everyday life by transfixing them in a phrase. This writer's only limitation is his tendency to censure indiscretion, overlooking its many benefits. For all expression, all art, Natalie continues, is an indiscretion which we commit against ourselves, and it is thus that we live the few hours of our lives in which we rise above ourselves. There are those who make masterpieces of their lives, leaving nothing behind but the story of their loves. Therefore, she believes, we should honor our dead with a bold epitaph recording their words and deeds instead of burying them in the oblivion of discretion. In writing this she may have had in mind Renée Vivien, who had died the previous year. More specifically she may have proposed to write an epitaph immortalizing Renée's indiscretions; in the front of *Éparpillements* she announced a work in progress which was never published, *Le Tombeau de Renée Vivien*. But even without this work, her manifesto explains and vindicates what she did in the best of her writing, which is not to be found in verse or dramatic form, but in her *pensées* and memoirs, the writings that are most revealing of her life and her indiscretions.

11
Remy de Gourmont

Natalie's most famous conquest was not a woman but a man, and a most unlikely one at that—an old, ugly recluse completely lacking in the social graces. Yet it was she who sought him out and exercised all her charms to win him, overcoming his shyness and reluctance. Eventually she succeeded so well that he fell in love with her, and for the five years that remained of his life she was his great love. This strange platonic courtship between youth and old age has been likened, somewhat ironically, to a similar relationship in the eighteenth-century, with Natalie playing the role of Horace Walpole to the doting old, blind marquise Du Deffand. But the marquise was a brilliant woman whose letters to Walpole did him honor. Similarly the *Lettres à l'Amazone* gave Natalie her nickname and the reputation, which she was to bear throughout life, of having inspired one of the finest intellects of her time.

Remy de Gourmont was one of the leading French men of letters of the period before the First World War. An enormously prolific writer, he turned out close to a hundred books of fiction, verse and essays in a relatively brief writing career. So voluminous was his output that for a time it was rumored that Remy de Gourmont was a pseudonym used by a group of writers. Although he acquired a reputation for his erotic fiction, it was primarily as a literary critic that he distinguished himself. He was the leading critic of the Symbolist

119

movement, one of the founders of the influential literary journal *Le Mercure de France*, and for many years its guiding spirit. Today his fame is largely forgotten, but in his day he was a kind of literary dictator—if such a term can be applied to a man who led a hermitlike existence—and the literary world deferred to his judgment. Since his time, his ideas have permeated English and American literature through the writings of T. S. Eliot and Ezra Pound, not to mention a host of other poet-critics, all of whom drew heavily on Gourmont's writings. And quite apart from his literary work, he had the wide-ranging mind of a Renaissance man who tried to encompass all the learning of his time, from science to philosophy. To Ezra Pound he represented nothing less than "the best portrait available, the best record that is, of the civilized mind from 1885 to 1915."

Unlike Natalie's other male friends, Gourmont was not a man of the world. On the contrary, he was completely withdrawn from the world and led a solitary, monkish existence in the book-lined study of his sixth-floor attic, writing, writing, writing. He even dressed the part in a coarse robe of monk's cloth. A neighboring apartment was occupied by his mistress of many years, Berthe de Courrière, a kind of witch who dabbled in occult practices and whose company was probably not the most comforting. A few—very few—literary friends came to call on Sundays, but Gourmont was antisocial and did not welcome many callers. For the most part he led the life of a bookworm, reading omnivorously and writing, it seemed, almost as much as he read. If he went out at all, it was only within a radius of a few blocks—to the office of the *Mercure de France*, to the booksellers on the quays along the Seine or, at most, to the Café Flore at Saint-Germain-des-Prés. Natalie lived less than ten minutes' walk from his apartment, but entirely outside his orbit in more ways than one.

He had not always been a recluse. In his youth he had been handsome and sociable, but when he was in his thirties he contracted lupus, a repulsive skin disease that left him so disfigured that he literally did not want to show his face. For years he only went out under cover of darkness and saw no one but his brother. This affliction left him feeling like a leper, isolated from ordinary human activities, prematurely aged and bearish, grumbling and muttering to himself. Yet, though he felt like a monster, he did not become one; despite his contemplative existence above the rooftops, he never lost touch with humanity. He remained fully alive emotionally, but horribly crippled in the exercise of his emotions. This was the forbidding personage Natalie met in the summer of 1910.

Her neighbor Edouard Champion introduced them—at first through books, appropriately enough. Champion, a young bookseller who was a friend of Gourmont's, sent him Natalie's poems on the death of Renée, which Gourmont then had published in the *Mercure de France*. Natalie wrote to thank him and enclosed her letter in a copy of her latest book, *Éparpillements*. Gourmont replied with a flattering letter, saying he found a kindred spirit in her epigrams. After these bookish beginnings, the next step was to beard the bear in his cave, and Champion offered to take Natalie to call on Gourmont on his "day," when he received a few close friends. Natalie and Champion were the first to arrive, and Gourmont met them at the door with a friendly handshake. In *Souvenirs indiscrets* Natalie remembers that she hardly noticed his scarred face but closely studied the shifting moods reflected in his pale blue eyes, detecting there a zest for life that had been repressed. Perhaps that is what she expected or wanted to find, for she soon made up her mind to bring this poor monkish soul out of his cloister. There was something of the missionary about Natalie; just as earlier she had decided to rescue Liane from the courtesan's life and to cure Renée of her death wish, so now she undertook the mission of bringing Gourmont back to life.

André Rouveyre, who knew Natalie and Gourmont intimately, analyzes their relationship at length in *Souvenirs de mon commerce*. To him it was a case of opposites attracting: Natalie intrigued by Gourmont's love for solitary meditation; he, by her love of vain pleasures; and both wanted to grasp what possessed the other. Though physically indifferent to him, she exercised her seductive powers because she wanted to be worshiped by the richest mind of his generation. Gourmont, according to Rouveyre, was a man of flesh and blood whose instincts and passions were intimately linked with his sensitive intellect. No amount of originality and intelligence would have affected him so profoundly if Natalie had not been beautiful. He fell completely in love with her, experiencing an emotional and sensual awakening that was like a total rejuvenation. But he knew that passion was forbidden, and he succeeded so well in disguising his feelings that Natalie never realized he was in love. Rouveyre documents the progress of their relationship by quoting from Gourmont's *Lettres intimes à l'Amazone,* at that time unpublished. These are the real letters that he addressed to her, as opposed to the *Lettres à l'Amazone,* which are really essays written for publication.

In one of these essays Gourmont characterizes Natalie in a way that tells something of the relationship that existed between them.

> I like the will to live, the appetite for pleasure in you, Amazon. You may be made to suffer, but nothing will destroy that vehemence which carries you towards beauty and towards love. Like all persons born to dominate and to bend others beneath their yoke, you do not give way beneath a disappointment, which only overwhelms you for a moment, and your woman-warrior's pagan heart is renewed thereby. It is a sight which enchants me like the renewal of the year; and what an example it is to me who am always ready to despair of myself and find only too many reasons for it.

Lettres à l'Amazone reflects the complete frankness of their conversation. The topic is almost invariably love, and though the letters often begin and end with gallant compliments, Gourmont does not write as a suitor but as an intimate friend who is well aware of his *Amazone*'s preferences. It is obvious that they have confided fully in one another how they feel about all the varieties and complexities of love, for his letters continue the conversation, responding to what she has said.

But the underlying story of their relationship is to be found in the *Lettres intimes à l'Amazone.* These are real love letters, centered on the two of them, seldom mentioning anyone or anything else, forming a continuous interior monologue in which he dwells constantly on her. They show what she meant to this sickly old man during the last years of his life and prove beyond a doubt that he truly loved her—shyly, humbly, tenderly, submissively. While his life is solitary and his thoughts are devoted exclusively to her, she is gadding about, involved in a constant whirl of love affairs. She is often away, and after the first two years she often neglects him, although he remains grateful, devoted and uncomplaining to the end.

But she was the one who made the first overtures and originally drew him out of his solitude. After their first meeting she went to see him again and invited him to go for a drive in the Bois de Boulogne one evening, something he never did. Gourmont resisted, Natalie insisted, and her will proved stronger. At the appointed hour she waited in the car below while her chauffeur walked up the six flights of stairs and brought the reluctant passenger down. All the way out to the Bois he said nothing, and she made no attempt to break into this intimidating silence. Finally, beside one of the lakes in the park, the moonlight on the water called forth a sigh of loneliness, to which Natalie responded with a sigh of her own, claiming loneliness herself since the death of Renée. Gourmont, who had read her writings, reminded her that she had other loves.

"How long and difficult is the conquest of a spirit," Natalie exclaims in *Souvenirs indiscrets,* and she goes on to say that this was a conquest worthy of all her resources. Still, she left town almost immediately, in pursuit of another person who also seemed worth the trouble, and the letter which Gourmont wrote after their drive reveals that he was only too willing to be conquered without further ado.

> . . . I am not in the habit of going out to the Bois de Boulogne with young women in the evening; that's why I only began to enjoy this situation when it was over. Not because it was unpleasant but rather because it was too pleasant and because it implied a state of mind on your part for which I had no evidence. And then in the Bois the moon looks too much like an electric-light globe. You intimidated me terribly, even though your voice was gentle and natural. Perhaps it was your natural ease that threw me off, and yet I expected nothing else of you. But since it is very rare for a woman to be unaffected, one has to be prepared for it.

Gourmont concludes the letter by timidly expressing a hope that this new acquaintance might develop: "Now something tells me that I may have found a friend to play with life a little more—occasionally, when you have a little time to waste?"

A few months later they are seeing each other frequently, taking walks together, going to the theater, exchanging little presents. He signs himself "Remy" and asks her to call him that, nicknames her "Natalis" and writes a poem about her portrait as a page. His letters begin to sound like love letters.

> Dear friend, you were so nice to me and so confiding that I want to write to you to have a pretext to go on thinking of that. I have hardly done anything but write all day long. That sharpens the impressions and makes them more vivid. I am so much a man of writings! No, that's not what I want to say. I am writing so that you will know that I think of you still more tenderly. Certainly you knew it, but we like best to hear each other say what we know best. Your presence is a sweetness which remains with me, permeating and coloring all the days that follow. You may even make me regain an interest in life that I have lost; if that's possible, it will come from you, because you are my own true friend and because I love you.

More declarations follow. "You are a present fallen from the sky at a time in my life when I was most depressed, when I no longer liked anything, hoped for anything, wanted anything." He makes this statement repeatedly, using more and more affectionate terms. In the *Midsummer Night's Dream* of his imagination, she is the enchantress Titania, and he is Bottom, transformed into an ass. Like any lover he is full of palpitations over meetings and partings, especially meetings anticipated or missed. He writes constantly, thinks of her incessantly, reports every tremor of his heart, full of tenderness and concern, overcome with joy at hearing from her, sadness when she is away, disappointment when she misses a rendezvous. Already she begins to take him for granted.

Natalie has described their meetings in his hermitage. At the sound of the doorbell—Natalie always rang twice, as a signal that she was there—Gourmont would rush to the door, all eagerness, and, seizing both her wrists, pull her inside, as if he were rescuing her from danger or, as Rouveyre puts it, tearing her away from the world in order to make her part of himself. Then, sitting down face to face, they would gaze into each other's eyes, and Natalie would reach out for his hands, which she found dry as old parchment and surprisingly warm. Once, to his dismay, she withdrew her hands, thinking he had improper designs on her, and he wrote a letter begging to be restored to favor. Soon all was forgiven, and she let him hold her hands again while they sat talking. At the end of her visit he would stand on the landing outside his door and watch while she went down the six flights of stairs; she never saw him close his door. Rouveyre likens their relationship to that of Socrates and his young disciples, but he also compares Natalie to Nero in her cruel domination of her fearful subject. He saw their encounters as episodes in a love affair and was convinced that Gourmont was consumed with passion, though, to his astonishment, Natalie assured him that she was not aware of any such feeling. Anyone reading the *Lettres intimes à l'Amazone* would conclude that she was either disingenuous or blind.

By the second summer of their acquaintance Gourmont was running all sorts of errands for his imperious Titania, only too willing to be of service, while she, who was accustomed to service, had no scruples about asking him. When she decided to give a masked ball in her garden, this most distinguished man of letters edited the text of her invitation, arranged to have it printed and supplied the address of his friend Guillaume Apollinaire, whom she wanted to invite. To her invitation in verse Apollinaire replied, also in verse, regretfully declining; but with Gourmont's assistance she had almost captured this literary lion, and she had his poem as a trophy. Gourmont himself came to the ball wearing Natalie's Arab gown with her green silk stocking wrapped around his head as a turban. Natalie dressed as a Japanese firefly-catcher, and the trees in the garden were hung with Chinese lanterns. The evening's entertainment included a harpsichord concert by Wanda Landowska and the performance of an eighteenth-century play, *Le Ton de Paris*, by the duke de Lauzun. But, for Gourmont, the extraordinary experience was in appearing at a social gathering of this sort, even behind a mask, and he philosophized in print about masked balls. He enjoyed the experience so much that he went to several other parties at Natalie's, and Rouveyre noted that the recluse appeared to be at ease in the midst of the agitation and music and perfume of beautiful women. Once he came dressed as a Chinese philosopher, a costume that matched his serenity.

During the same summer, 1911, Natalie decided to cruise up and down the Seine, and Gourmont acted as her factotum, making inquiries and arranging for the rental of a boat. As his reward he once again shared in her pleasures and for three days of perfect bliss sailed down the river with her, disembarking every evening to stay at a local inn and rising early every morning to write his daily newspaper column, which he then mailed off to Paris. Along the way they stopped off to visit the Symbolist playwright Maurice Maeterlinck in his Gothic abbey. After talking with Gourmont, Maeterlinck remarked to Natalie, "Why, that man's nothing but a bottle of ink." She retaliated in her memoirs by characterizing Maeterlinck as "a mystic on a motorcycle" and describing him shooting at birds from his balcony while a young woman reloaded his gun, an arrangement that struck Natalie as too comfortable to be sporting. After three enchanted days on the river, Gourmont left the boat and, as Natalie sailed away, began writing to her again.

> How sweetly the days passed with you, my friend! And how natural it seemed to me to live near you thus, and how I love to look at you, listen to you, cherish you. Only with you do I speak at all readily, and very poorly at that, of the things which I value in life and which underlie my thinking. I am so accustomed to solitude and silence that I hardly know how to talk any more, but what a profound accompaniment is the presence of Natalis, even when she is silent too and dozing in her hammock! . . . It seemed to me that those three days would never end, and that's how I spent them, like a little eternity. Last night I was still rocked by the gentle rolling of your boat.

After that summer Natalie sometimes took him for other boat rides, rowing him around the little lake in the Bois de Boulogne.

In December, 1911, Gourmont launched the project of writing his *lettres à l'Amazone,* to be published in the *Mercure de France.* This title was suggested to him when Natalie stopped by to see him on her way home from a ride in the Bois, dressed *"en costume d'amazone,"* that is, in a riding habit. He found the costume charming and the term convenient in another sense, denoting that she belonged to a special breed of woman. In his personal letters he never addressed her as "Amazone" until much later, and then in jest, when this form of address had become public property and he was being propositioned by other ladies who fancied themselves as his *Amazone*. In May, 1912, he sent Natalie a newspaper clipping about a singular combat between two Amazons of letters, Mme. Aurel, defending outraged morality, and her well-known opponent, defending the school of Lesbos. What right, he asks, has Aurel to call herself "Amazone" when that name is his to confer and belongs only to his Natalie? More frequently, though, he calls her Titania, saying that he would gladly eat oats and thistles from her hand and signing himself "Bottom."

The *lettres à l'Amazone* were particularly dear to his heart because they involved him in collaboration with his beloved Muse. These epistolary essays were inspired by their conversations—were, in fact, a continuation of their conversations, incorporating many of her ideas. He planned the series as a little book written especially for her and filled with her *pensées*. Before delivering the individual installments for publication, he submitted them to her for approval, watching closely as she read them and rejoicing when she was pleased. And in this he was not only motivated by love but by a genuine respect for her intellect. Rouveyre's judgment can be reversed: Natalie's beauty would not have affected Gourmont so profoundly if she had not also been possessed of originality and intelligence. In a personal letter he confessed, "You are the only person to whom I have ever submitted, not emotionally, but intellectually. If I dared, I would have you read everything that I write."

While his public *lettres à l'Amazone* were appearing in print every two weeks through most of 1912 and 1913, he continued writing his private letters to Natalie. Gourmont was capable of writing a letter to her minutes after they had parted, even if they were to meet again the following day. But many of his letters were written in her absence, for during this period of her life Natalie came and went constantly, often on a sudden impulse, usually in pursuit of love. At the beginning of 1912 he saw her off at the train station as she left for the Riviera, and she gave him her fur muff to keep him company. Walking home with his hands in the muff, Gourmont wished her hands were there too: "When you are not here, Paris seems depopulated." In July she was in a serious automobile accident in the provinces, and her chauffeur was killed. Gourmont read the news in the papers and spent a day and a night frantic with worry, until he received a reply to his telegram that Natalie was all right. He was sorry about the poor chauffeur, but what really mattered was Natalie's safety. During 1913 she was away most of the time, in England or in Normandy or sometimes, even, in Paris, but not at the Rue Jacob. She sent him flowers but did not see him much.

The last *lettre à l'Amazone* appeared in August, 1913, and as the collection went to press, he wrote that this was the first book he had ever finished with regret, for it marked the end of a phase in his life. These words were truer than he realized, or perhaps he knew that his days of intimacy with his Natalis were practically ended. In the two remaining years of his life, he saw her infrequently and wrote far fewer letters to her. An invalid much of the time, he looked forward to her visits but was often disappointed. Thus, anticlimactically, ended this love story of beauty and the beast. After courting him and making him fall in love with her, she let him drop, and there are those who claim that her neglect caused his decline and death. But Gourmont would hear no criticism of his beloved Natalis—he could hardly forgive Rouveyre for publishing a caricature of her with stubble on her chin—and he remained devoted to her to the last, grateful that the end of his life had been blessed by this radiant presence.

He would not agree with those who said she got the best out of their friendship, though he realized that his *lettres à l'Amazone* had immortalized her: "For you are the Amazon and you will remain the Amazon as long as that does not bore you, and perhaps even after that in the ashes of my heart." Natalie, who had a well-developed ego, never tired of her fame as the Amazon. A painting of Gourmont, which she had commissioned, hung prominently in her salon from that time forth. Yet she had surprisingly little to say in the brief chapter she devoted to him in *Aventures de l'esprit;* and later, when she expanded her literary memoirs in *Souvenirs indis-*

Natalie on Tricksy

THE BARNEY FAMILY

Albert Clifford Barney *(portrait by Alice Pike Barney)*

Alice Pike Barney, circa 1914
(Collections of the Library of Congress)

Laura and Natalie, 1915

EARLY PORTRAITS
OF NATALIE

by Carolus-Duran

by Lévy-Dhurmer

by Alice Pike Barney

**"PALE AS OPHELIA, GRAVE
AS HAMLET"**

Natalie as a young lady of fashion

Eva Palmer

Liane De Pougy *(Anciennes collections Nadar, Bibliothèque Nationale)*

Berthe in the salon (one of Besnard's nymphs overhead, portrait of Gourmont in background)

Remy de Gourmont *(portrait by Henry de Groux)*

Natalie and Romaine, circa 1915

Romaine and Natalie, Beauvallon, 1936

Romaine and Natalie in Florence, 1945

Jean Chalon and Natalie toward the end of her life

crets, she merely revised what she had written earlier about him, adding a gerrymandered selection of his *Lettres intimes.* Actually, her chapter on Gourmont is one of the best things she ever wrote, which may demonstrate that she was a better writer when less personally involved. Her memories of Gourmont were graceful and eloquent but not profoundly moving. She claimed her right to mourn as she chose, but it was evident that she cared more about her legend as the Amazon than about Gourmont's affection or the ashes of his heart.

12
The Legend of Lorély

Remy de Gourmont died in 1915, in the midst of the great war that obliterated so much. The date of his death may explain why he so quickly sank into oblivion, as the postwar generation did its best to forget the past and tried to create the world anew. Thus, a few years after his death, Gourmont seemed to belong to a prehistoric age. That is, Gourmont the man was regarded as a dim figure in the remote past; actually, his ideas were more widely disseminated in the 1920s than during his lifetime, not only in France but in England and America as well. In 1922 he was the best-selling author in France, and during the twenties some fifteen volumes of his works were translated into English by such prominent writers as Ezra Pound, Aldous Huxley and Richard Aldington. The last of his books to appear in English was *Letters to the Amazon,* translated by Aldington and published only in England, in 1931. By then another international disaster was under way, the Great Depression, and the world of Remy de Gourmont seemed more remote than ever.

All this may explain why the name of Natalie Barney was unknown in her native land. But she was well known and respected as Gourmont's Amazon in Anglo-American literary circles abroad, and in France her name became a legend even before Gourmont's death. His *lettres à l'Amazone* had made her famous while they were appearing regularly in the *Mercure de France,* during 1912–1913, and had succeeded so well in immortalizing her role in the old invalid's personal saga that after the war, the Amazon was sometimes regarded as a survivor from another era. Although she and her salon were in their prime during the period between the wars, this was also the period when she became a mythical character. Needless to say, the legends of Renée Vivien, Liane de Pougy and other Sapphic romances did nothing to diminish her aura.

Natalie's name appears in many books of memoirs that deal with the first half of this century, but more often than not it is her legend that is remembered. Oddly enough, the novels in which she appears as a character generally give more reliable portraits than the memoirs, and this is true even of memoirs written by people who knew her well. The most striking examples are provided by André Germain, a social and literary butterfly who met her shortly after she moved to the Rue Jacob and who was one of the regulars of the salon during almost the entire period of its existence. A frail little man who looked as if a puff of wind would blow him over, Germain was afraid of everybody but got along with Natalie because, some said, he was as feminine as she was masculine. In one of his books of reminiscence Germain claims that for years she carried on a flirtation with him that hovered between friendship and love. And although his pose as a lover cannot be taken seriously, he certainly knew her well and felt her magnetism. Yet he was by no means uncritical in his appreciation. He comments a good deal on her fickleness, and he is one of those who blame her for the death of Renée. Ever since the appearance of his biography of Renée, in 1917, that charge has stuck.

Natalie turns up in several of Germain's many books of literary reminiscence. Usually he refers to her by one of her legendary names, calling her "Amazone" or, more often, "Lorély" or "Undine," following the precedent of Renée's novel. Invariably he characterizes her as a siren, and a siren she undeniably was. But Germain is not the most reliable historian, for his information often comes at second hand and is sometimes colored by his fondness for gossip. Yet his impressions tell much about the effect created by this

woman, whom he saw as a legendary enchantress, from the moment
that Lucie Delarue-Mardrus first brought him to 20 rue Jacob.

> I shall remember that first encounter all my life. My pretty guide
> and I walk up the long courtyard bounded by eighteenth century
> buildings which serves as a vestibule to that extraordinary *pavillon.*
> We knock at the door of the *pavillon,* which they say was the dwell-
> ing of Adrienne Lecouvreur. Heavy hangings are raised, allowing us
> to enter into the dim light of a strange room. There are candles and
> lilies which would be tasteless elsewhere but which the beauty of
> Lorély lends a magic power. On the backs of the chairs are ancient
> and faded chasubles which yearn for the incense of cathedrals. It is a
> solemn place, strange and somewhat enchanted; instinctively one
> lowers his voice.
>   An extremely graceful gesture raises a door-hanging. A look and a
> voice settle on us without the preliminaries of introductions. The
> voice has a crystal sound, touching and caressing like the wind pass-
> ing over flowers. "Who is this Pre-Raphaelite?" she asks, instead of
> saying hello. And she designates me as if she were subtly and imperi-
> ously taking possession. Something in my longish hair and in my
> old-fashioned clothes has given her the clue. But her antennae are as
> marvellous as her coquettishness. She has gone beyond appearances;
> she has felt my soul and begun to play with it.

This first impression conveys a sense of Natalie's extraordinary
intuitive powers and of the magic spell that she cast on almost everyone who met her. That magic may have affected Germain's
imagination, for the room he describes sounds more like a Pre-
Raphaelite decorator's dream than anyone else's description of Natalie's drawing room. Or, under the same influence, he may have had
a vision of Renée's apartment, which was dim, like this, with heavy
hangings and candles and incense; and lilies were flowers that Renée had dedicated to Natalie. This would have to be a vision, because
Germain, though infatuated with Renée, had never known her. The
church vestments yearning for cathedrals may be a pure figment of
his Catholic imagination; conceivably, Natalie could have draped
chasubles over her furniture, but she never in her life had any yearn-

ings for religion. All of which merely goes to show legend in the making.

The ghost of Renée seems to have haunted Germain when he first met Natalie.

> Several days later she comes to dinner at my house. To celebrate her coming, I have dimmed the lights and scattered innumerable violets on the table cloth. The allusion is subtle, and I wonder if she will recognize it. But although her mind is forever wandering, nothing escapes her. The moment we enter the dining room her keen look plucks the flowery compliment.
>
> "Renée Vivien liked violets," she says. "Is that why you have spread so many of them around?"

Natalie's version of this dinner is somewhat less romantic. To her the dying violets looked like so many dead flies sprinkled on the tablecloth. Not everyone can be a poet, she remarks dryly, and goes on to quote Colette advising Germain to purge his style of its beauty. His real talent, Natalie thought, was for malice rather than poetry, and she called him her "elf" to indicate his malicious spirit. (Germain, misinterpreting her intention, took the nickname as a compliment.) Natalie noticed that he had organized the dinner party for a number of people who were not getting along in order to watch the results. Amused at his amusement, she played her part in the comedy by providing the kind of repartée he wanted to hear. When Dr. Mardrus, seated next to his enemy Mme. Mühlfeld, warned her not to start hostilities or his friend the Amazon would scratch her eyes out, Natalie promptly conciliated the lady by saying that she would try to open her eyes instead. Germain admired her ability to blunt an insult with her ready wit. Once, when asked about one of her lovers, the baroness Deslandes, Natalie replied, "She is one of my friends who is very vain," immediately adding, "and with good reason, for she is charming."

Germain and his friends admired the Amazon's brilliant wit and never tired of quoting examples, counting these among her exploits as well as the episodes from her love life which they were forever

embroidering. Like almost everyone who wrote about her, Germain
could not resist the temptation to pun on the metaphor of the Amazon's bow and quiver and breast, which Gourmont had invented and
later writers had made stale with repetition. The Amazon was not
aggressive, Germain noted, but no one daunted her.

> She fought but seldom and with elegance. One day in the studio of
> the painter Barbier we saw her at odds with Baroness Deslandes, who
> was sometimes a very irascible friend. Those ladies were so exer-
> cised that they went off into the painter's bedroom to settle their quar-
> rel. With terror we heard frightful outbursts in a foreign language.
> The angry Baroness, who was half German, had a "complex" which
> in the confusion of rage caused her to lapse into her childhood tongue
> and insult in German an adversary who hardly knew that language. It
> was all the more remarkable that this took place in wartime.
> After some time the belligerents reappeared without having done
> each other any apparent harm. When the moment of leave-taking ar-
> rived, Baroness Deslandes passed near Lorély and nodded her head
> slightly as if she scarcely knew her. But Lorély, dominating her with
> all her skill at fencing, caught that insolent farewell on the wing.
> "That won't do, Ilse," she said. "Either you say goodbye nicely, or
> else it's goodbye forever." For once, the furious woman was sub-
> dued.

Although he often romanticized, Germain was also capable of
seeing Natalie as the mortal woman that she was. One of his portraits, less flattering but all the more realistic, shows a woman who
has lived. This is the most balanced portrait available of Natalie in
her middle thirties, some ten years after her affair with Renée.

> Those ten years, lived to the full, had modified the subtleties of her
> charm. A voluptuous lassitude turned down the corner of her mouth
> and emanated from the almost heavy lines of her body—which the
> spirit nevertheless visited, transformed and rendered ethereal. Her
> desire to please was as fresh as on the first day, and a youthful co-
> quettishness enveloped her. And besides, a noble soul governed that
> passionate body. the adventures she confessed with haughty frank-
> ness had not soiled her or left their mark. Her great distinction and

perfect correctitude, which were not artificial but genuine reflections of her true self, renewed and disguised her.

Germain continues with an amusing anecdote that demonstrates how proper Natalie could appear to the stuffiest people.

I can understand the memorable mistake of my brother-in-law Fabre-Luce. My brother-in-law, who liked order and established values, who liked three percent of Life, would have liked my sister to exercise her great charm to attract the company of ambassadors, duchesses and presentable ministers of state. Instead of that my sister preferred taking chances with fate and invited actresses, poets, roughnecks and repentant courtesans. My brother-in-law had suffered much during a reception at which the ladies had been particularly painted and scarcely titled. His brow was furrowed. Even the arrival of Valéry, that sun of Parnassus, did not remove the wrinkles. How could my brother-in-law, who had never read a line of verse, see the very image of Poetry on Valéry's intelligent forehead? He saw only two ladies hanging on his arms, two great actresses, but they were quite drunk. He grew even gloomier. Suddenly he brightened as he saw a different kind of lady entering. "Here at last is a normal woman," he declared. It was Lorély.

Part of Natalie's legend was created by the atmosphere in which she lived, in her own little world removed from the city, with her cobbled courtyard, her pavilion and her temple of friendship in that surprising garden of tall trees. During the years immediately before the war, she gave memorable parties, creating a magic world in her garden.

She could indulge in enchanting entertainments that would have suited no one else. Sometimes, as though ordered by her wand, marvelous lilies appeared in her garden. On June nights especially, they were arranged in a circle around her lawn. Each one of these lilies had at its feet something like a drop that had fallen from the wise virgins' lamp, a little votive light that illuminated it. They seemed to dance a charming nocturnal ballet.

Germain provides the best illustration of Natalie's legend when
he writes about Remy de Gourmont. Though professing to write
memoirs, he actually fictionalized more than most of the novelists
who wrote about her, partly because he wrote from hearsay, partly
because he improved on the truth in order to tell a better story. Yet
there is a basic element of truth in what he wrote, for though he
stretched the facts, he understood from his own experience how
Natalie courted and captivated people, than absentmindedly ne-
glected them. It is easy to understand why so many legends grew up
around her.

Of all those who were in love with Lorély, none was more patient,
more devoted and tender than Remy de Gourmont. This remarkable,
wild and sensitive man, who under his shy exterior concealed, I believe, a great spirit, was suddenly won over by this Undine and spent
the last ten or fifteen years of his life at her feet. His love was so powerful that it made him depart from all his usual ways. He who never
went out answered all the summons of his new friend and became almost sociable. He would often be seen, huddled up, protesting, but
heroically present in a corner of that salon where he would have liked
to be alone. One would have said he was an owl in love with a Fairy.

In spite of the cruelty that was part of her charm, Lorély hardly tormented this old loving friend. For his sake she even cultivated the
virtues of which she seemed least capable: patience, a soft tenderness, a sort of fidelity. Only she could not help subjecting him to tri-
als. I remember one of the more picturesque instances.

That summer Lorély led a strictly watery existence. In June she
had muttered to me in an offhand way: "Why use the roads on land
when they are so dusty? There are also river roads."

I had attached no great importance to this passing remark, which
had kindled a sudden dream and gone off to die with all the petals that
she discarded at the bottom of that little water nymph's pool, which
even more than her *pavillon* and her garden seemed her constant
dwelling place.

But a month later I discovered that the epigram had taken shape
and life in the form of a smart little yacht on which Lorély glided,
dreamed, dined and slept. This peaceful craft never went very far. To
begin with, it was not swift, and above all, the locks limited its travels, perhaps the only obstacles that my imperious friend could not

overcome. In connection with this yacht, Lorély sent out complicated invitations whose beneficiaries often became victims. She refused to take account of the difficulties in navigating and made rather unrealistic rendezvous with her many admirers in the nautical centers of suburban Paris.

Those who took prompt means of transportation—train or car—arrived punctually at the appointed place and were subsequently reduced to boring themselves for hours in the local inn or bistro. For the slow-moving Siren arrived in the evening instead of the morning, or did not arrive at all. And yet, she would do it again, careless about her schedule and despotic in her whims.

I for my part have the most pleasent memory of a voyage that on the other hand was fatal for Remy de Gourmont. I was among the privileged persons who sailed with Lorély from the bridge of La Concorde.

Germain describes the confusion of that departure, Natalie remembering one passenger, a pretty young woman, but absentmindedly forgetting another, her own mother, who arrived too late to catch the boat. Still another passenger, less privileged, was to meet them later, some distance outside Paris.

. . . while the boat, capricious as a young woman, slowly cleaved the beautiful warm September day, Remy de Gourmont committed himself to the sweat and dust of the train. On the deck of our boat everything was balmy. I forgot the plans. They were lost in the brightness of summer's end, and I only knew that they were light and airy.

In the train Remy de Gourmont sweated and suffered. A magic name counteracted the heat, the discomfort, the impatience: Nogent-sur-Marne. There at an appointed hour of the afternoon he was to regain possession of that which he loved most in the world. And since the name of a hotel is a dull thing to mention, he had been told more poetically: "On the bridge."

We arrived at Nogent-sur-Marne several hours late. As we approached, Lorély was attacked by pangs of remorse. But quickly she dismissed them. "I know the ways of Monsieur de Gourmont well," she said. "He will have taken refuge in some bistro."

Alas, how poorly she knew the ways of his heart. She did not take into account the humble fidelity of love. When Nogent came into sight, a venerable bowed silhouette appeared at the same time as the arches of the bridge. Conscientious as a schoolboy lover, Remy de Gourmont was waiting there where he had been told to wait.

For ten years or more the great writer lived on something like the bridge of Nogent. Every hour he hoped for a little boat, a sign, a message. He lived in a state of perpetual expectation and perhaps even died of it.

13

Lily de Clermont-Tonnerre and Romaine Brooks

When war broke out in 1914, Natalie was urged to go home to America. But though she packed and shipped her baggage, she discovered that she could not bear to leave her adopted country in its hour of need. This was not exactly patriotism—an abstraction which meant nothing to Natalie—but France was the land of all her loves and friendships, and she could not tear herself away from these personal attachments that meant so much to her, simply to return to a country which was no longer home. So she remained in France throughout the war, most of the time in Paris, even while it was being bombarded.

At the time the war broke out, the person who mattered most to Natalie was the duchess de Clermont-Tonnerre. Elisabeth de Gramont, or Lily, as she was called, was a woman of character and intelligence who made a deep impression on all who knew her. Though associated by birth and marriage with the noblest names of France—her lineage descended from Henry IV—she was unimpressed by the aristocracy of birth and preferred the aristocracy of merit. In her memoirs she recalls growing up in the Faubourg Saint-Germain, in a household that was run on a lavish scale, and calculates that in their lifetime her parents entertained some ninety thousand guests. Yet she lived to see her own means so depleted, first by separation from her husband, then by the war, that she was reduced to earning her living with her pen. None of this distressed her in the least, however, for she was a person of indomitable courage and independence who lived according to her own rules instead of following those of her class. When convinced that communism would benefit mankind, this duchess did not hesitate to espouse the cause.

Natalie, who was extremely conservative and who detested politics anyway, was amused. For everything that Lily said or did reflected an original spirit that appealed to her. Temperamentally Lily suited her better than any other woman she had ever known. The chapter on Lily in *Souvenirs indiscrets* gives a fine sense of the originality and humor that were an endless source of delight to Natalie. This portrait explains why Lily was one of Natalie's most beloved friends for so many years and why Natalie was devastated by her death. But it tells nothing about their early love, and the only evidence that remains is to be found in a few love poems dedicated to "L.," which could just as well have been addressed to Liane or Lucie. There is one, "A Sonnet to My Lady with the Jaundice," in which the lady can be identified as Lily because there is also a French poem on the same subject in which she is addressed by name. And another poem mentions lilies in the punning fashion of the Elizabethan sonneteers. But love poems are not very informative, and all that can be said with any assurance is that Lily was Natalie's strongest attachment to France when the war broke out. Apparently their love had begun a number of years earlier, and they were very close during the years of Natalie's friendship with Gourmont, 1910–1915.

In her memoirs Natalie says that Lily personified the best of France, and it is clear that she loved France in the person of Lily. When Paris was threatened by the invading German army, Natalie stayed there with Lily until the danger appeared too great. When Lily went off to join her family in Deauville, Natalie went to nearby Honfleur to stay with Lucie Delarue-Mardrus. This was the time when everyone volunteered for war service. Lucie, now divorced from Dr. Mardrus, was working as a nurse in a military hospital, and he was serving in the army as a doctor. Lily, after helping with the wounded in Normandy for a few months, returned to Paris to work at a distribution center where the wounded arrived from the front. Americans living in France also volunteered, serving with the Red Cross and the Ambulance Corps. Natalie's sister Laura, now Mme. Hippolyte Dreyfus, served in both organizations and was decorated with the Legion of Honor.

The war changed the lives of many of these women. Lily developed an interest in politics and wrote editorials for a radical newspaper; later she also gave lectures. Laura became a busy committeewoman and, after the war, represented the International Council of Women at the League of Nations. But Natalie refused to be carried away by the war fever and even went so far as to organize pacifist meetings in 1917, when the war was at its worst and the French Army in a state of mutiny. That was the year that Henri Barbusse, who had fought in the trenches and written a bitter antiwar novel, appeared at 20 rue Jacob. However, when the United States finally entered the war, Natalie celebrated the occasion with a very bad poem which was published in the New York *Herald* under the title "D'Une Amazone américaine." But that was an uncharacteristic gesture.

Generally speaking, Natalie was profoundly opposed to the war. *Pensées d'une Amazone* (1920) includes a section that might be read as her wartime notebook, with precisely rendered scenes from the war, such as the description of the military hospital in Honfleur, where Lucie worked, and a wartime dictionary listing all the new expressions that everyone learned from the news of the day, many of them transparent falsifications. The book also reflects her complete skepticism about politics and strategy, her refusal to succumb to propaganda or hysteria, to surrender everything she valued to a questionable military necessity. Far more space is devoted to love, "that outmoded form of heroism," than to war, and the proportion tells something about her scale of values. At the time her outlook must have seemed unpardonably cynical and selfish; now it may appear more clearheaded and, considering the circumstances, courageous; actually she was both selfish and rational during a crisis when everyone else was being selfless and irrational.

For the most part Natalie ignored the war as much as possible and tried to lead her life as before. All through the war she continued to receive guests in her salon, preserving an island of sanity in a world gone mad. Several of her friends remember with gratitude those moments of respite from the anguish and anxiety outside. Magdeleine Wauthier, a newcomer to the salon, reminisces about those Fridays during 1916, 1917, and 1918, when tensions relaxed and hardships were forgotten in a civilized atmosphere of intelligence, calm, and beauty: "Freedom of thought, opinion and expression ruled in that society, and that also gave it an incalculable value." Another newcomer, Paul Morand, found himself transported to a different world, which he viewed somewhat ironically at a Christmas party for a hundred aesthetes at which Darius Milhaud played Debussy. Later Milhaud could not recall that he had ever played at Miss Barney's, so perhaps it was all a dream; Magdeleine Wauthier said that returning to the grim everyday realities from Natalie's salon was like waking from a beneficent dream. Alan Seeger, the American poet who wrote "I Have a Rendezvous with Death," sent Natalie a letter shortly before he was killed in action, praising her for remaining loyal to Paris in these sad times: "I fancy in your charming retreat you can make an atmosphere where things do not change so lamentably." André Germain remembers that in the bomb-shattered winter of 1918 it was still possible to escape from the war in the peaceful, poetic climate of the Rue Jacob. From these testimonials it could be argued that Natalie kept alive the civilized values for which the Great War was supposed to be fought.

All through the war she continued to cultivate her literary friendships and to conduct her love affairs. She often went to lunch or dinner with Anatole France during those years, sometimes accompanied by a love of the moment, the Persian dancer Armen Ohanian. She kept in touch with her regulars when they could not come to the salon, going to Chartres with Lily to visit Edouard Champion, who was stationed there in the army, and visiting José de Charmoy in a nursing home outside Paris, where he was wasting away of consumption. She renewed her friendship with Pierre Louÿs, who was going blind, and brought friends to call on one occasion, two women who shared her interest in the *Chansons de Bilitis;* on another, Bernard Berenson, whom she had just met at the home of Salomon Reinach. At this time, in 1917, she also met Louÿs' old friend Paul Valéry at the first public recital of his new poem, "La Jeune

Parque.'' This event took place in a bomb shelter at Lily's house, where Natalie often went during the war. For a brief time she even moved to Lily's neighborhood when Big Bertha was bombarding Paris and the Rue Jacob seemed unsafe. But most of the time she was quite fearless and fatalistic. There was a good deal of the stoic about Natalie.

Certainly she made few concessions to the war. In her bilingual book of poems, which appeared in 1920, there are only a few passing references to indicate that she had lived through those four cataclysmic years in Paris. The opening ''Apology'' explains,

> While blue and khaki share the heroes' mud,
> And women tend in white or weep in grey,
> Though all expressiveness seems over-dressed,
> Yet some must wear the colours of their hearts
> Upon their sleeves, like troubadours, of old;
> And sing, and sometimes write their singing down.

One poem, entitled ''A Parisian Roof Garden in 1918,'' proposes an evening of music and feasting and love under the night sky,

> And if the enemy from aerial cars
> Drops death, we'll share it vibrant with the stars!

The roof garden was no doubt her Persian dancer's, and, apart from these last two lines, the poem evokes the world of Omar Khayyám rather than the world of war. Another poem, ''The Near Enemy,'' employs the language and imagery of trench warfare to describe the wars of love, likening lovers who have become enemies to treacherous Prussians. And one of the French poems, ''Mes Morts,'' is not, as might be expected, about the war dead but about her dead lovers, ending specifically with ''my first love, my dead one'' buried in the cemetery of Passy.

There is something chilling about Natalie's disregard of the anguish of war. She expresses no feeling for the millions who died horribly during those four years. Yet her actions during that period reveal solicitude and compassion for her friends, and she almost breaks down at the heartrending sight of Charmoy on his deathbed. It was ironic that he should be dying of a peacetime disease while in the barracks next door, bugles were summoning others to die in battle; doubly ironic that this civilian should be dreaming of one last monumental sculpture of Victory, which he had hoped to complete for France before he died; and trebly ironic that Natalie should be overcome with emotion at this spectacle when she had been unmoved by so many others. But Natalie was so constituted that she could only feel deeply for those she knew and was incapable of feeling emotion for the mass of humankind. Perhaps she was not unfeeling after all but merely more honest that most in facing the fact that one can only love individuals, not abstractions. Hypocrisy had no part in her nature, and what appears to be callousness may really be unflinching honesty in refusing to adopt secondhand sentiments simply because they happened to be universal at the time. But the voice of cold reason may sound like indifference to those who think in the clichés of a great cause.

Certainly she saw no reason to suspend her love affairs in time of war, and it was during this period that she found one of the great loves of her life. Romaine Brooks was an American painter who had lived most of her life in Europe and had been in Paris for ten years before she met Natalie. It is surprising that they did not meet sooner, for they traveled in the same wealthy international circles and had quite a few acquaintances in common. Romaine had known Renée during her last years and knew perfectly well who Natalie was, but for that reason may have kept her distance. She was serious about her painting and hated to waste her time in social frivolity or love intrigues. In her unpublished memoir, "No Pleasant Memories," she recalls what she had heard and seen of Natalie before they met.

Renée Vivien had often spoken to me of Natalie Barney and I found little interest in listening to those endless love grievances which are so often devoid of any logical justification.

Before I knew Natalie I often caught glimpses of her from my car solemnly walking in the Bois de Boulogne followed by a pretty but insignificant little woman dressed in Oriental clothes with a shawl on her head. This left me wondering till I knew and understood Natalie. She possessed, along with many other literary people, the capacity of endowing the commonplace with her own poetical fancies. She told me that when this little woman danced (and very second-rate dancing it was) it brought to her all the splendors of the East. It was the same at another time with a Chinese girl. This young person who looked Chinese except for a long nose, had been educated in Belgium and during the process lost all the natural reticence and dignity of her race to become like some over-free and crude Westerner. But Natalie would thrust a sword into her hands and tell her to jump about in Chinese fashion and that sufficed to create an illusion.

Romaine had also heard about Natalie from the stuffier element of Anglo-American society.

Now everyone in Paris knew of Natalie Barney. Her spirit, her writings in the form of "Pensées" and her poetry. But as usual it was her reputation rather than her that was commented upon.

One afternoon before the war for some unknown reason I accompanied Aunt Minnie to a reception given by an American society woman of the pouter-pigeon variety. There were many of these pigeons, all looking very much alike and they were assembled to drink tea, eat cakes and play cards. One of these was talking to Aunt Minnie when my attention was attracted by hearing her mention Natalie Barney's name. "She will be received again in society when she returns to her Mother's friends" I heard. Looking round at these smug and puffed out members of society I decided that Natalie Barney had doubtless made more inspiring friends elsewhere.

The "Aunt Minnie" referred to here was Lady Anglesey, now well along in years but formerly a pretty American heiress who married an English lord. Like Princess Edmond de Polignac, she seemed to know all the attractive young women in Paris. She had known Natalie since the days of her love affair with Renée and had introduced Renée to Baroness van Zuylen. It was she who introduced Romaine to Natalie, probably in 1915, when the war had given Romaine a good excuse to withdraw from the social life that she despised: "Except for war work I was now living in Paris in seclu-

sion and completely detached from all former acquaintances. It was
a relief to be once again adrift and alone. I thought that like myself
everyone was occupied with the war.'' Though probably reluctant
to accept Lady Anglesey's invitation, she was in for a pleasant surprise. After hearing so much about Natalie from Renée and the
pouter-pigeons, she finally found the person nothing like her reputation: "Natalie herself was a miracle. Though she had lived many
years in dank unhealthy houses, among many dank unhealthy people, she remained uncontaminated, as fresh as a Spring morning.
The finer qualities of her intellect had allowed her to rise above rather than remain within her chosen 'milieu.'" Romaine had found a
kindred spirit, a woman who was in every way her equal and who
shared her attitudes toward conventional society but who lived more
comfortably with those attitudes.

> Her rebellion against conventions was not combative as was mine.
> She simply wanted to follow her own inclinations—these not always
> bringing credit to her. In those days Bohemia was the only refuge for
> the independent, and when I first knew Natalie she was certainly one
> of its members. But later, after the war, when points of view had
> broadened, she actually became popular and this was a sore disap-
> pointment to me.

Natalie was to disappoint Romaine many times over the years,
not only in her social life but in her many love affairs. "But I had
never found a real woman friend before," Romaine continued,
"and Natalie brought me a wealth of friendship which I gratefully
accepted and fully returned." Much of Romaine's life had been unhappy, with utterly Dickensian episodes in childhood and adolescence that had left her so traumatized that she could not readily open
her heart to others. She had been married for about a year to a handsome homosexual and had had several brief involvements with men
and women; the list is impressive, including Lord Alfred Douglas,
Princess Edmond de Polignac, Gabriele D'Annunzio and Ida Rubinstein, but on the whole these affairs—if they even amounted to
that—had been as unsatisfactory as her marriage, and she had never
succeeded in forming a lasting relationship. As a rule she had been

the pursued rather than the pursuer, and she had never known a love that was mutual. Whether lacking in passion or afraid of sex, she seems generally to have regarded the proceedings with distaste or with a sense of defeat.

Natalie was just the person to change all that and to bring into her life the kind of intimate love that she had never known. The word Romaine uses in her memoirs is "friendship," but she was always extremely reticent about her personal feelings, and the brief, understated chapter she devotes to Natalie tells next to nothing. Nor do any letters survive from the period before 1920, so again, as with Lily, there is nothing like the account of Natalie's early love affairs with Liane, Renée and Lucie. But some six hundred letters survive from the period between 1920 and 1968 to show what they meant to each other. Romaine's biographer, Meryle Secrest, was allowed to read these letters and to quote excerpts. Here is how she described Natalie's side of the correspondence:

> Natalie in love was anxious, tender, placating. She gave Romaine repeated assurances of her uncritical admiration. There was no greater painter. There was no more beautiful or desirable woman. Even Romaine's voice suited her physique to perfection, unlike those of some lesser woman, and Natalie adored listening to it. She idealized every aspect of Romaine, as if Romaine were a goddess to be worshiped, or a god whose displeasure meant the end of her existence. Although the facts of their frequent separations indicated otherwise, Natalie believed that what she wanted was union: "Alas to be one," she wrote to her "Angel darling" in Venice; "we who are so agreeably, so irreplaceably two together—a stronghold above the bleak and bland and banal world."

The latter remark sounds more like Romaine's view of the world than Natalie's and reflects the constant solicitude behind Natalie's efforts to bolster Romaine's morale. Natalie was not deceiving herself in wanting to be united with Romaine, but for her that did not mean being together all the time; nor did Romaine want to live with Natalie, for she kept her own house in Paris, and during most of her later years lived in Italy or Nice. So they were often apart; and Nata-

lie was often jealous or afraid of losing Romaine, as Meryle Secrest
points out, quoting several passages to this effect, like this one,
written when Romaine was on Capri: "I know that you have not
bathed without everyone on that hot island desiring you—that they
could follow the glimmer of your perfect form to the ends of the
earth." What that declaration really shows is that Natalie wanted
Romaine to appear desirable to others. Her own desire was increased by jealousy and the fear of losing her beloved, and she preferred such agitated emotions to the monotony of perfect constancy.
Yet, paradoxically, she also wanted a love that would last forever
and succeeded in achieving it.

Lily and Romaine were the two greatest loves of Natalie's life,
the two women with whom she had the deepest and most enduring
intimacy. This kind of love was not a flaming passion which soon
burned out, and even if it began thus, it grew into something far
more profound and meaningful. These two loves of Natalie's middle years were quite similar: they were loves between mature individuals who had lived and grown with experience, between equals
who respected each other and never tired of each other's company.
Romaine and Lily were both strong-minded, independent women,
and Natalie appreciated a strength which matched her own. Lily was
more her type, with a quick wit and an easy offhand way with people, while Romaine was more intransigent and intractable, disliking
the salon and wanting Natalie to herself or at most in the company
of a select few. With Romaine there were sometimes scenes, and
Natalie had to be more accommodating. Some of the scenes were
undoubtedly caused by Natalie's other love affairs, for nothing, not
even undying fidelity, could keep Natalie from having other affairs.
Romaine could not understand this contradiction, Lily was probably
amused by it, and Natalie saw no contradiction. She had always believed in having several loves at once.

Whether she liked it or not, Romaine was forced to accept Natalie
as she was, which meant accepting Lily too and sharing Natalie with
her. Fortunately Lily was the kind of person she could respect, honest, straightforward and at the same time thoroughly civilized in her
behavior. Besides, they were all beyond the stage of melodrama in
their love, though not beyond the point where other loves could

cause them pain. Natalie had grounds for jealousy just as Romaine did, and sometimes even friends could come between them. They often joked about these matters, but in times of crisis Natalie was the one who had to placate and conciliate, while Romaine was inclined to sulk. She had always been uncompromising in her likes and dislikes. When she developed an antipathy for Jean Cocteau, for instance, all his attempts at reconciliation failed, and nothing could mitigate her scorn. In this instance she may have influenced Natalie, who wrote a wicked satirical sketch of Cocteau which betrays little understanding of his real talent. On the other hand, for all her loving admiration of D'Annunzio, Romaine could not prevail upon Natalie to take him seriously; D'Annunzio was too Italian for Natalie, too operatic in his gestures and poses, too compulsive a Don Juan, "a little object in old ivory polished by so many women's hands." Generally, though, Romaine and Natalie shared friends, especially during their summers on the Riviera, where their neighbors included Colette and Somerset Maugham, and all sorts of friends came to visit.

In 1927 they built a house together near Beauvallon and called it the Villa Trait d'Union, the "hyphenated villa," because it was really two separate houses joined together by a common dining room; thus each could lead her own life, respecting the other's privacy and coming together only for meals. This arrangement, which suited both of them, had occurred to Natalie many years before, when she rented a house in Neuilly with a separate apartment for her friends, and again on Lesbos, when she and Renée rented two little villas joined by a common orchard. In Beauvallon Natalie and Romaine spent their summers from the late 1920s through the thirties, getting along as well as their different natures permitted. But Natalie had another tandem arrangement and usually spent part of her summers in Honfleur, with Lily. And though she repeatedly wrote letters reassuring Romaine that she was her one and only love, Natalie could never have given up her loving friendship for Lily. So she moved with the seasons between the three fixed points on her map: from her salon in Paris to Romaine on the Riviera to Lily in Normandy. Romaine never liked the salon, and with the passing years she liked Paris less and less. In one letter she complained that she had only remained there for Natalie's sake and had wanted to leave fourteen years before. This suggests that she stayed in Paris all through the twenties, though in fact she was often elsewhere.

Those years might be dated by several works in which Romaine and Natalie paid tribute to each other. The first is a poem called "the Weeping Venus," which takes its title from a cadaverous nude of Ida Rubenstein which Romaine painted in 1915; to her that "fragile and androgynous beauty" represented the death of the old gods amid the mutilations of the war. Natalie's poem gives the painting another interpretation, ending with a characteristic feminist twist.

> No crown of thorns, no wounded side,
> Yet as the God-man crucified,
> Her body expiates the sin
> That love and life with her begin!

Fifteen years later Romaine repaid the compliment by providing two illustrations—the only ones she ever did—for Natalie's strange Gothic novel, *The One Who Is Legion, or A. D.'s After-Life* (1930). The story concerns a suicide who is resurrected as a sexless hermaphrodite, and the figures in the illustrations are gaunt and epicene; but Romaine always liked her nudes thus, and there is reason to suspect that she had influenced this weird tale. Its dreamlike atmosphere seems to be haunted by the same spirit that possessed Romaine in 1930, when she produced a series of harrowing line drawings torn out of the depths of her tormented psyche. The novel was also influenced by Balzac's *Séraphita*, a "mystical" work that Natalie had always admired and that she explicitly acknowledges in a poem epitomizing the novel's theme.

> A double being needs no other mate—
> So seraphita-seraphitus lives:
> Self-wedded angel, armed in self-delight,
> Hermaphrodite of heaven, looking down
> On the defeat of our divided love.

Still *The One Who Is Legion* sounds more like a work of Romaine's imagination than of Natalie's and suggests that for a time, at least, she made Natalie share her vision.

At the time they first met, Romaine was producing some of her finest work: the portrait of Cocteau, one of D'Annunzio as poet-in-exile and another of him as warrior, several of Ida Rubinstein, including the allegorical figure of France as a Red Cross nurse against a war-torn landscape. In the early twenties she turned out a series of striking portraits, including several depicting members of Natalie's circle: Eyre de Lanux, Una Lady Troubridge, Lily, Natalie, and Romaine herself. The portraits of Una Lady Troubridge and of herself in male attire expose their subjects remorselessly. The others are blank masks that tell nothing of what lies beneath the surface: Eyre de Lanux rather allegorical as a bare-breasted Alpine huntress; Lily a handsome middle-aged aristocrat in front of her ancestral home; Natalie a correct society matron in a fur stole against a dim backdrop of 20 rue Jacob, with only the figurine of a horse as an emblem of her equestrian and Amazonian past. Like the sketch of Natalie in Romaine's memoirs, this portrait is deliberately and disappointingly noncommittal. The only thing it tells is that in middle age Natalie had begun to appear respectable.

14

The Patroness of Letters

As her mother's daughter, Natalie grew up with the assumption that the arts were an integral part of life. Alice Pike Barney was not only a creditable painter, she was also a generous patroness of the arts, as her father had been before her. Thus it was natural that Alice's daughters should take the arts for granted and dabble in a casual fashion that was halfway between the genteel dilettantism of their class and the dedication of the true artist. Laura, who betrayed no talent to speak of, nevertheless wrote a historical drama and sculptured portraits in bronze. Natalie was a fairly serious student of music in her youth and showed a taste for all the arts throughout her life. Like her mother, she sought the company of creative people and took a genuine interest in their work.

Natalie was not remarkable for her generosity, but her salon served a useful purpose in the promotion of the arts, both as a meeting ground and as a theater where new works could be tried out before a discriminating and influential audience. Paul Valéry's *La Jeune Parque* was read there before its publication; Colette appeared as an actress in the premiere of her own play, *La Vagabonde;* and George Antheil's First String Quartet was first performed at 20 rue Jacob. In addition to organizing such programs as these, Natalie actively applied her practical sense in efforts to support worthy causes, notably in a scheme to subsidize Valéry, Eliot and other writers. She also founded an "Académie des Femmes" where women writers gave readings from their work, a counterpart and perhaps a reproach to the venerable Académie Française, from which women were excluded. Most of these activities date from the 1920s, when the salon was in its heyday, with its most distinguished visitors and most active patronage of the arts.

Since the main business of a salon is talk, not much remains of the best that was thought and said at 20 rue Jacob. The salon had no Boswell, and Natalie's memoirs give her impressions of those who came to the salon rather than a history of its proceedings. Her three volumes of *pensées* give an excellent impression of her wit but not of real conversation. The closest thing to conversation is to be found in letters, and her correspondence with certain individuals sheds a good deal of light on her role as the hostess of an international literary salon. This is best seen in her relationships with three Americans living in Europe: Bernard Berenson, Ezra Pound and Gertrude Stein. Each of these friendships engaged her in a different way; each correspondence brings out a different side of her character and presents her role in a different light.

Her friendship with Berenson can be seen as a sequel to her friendship with Remy de Gourmont, revealing once again her appeal to men of complex and subtle minds. Natalie and Berenson met during the war, at the home of Salomon Reinach, the classical scholar who was a good friend to both and a habitué of the salon, as were other men of learning. To run a successful salon, she had to be more than a gracious hostess, and it is clear that she was esteemed by such men for her intelligence rather than her wealth and good looks. To say that they were attracted by her wit and charm makes her sound superficial and does justice neither to her nor to them. For her wit was the articulation of an original mind that quickly seized the complexity of an idea, her charm an intuitive response to people who interested her. Men of ideas—scholars, philosophers, statesmen, critics—found her remarkably easy to talk to and capable of establishing close rapport in short order. Men of ideas are human, too, and therefore all the more susceptible to an attractive woman who can put them at their ease, listen intelligently to what they have to say, and respond in kind.

The correspondence with Berenson illustrates the affinity that existed between Natalie and a number of learned intellectuals. In the case of Berenson it would be no exaggeration to call it intimacy, and in many ways this relationship resembled the earlier intimacy with Remy de Gourmont. Both men were fifty-two when they first met her; both considered themselves old, thought of her as young and were dazzled by her presence. Natalie was never a real beauty, but she had a physical radiance in her youth that persisted as charisma or glamour in her middle years. Everyone found her striking, and many fell in love at first sight. There was, of course, no question of physical intimacy with the men she liked, but both Gourmont and Berenson expressed passionate feelings that may have been genuine, though they could also be taken as gallant compliments. Berenson's biographer, Ernest Samuels, says that Berenson liked to court and caress the ladies but seldom carried his flirtations further. Yet he was obviously infatuated with Natalie during the first year or two that he knew her, and to the end of his life he remembered his early emotions. In the final letter of the correspondence he wrote, "The last visit, short as it was, brought back the Natalie I was so much in love with nearly forty years ago. Thank you for letting me recapture a glimpse of those bitter-sweet days of intense living."

There was also a good deal of playfulness in their relationship. Berenson enjoyed flirting with a woman of spirit, and Natalie responded playfully to his advances. In one letter she appears flirtatious herself as she writes, "I am too perplexed in all my feelings and sentiments to know what or how I am myself just now. . . . B. B. what shall I say—Just sans phrases, or verbal agility that I'm glad you're here and that I know you; and surely 'the wild girl from Cincinnati' and the 'sauvage de Danube' were meant to meet!" (Both epithets had been conferred by Reinach, who also showed a sense of fun.) She appears to have been as frank with Berenson about her sex life as she was with Gourmont, for in another letter she observes, " . . . you have so many ladies . . . more than I. . . ."

They wrote more seriously at times, he about his researches, she about writers she wanted him to meet, like "the most subtle of French poets Paul Valéry," or Colette, who "would perhaps shock you more than Berthelot please you." Berenson had already met Proust, who acknowledged a debt to Berenson's book on the Venetian painters of the Renaissance. Now Natalie was to meet him.

> I'm having a "hide and go seek" correspondence with Marcel Proust. We may meet and end it, as you did? I've already warned him that he may be of those qu'on rencontre tout d'abord pour la dernière fois? But as he seems to spend his life between colds and fevers our meeting may be deferred long enough for us to become great friends. You B. B. stand the double test of time and infidelity. Hence I welcome your ever fresh returns.

They discussed books, especially their own, which they exchanged. She admired his connoisseur's vision of Renaissance art, for which she professed great enthusiasm. He in turn appreciated her writings, though by no means uncritically.

> I thoroughly enjoyed your "Actes et Entr'actes." Truth to tell I did not expect to, for most contemporary verse bores me to tears, and none more so than the vague vanities of the neo-Latin muse. . . . Your verses strike a singularly vibrant chord of my own lyre. For though in French they are essentially due to the impulse of the passionate pilgrim come from America home to beauty. . . .
> I wonder how many people there are who can enjoy you as I do. In the first place one must know English as well as French. Then one must be American. Then one must enjoy the artistic effort of a person who enjoys the illusion of attaining to a less hackneyed form of expression than is possible with the worn out idiom of one's mother speech. And finally one must sympathize with the point of view, and it is one which can be entertained by a very few renegade Americans and no others.
> Am I all wrong?
> I want to read all you have written, because you interest me. I dare say I shall be again rewarded beyond my expectations.

He appreciated her poetry most of all, not so much for its literary merits as for what it meant to him personally.

Your verses which I return on the understanding that you will send me back those that I have marked as to my taste, interest me much more on your than on their own account. Most of them are like humming which means little to others but helps to bring back the physical joy of music one has heard. Only in your case the music is your life's experience. . . .

I can't tell you for instance how the theme you treat several times, anxious waiting, calls up memories of days when one used to get faint and a heart burning as with live coals because one was made to wait. . . . Then you have for me a great advantage over most versifiers, and it is that you always have something to say that cogs in with the wheels of my own life. Even when your form is ungracious you always appeal to my experience, and that, by the way, is why you must send everything you have written, whether printed or in manuscript. You must omit nothing, for all of it is sincerely you, and it is you I wish to get to know.

For all his scholarship, Berenson was a man of the world, not a recluse like Remy de Gourmont. Yet Berenson, too, sometimes felt like an owlish drudge as he contemplated his fairy princess, a man immersed in studies while she was in the midst of life. He, too, felt like Bottom in love with Titania, and as he regarded his love from afar, his musings were reminiscent of Gourmont's constant thoughts about his Amazon. Berenson writes,

I must interrupt work, although it is almost feverishly difficult, to send you a word—a word among the millions that my spirit wafts to you each day and every day. If you could realize what converse I hold with you through all hours of the 24, you would understand how absurd it seems to come down to a few aphasiac scratchings on a sheet or two of paper. You understand for your heart is intelligent and has stored up wisdom, and you know what symbols are, and what facts mean, and many a hysop grows therein whereof you have sung at times. . . . Quite extraordinary is the joy the words from a life enhancing person give one, and while one writes to such an one, suddenly one gains vitality and zest.

Finally, one rather long discursive letter is worth quoting in full, for it reveals Berenson's stream of consciousness as he thinks of

Natalie and demonstrates how fully he confided in her. This reads like another *lettre intime à l'Amazone.*

I should have perhaps given a more cordial welcome to "The Woman Who Lives With Me" if on the fly-leaf it had not in language aromatic and flattering led me to infer that its author was going to disappoint me of her visit. For disappointed I am—at least one great part of me, the whole of me that still thirsts for experience as experience and receives it always with ardour and never looks back with regret. That part of me had, I confess, taken the upper hand. But there is another great part of me which has always been the greater part of me and now has grown to be the greatest part which ever so much prefers to dream: to dream intensely, and ask of the not-me no more than that it should come just enough in to my ken for me to dream about. And either as subjects or objects of ideation I should perhaps have left all human contacts if unlike me they had not taken the lead and rapt me out of my revery. So whatever happens I always win. If you insist on becoming an experience, it will be stimulating and vitalizing, but you no longer can avoid remaining an image about which a great deal in me that hitherto has remained instable can now and at last crystalize. This is very egoistical, and would be thin and poor if it were all of me, but there is ever and ever and ever so much more—so much in fact that looked at from within I can come to no conclusion with regard to myself. Can any one? Except in action, surely not. And we are impelled to action in order to find rest, that is to say determination. For myself I know that most of the stupid things I have said and all the stupid things I have done have been due to a panic dread of the indeterminate and an anguishing need of something to cling to or to hide in, etc. etc. etc. *ad infinitum.* Who is industrious and energetic enough to remain inactive, and grown up enough to be unproductive?

You not, quite clearly no more than I. I grind out pedantic studies which waste my soul, and you who are much more exquisite and above all ever so much more of an artist, you write cryptic short stories like the one I am now returning—with regret for I should like to keep it. Not that it has so very much intrinsic value but because of you who interest me. Evidently it shadows forth one of your *vous,* and I want to know as many of them as will not kill and devour me. For of course you have such too. We all have cannibal selves. I only fear that mine are too few and of too feeble appetite.

What epigrammatic things you say in this story, chiming so well
with notions of my own: — "I love the love of those who are far
enough away, it becomes whatever I wish to believe it" — "We
have no scenes: we do not care about the same thing" — "It is easier
to love than to like" — "Life is as others spoil it for us" — "She
worries a great deal over little things but this is not because her nature
is small but because it is sensitive" —

No, I find I can't return it, unless you have no other copy and must
have it back. Do send me more—please— — —

Salomon clamours for news of you and supposes you are here. I
wonder what you are to him. What I am to him I know fairly well.
All that he knows of me is me—how should it be otherwise! Only he
supposes it is all of me—at least all that what he does not wish to
know of me. But you—I wonder what grotesque figment of his gram-
marian mind you have become, and how he would publish you if you
became the theme for one of his "Mythes, Cultes & Religion." Dear
Salomon, to him you and all other women are but glosses to mutilat-
ed lines of Sappho, and obscure ones of Virgil. And he too is right.
Why not? Much more romance, and yearnings, and even passion
hides behind his pedantries than many a professed *homme à femmes*
has ever known. So I feel full of *tendresse* for him, and while I laugh
at him a great deal it is always with pure affection.

How much nicer it would be to talk to you than to write, for the
pen is not my instrument. It is yours ever so much more. So pray use
it for my delectation.

    B. B.

All of these letters date from the first two years of the correspondence, 1917–1918. After that the correspondence was far less frequent and intense, but they kept in touch and continued to see each
other whenever Berenson was in Paris or Natalie was in Florence.
The initial courtship was over, but friendship endured, one more
proof of Natalie's great gift for friendship.

With Ezra Pound she had a different kind of friendship—breezier,
less intimate, and more practical. They collaborated on several enterprises that were typical of Pound, who was as generous in his patronage of the arts as he was impecunious. For Pound, Remy de

Gourmont was the most important French man of letters of his day, so he was predisposed to like Natalie. They probably met in the spring of 1913, when Pound came to Paris for a visit, during the period when the *lettres à l'Amazone* were appearing in the *Mercure de France*. They began corresponding later in that year about a translation of one of Gourmont's novels that Pound was trying to get published. Natalie had a hand in this scheme, for the translator, Cecile Sartoris, was one of her loves; Gourmont reported to Natalie that Mme. Sartoris spoke of her as "the Saint of Saints" and with the slightest encouragement would have confided much more.

After the war, when Pound was living in Paris, he and Natalie saw a good deal of each other, played tennis together and became good friends. In 1919, when she was preparing a bilingual volume of poetry for publication, she submitted the English poems to him for editorial comment. Pound proved to be a more severe critic than she wanted. Her writing had always been full of outmoded "poetic" phrasing that belonged to the early nineteenth century rather than the twentieth. After living in France for twenty years, she was somewhat out of touch with her native idiom and hence inclined to translate some expressions literally from the French or to quote clichés as if they were epigrams. Pound was just the schoolmaster to correct such tendencies and tighten up her syntax, but she was not the pupil to learn from him; careless and unwilling to take the necessary pains, she never really submitted to his discipline. In the end they agreed that he should not revise her poems, and she was satisfied to publish them with all their imperfections instead of having them improved beyond recognition.

Pound admired her epigrams more than her poems and published his opinion in a "Paris Letter" which he wrote for *The Dial* of October, 1921.

As an American one has the more intimate contrast between two female expatriates: Mrs. Wharton, who in conserving the Salem–to–New York attitude beneath her formal novels has ended by becoming less readable and Natalie Barney who has published with complete mental laziness a book of unfinished sentences and broken paragraphs, which is, on the whole, readable and is interesting as documentary evidence of a specimen liberation. The *Pensées d'une Amazone* contain possibly several things not to be found in the famous *Lettres* addressed to that allegory and at least one sublime sentence running I think, "Having got out of life, oh having got out of it perhaps more than it contained."

This comment is not as uncomplimentary as it is usually taken to be, for Pound's bantering humor tempers the criticism, making it sound like a private joke addressed to his allegorical friend. Oddly enough, those who cite Pound's remark as an insult are likely to find a compliment in Gide's: "Miss Barney is one of the few people that one ought to see—if one had time." Clearly Gide intended this as a left-handed compliment.

During the early twenties Pound was actively involved in promoting several literary magazines, to which Natalie was induced to make literary as well as financial contributions. As Paris editor of *The Dial*, Pound not only wrote a column on the literary scene but recommended material for publication. No doubt it is he who submitted her translation of Valéry's "An Evening with M. Teste" in 1922 and a poem of hers in 1923. He carried collaboration even further when he published two of her poems in the *Transatlantic Review*, a little magazine that he helped to found. These poems were "Arranged by Ezra Pound," a caption explained, without explaining exactly what that meant, but there is a distinctly Poundian ring to the sardonic humor of one.

REPERCUSSIONS

Because the cows have fed on garlic,
    With cowslips and buttercups,
On the hill-side pasture—
The millionaire must taste at breakfast
A butter that stinks of this herb.

Natalie contributed money to the *Transatlantic Review* when it ran short of funds, and its editor, Ford Madox Ford, frequented her salon while he was living in Paris. Her association with Ford and Pound probably gave her the idea of launching a bilingual literary magazine, with Sinclair Lewis as coeditor, but this publication never materialized.

The most ambitious enterprise in which she collaborated with Pound was "Bel Esprit," a scheme to relieve selected writers of their financial worries so that they could devote all their energies to writing. The disinterested generosity of the scheme was typical of Pound; its businesslike operation sounds like Natalie's doing. In 1922 they drew up a prospectus and had it printed in a brochure, with a picture of the Temple à l'Amitié as a trademark. Here is the opening paragraph of the French text, quoted in *Aventures de l'esprit:*

> Recognizing that there are no longer patrons for writers, that the public generally supports literature only at its level, that prizes are but a temporary measure, we, friends of literature, have resolved to found an association, pledging to subscribe annually thirty shares at 500 francs, or 15,000 francs a year, to be paid to the chosen author. (If necessary, five persons may divide a share among themselves.)

Pound also advertised the scheme in *The Dial* by announcing in his "Paris Letter,"

> The society of Bel Esprit has been founded in Paris, a sort of consumer's league to pay for quality rather than quantity in literature and the fine arts.

The first two writers they proposed to support were his friend T.S. Eliot and her friend Paul Valéry. Friendship was not a consideration, however; each poet was chosen as the best in his language. Eliot published *The Waste Land* that year, which Pound immediately hailed as the greatest modern work of poetry and the best argument for liberating Eliot from his job in a bank. Though more interested in Valéry, Natalie took up the cause as part of their joint venture, and by the end of the year she had raised considerable sums. A few months later she wrote Eliot a very businesslike letter, not neglecting her own interests in the process.

4th of April 1923
"April is the cruelest month"

Dear Mr. Eliot,

I'm to be in London Monday 16th at 97 Cadogan Gardens S. W. and should very much like to see you one of the days you're free of Lloyds Bank after 5 or evenings of that week: about the "Bel Esprit" idea, we are trying, first, on Paul Valéry, under the present forms which you will kindly return to me when we meet. I am also seeking an Anglo-American editor for my "Pensées d'une Amazone" que voici—and which have been translated by Pound, Reinach and other friends. Can you suggest any likely publisher I could make arrangements with during the short week I'm to be in London?

The "Criterion" and "Dial" have both brought me your "waste lands" and I wish, indeed, that the energy of so stimulating a poet might be liberated. Lady Rothermere tells me that this is not so easy a matter as Pound and I first hoped—because of the many occupations you seem to be interested in. Il n'y a en effet rien de plus délicat que la "gérance du génie!"

But let us meet and further some of these conclusions—and so that I may not regret taking a few hours of your time, benefit the future use of it, by an understanding of how we may best serve so rare a delight.

Yours sincerely
Natalie Clifford Barney

In a postscript Natalie asked if Eliot could put her in touch with Richard Aldington, who had translated a novel by Gourmont. Subsequently she had a good deal of correspondence with Aldington about further translations of Gourmont's work, including *Letters to the Amazon.*

Bel Esprit embarrassed Eliot, and he refused to accept this charity. In any case he was soon relieved of the need to work in a bank when Lady Rothermere became his patroness. Natalie's efforts to relieve Valéry of his financial worries had a similar consequence.

Others who should have been more concerned about the poet's welfare resented this officious American intervention and were incited to compete. Adrienne Monnier, who ran a literary bookstore, organized a rival organization to raise funds for Valéry; the literary magazine *Nouvelle Revue française* and the publisher Gallimard assumed the responsibility of looking after their poet with a subsidy of up to fifteen thousand francs a year. The whole business was resolved over lunch at what sounds like a board of directors' meeting, except that it was attended mostly by writers: Valéry, Cocteau, Léon-Paul Fargue and Valery Larbaud. The meeting was called by another American patroness of the arts, Marguerite Caetani, the princess di Bassiano, who had been a generous subscriber to Bel Esprit and who gave Natalie credit for the whole idea of solving the poet's financial problems.

As a rule Natalie did not engage in literary politics, but sometimes she was unable to avoid them. As Remy de Gourmont's *Amazone,* she was naturally aligned with the *Mercure de France* in the minds of most French writers and therefore regarded as the enemy by those associated with the rival *Nouvelle Revue française.* Gide was an extreme example. Through their mutual friends Pierre Louÿs and Dr. Mardrus, she had known Gide before she ever met Gourmont, yet Gide was so obsessed with Gourmont that as late as 1947 he declined her invitation to the salon. Gide's fear of falling under Gourmont's shadow was no doubt aggravated by a book comparing Gide unfavorably with Gourmont; the author was André Rouveyre, who had been a close friend of Gourmont and who remained Natalie's closest male friend for almost fifty years after Gourmont's death.

Literary politics often originated in the salons, as the hostesses sought to promote their protégés to literary prizes or to the Académie Française. (The most famous example was Anatole France, who was a lazy writer and a slovenly man until Mme. Arman discovered him; she forced him to write some of his best works and literally groomed him for a seat among the immortals.) Natalie seems to have had no interest in such activities and no reverence for that august body. She preferred Valéry as she first knew him, during the

war and shortly after, when he addressed playful poems to her and
gave her editorial advice on her French poetry, much as Pound had
done in English. And though she organized readings of his work in
the salon and otherwise helped him prosper in his career, she
thought he took himself too seriously after his election to the seat
vacated by the death of Anatole France. She joked that he behaved
as if he had just given birth to a child and noted that his poetry
subsequently went into a decline. This could be the resentment of
one who had known him when, but it is just as likely that she resented the Académie as a self-important and exclusive masculine club.
When Cocteau was elevated to the Académie she wrote a wicked satirical sketch presenting him as a clown, "Harlequin à l'Académie," and when her friend Paul Morand, after waiting many
years, finally became immortal, she quipped, "Better never than
late."

The salons played an even more important part in helping composers advance their careers by providing auditions for their works
and commissions for new compositions. As a general rule Natalie
was not interested in running a musical salon, but on a number of
occasions during the twenties, the Fridays were enlivened by concerts. Once again Ezra Pound enlisted her support for his good
works. To begin with, she let him use her piano when he was composing his opera, *Villon*. Then Pound prevailed upon her to allow
the young American composer George Antheil to perform at 20 rue
Jacob. Antheil, with his percussive experiments, was not the sort of
composer calculated to appeal to Natalie's nineteenth-century tastes
in music, but he performed in the salon a number of times, including one New Year's Day when she thought this a rousing way of
celebrating the occasion. In addition, she and Romaine Brooks sub-
sidized the composition of his most famous work, *Ballet mécanique*, which was subsequently performed in the salon, and Lily de
Clermont-Tonnerre asked him to play in her salon. Some years later
Antheil gratefully remembered those performances, which had been
the first to encourage him. And many years later Pound, in his *Cantos*, remembered Natalie and the Rue Jacob and the Temple à l'A-
mitié in a collage of prewar memories of Paris, including one about

an adventure she had in a lower-class bistro when she was robbed but not daunted. He also echoed a scrap from his review of *Pensées d'une Amazone* in writing about his old great-aunt, who had got out of life,

> like Natalie
> 'perhaps more than was in it'

During the twenties the salon became one of the standard tourist attractions for the American writers who flocked to Paris. Morrill Cody, a journalist who has been in Paris since the Hemingway era, compares the salon to Gertrude Stein's studio, saying of both, "It was considered quite an honor and part of one's education, but was really quite a bore." He went to the salon once and to Gertrude Stein's twice, "which was once too much." Among the Americans who went to the salon were Hemingway, Scott and Zelda Fitzgerald, Sinclair Lewis, Glenway Wescott, Louis Bromfield, Sherwood Anderson, Janet Flanner and Edna St. Vincent Millay. Previously Natalie had received mostly French writers, with a scattering of other Europeans. Now she prided herself on introducing them to American and English writers, emphasizing the international character of her salon. A letter to Gertrude Stein indicates how Natalie set about bringing French and American writers together and how she organized programs for her salon.

Dec 16, 1926

Dear Gertrude Stein,

The other night "au Caméléon" I realized how little the French "femmes de lettres" know of English and Americans and vice versa (orful expression—only such clichés remain!) I wish I might bring about a better "entente," and hope therefore to organize here this winter, and this spring, readings and presentations that will enable our mind-allies to appreciate each other. As you will see, by enclosed card, je fête à mes prochains vendredis les 2 femmes qui m'ont si aimablement et humouristiquement exposés—and "Colette" has promised to act a scene from her "Vagabonde" which is to appear

later in a theatre in Paris. I should like to add at least one Anglo-Saxon to this first group, and thought that *you, presented by yourself*
would make a good representation—and balance the French trio.
Will you! Shall we? And may I announce you, in the invitations I am
sending out Saturday for either the last Friday of January—the
28th—or the 4th of February? Wasn't the 4th of February celebrated
in some way by Americans in history, if so we must surely cling to
that date! I'm at home, dans l'intimité, to-morrow Friday all afternoon and we could talk it over, or I could drop in and see you (if you
don't come here to-morrow) this Saturday about 3:30 or 4 o'clock.

Hoping my "petit projet" may meet with your approval and receive your participation. With affectionate greetings to you and your
friend, in which Romaine Brooks joins me—

Yours most appreciatively
Natalie C. Barney

Enclosed in this letter was a card listing the writers who were to be
featured on the first three Fridays of 1927 and inviting Gertrude
Stein to become the fourth by repeating the lecture that she had delivered in England the previous spring.

January 7 in honor of Madame Aurel
January 14 in honor of Madame Colette, who will play a scene from *La
Vagabonde* with Monsieur Paul Poiret
January 28: Lucie Delarue-Mardrus, poet and novelist
February 4 Gertrude Stein presented by herself (as at Oxford?)
R.S.V.P.

Another card, sent out later in the same year, outlines four more
programs.

May 6 in honor of the Duchess de Clermont-Tonnerre and the English po-
etess Mina Loy
May 13, a novelist, a poetess, an unknown, etc.
June 3, Rachilde, then Ford Madox Ford will discuss American women
of letters, including Djuna Barnes
June 10, retrospective of the works of Renée Vivien and Marie Lenéru

Most of the time Natalie had no planned program for the salon but
merely a weekly gathering of invited guests and the habitués who

had a standing invitation. But in 1927 she made a concerted effort to organize a series of special meetings featuring women writers. The programs outlined above appear to be fairly representative of the Académie des Femmes, whose membership and proceedings are reported in the second half of *Aventures de l'esprit.* This feminist society seems to have had its orgins in the anti-war meetings held on the steps of the Temple à l'Amitié in 1917 and attended by professional journalists and critics like Aurel, Rachilde and Severine, who wanted to stop the killing. The Académie des Femmes included these women and others, presenting the leading French women of letters in a series of discussions and readings from their work. The purpose was also to introduce them to English and American women writers, some of whose work was translated for these readings. The French writers included Colette, Aurel, Rachilde, Lucie Delarue-Mardrus and Elisabeth de Gramont (the pen name of Lily de Clermont-Tonnerre); the Anglo-Saxons were Djuna Barnes, Mina Loy, Gertrude Stein and Anna Wickham. There were also "retrospectives" of Renée Vivien and Marie Lénéru, who had inspired the pacifist meetings in 1917, and Romaine Brooks was also included, the only painter and at the time an aspiring writer of memoirs.

Gertrude Stein was celebrated at one of these special Fridays in a program that reflects a good deal of thoughtful planning, with an opening presentation by Mina Loy, readings from Gertrude Stein's work and a performance of several songs which Virgil Thomson had composed on texts by Gertrude Stein. To introduce the author's work to a predominantly French audience, Natalie had translated passages from *The Making of Americans,* no easy task, and asked Mme. Langlois, a friend of Virgil Thomson, to read her translations of Gertrude Stein's poems. The author was to invite her friends, and everything about the program was calculated to please her.

Surprisingly enough, the friendship between the two literary Amazons did not begin until 1926, although Gertrude Stein had lived in Paris since 1903 and they had many common acquaintances, including Laura Barney. But they lived in different worlds. The bohemia of Montparnasse could have been centuries removed from a salon in the Faubourg Saint-Germain instead of an easy half hour's walk. In *What Is Remembered* Alice Toklas recalls their first encounters and "the beginning of a long and warm friendship." But Natalie's early letters to Gertrude Stein suggest that, for once, friendship did not warm up immediately. Perhaps Gertrude Stein was wary of lesbian notoriety or afraid of becoming a tame lion in a salon. Apparently she declined several invitations to perform. Natalie wanted her to rehearse her lecture at the salon before going to England, but Gertrude seems to have limited herself to asking the professional advice of a professor she met at the salon. The following year Natalie wrote, in planning her programs for May and June, "Ford Madox Ford is to speak about les femmes de lettres—and if you won't speak about yourself, as I've so often begged you to, he should mention you and your influence foremost."

Natalie was extremely patient in cultivating people who seemed worthwhile, and eventually she managed to overcome Gertrude Stein's reluctance. The program in her honor may have softened her resistance, or she may have discovered that she had nothing to fear, or that there was more to Natalie than she had suspected. Gradually they became good friends, visiting back and forth and introducing friends whom both appreciated: Romaine Brooks, Lily de Clermont-Tonnerre, Ford Madox Ford, Carl Van Vechten, Sherwood Anderson, Dolly Wilde, Edith Sitwell, Thornton Wilder. During the summers they made many plans to meet, usually at the country home of Gertrude Stein and Alice Toklas when Natalie was en route to her villa on the Riviera. And in 1937, when Gertrude moved to the Rue Christine, a few blocks from the Rue Jacob, their friendship deepened. In her foreword to Gertrude's posthumous *As Fine as Melanctha,* Natalie remembered:

> Often in the evening we would walk together; I, greeted at the door of 5 rue Christine by Gertrude's staunch presence, pleasant touch of hand, well-rounded voice always ready to chuckle. Our talks and walks led us far from war paths. For generally having no axe to grind nor anyone to execute with it, we felt detached and free to wander in our quiet old quarter where, while exercising her poodle, "Basket," we naturally fell into thought and step. Basket, un-

leashed, ran ahead, a white blur, the ghost of a dog in the moonlit streets. The night's enchantment made our conversation as light, iridescent and bouncing as soap bubbles, but as easily exploded when touched upon—so I'll touch on none of them for you, that a bubble may remain a bubble! And perhaps we never said *"d'impérissables choses."*

From other comments in this reminiscent forward it is evident that both these strong-minded and independent women respected each other. Everyone who knew Gertrude Stein would agree with the first part of the following statement, but few would agree with the second: "Although the most affirmative person I ever met, she was a keen and responsive listener." Evidently Gertrude found Natalie worth listening to. And Natalie in turn paid rare tribute to Gertrude's judgment.

Even I, who am not in the habit of consulting anybody about my dilemmas, once brought a problem of mine to the willing and experienced ear of Gertrude. In a moment, in a word, she diagnosed the complaint: "Consanguinity."
She never appeared to hesitate or reflect or take aim, but invariably hit the mark.

Since Natalie herself was known for her willing and experienced ear and her unerring aim, this praise is all the more creditable.

As writers they were totally different, and Natalie had serious reservations about Gertrude's method. "Being a writer of *pensées,* I like to find a thought as in a nut- or seashell, but while I make for a point Gertrude seems to proceed by avoiding it." Amusingly enough, Natalie manages to make Gertrude sound aphoristic by quoting fragments from her writing. Further she comments, "I have always had a predilection for what is short, and especially novels and long stories often seem to me much longer than life and far less interesting." She liked one of the novels in *As Fine as Melanctha,* but only because it was not like a novel at all. Still she was interested enough to keep up with Gertrude Stein's writings as they appeared, even though she could not have derived much pleasure from them. Out of loyalty to her friends she followed their careers in this way and displayed their books in the salon. Her own she did not take too seriously. "What are you writing?" she asked in a letter to Gertrude, adding, "I, having produced a book, will now rest ten years more."

15
The Matron Saint of Lesbos

By the 1920s Natalie Barney was as famous for her avowal of lesbianism as she was for her literary salon. Her *Pensées d'une Amazone* (1920) published, for all the world to see, the conclusions that she had reached about Sapphic love during her stormier years. This book must have done a great deal to establish her as "*l'impératrice des lesbiennes.*" Two novels published in 1928 clearly portray her in that role—Radclyffe Hall's *The Well of Loneliness* and Djuna Barnes' *Ladies Almanack*—one solemnly, the other satirically. And Sylvia Beach, in her quiet, understated book of memoirs, *Shakespeare and Company,* sketches a milder version of the same portrait, remembering Natalie as she appeared in her prime.

One of the people who always took a great interest in my bookshop and also Adrienne's was my compatriot Miss Natalie Clifford Barney, the *Amazone* of Remy de Gourmont's *Letters.* She rode horseback in the Bois de Boulogne every morning, hence the name. She wrote poetry, and her *salon* was famous in the Paris literary world, but I wonder if she ever took literary things very seriously. As an amazon, Miss Barney was not belligerent. On the contrary, she was charming, and all dressed in white with her blond colouring, most attractive. Many of her sex found her fatally so, I believe.

171

And a little further on, Sylvia Beach adds:

> At Miss Barney's one met the ladies with high collars and mono-
> cles, though Miss Barney herself was so feminine. Unfortunately, I
> missed the chance to make the acquaintance at her *salon* of the
> authoress of *The Well of Loneliness,* in which she concluded that if
> inverted couples could be united at the altar, all their problems would
> be solved.

Radclyffe Hall's novel was in its day the great controversial novel
about lesbianism, banned in England but a best-seller in the United
States, translated into French and a dozen other foreign languages.
The plot traces the sexual biography of Stephen Gordon, a girl born
into the English landed gentry, the only child of parents who wanted
a son. After many traumatic experiences Stephen achieves a measure of peace as a successful novelist living in Paris. Here she becomes acquainted with Valérie Seymour, whom she both admires
and deplores for the candor with which she accepts lesbianism, for
her cool dignity, not to say coldness, in judgment and demeanor, for
the entire way of life she has created. Radclyffe Hall gives a very
full, scarcely fictionalized portrait of Natalie, who epitomizes for
her a diametrically different view of life, classical rather than Romantic.

While Valérie Seymour has come to terms with lesbianism—sto-
ically or cynically, depending on one's point of view—Stephen
Gordon continues to struggle against it and to suffer in the process.
Hers is essentially a tragic view of lesbianism as an abnormal state
doomed to ostracism, guilt and unhappiness. The last and longest
section of the novel is devoted largely to the varieties of homosexual
anguish in Paris: alcoholism, promiscuity, rootlessness, bereave-
ment and suicide. But Valérie Seymour rises above all this suffering, aloof and serene. Toward the end of the novel Stephen Gordon
turns to her for understanding, "as many another had done before
her. This woman's great calm in the midst of storm was not only
soothing but helpful to Stephen, so that now she went often to the
flat on the Quai Voltaire . . . to unburden her weary mind of the
many problems surrounding inversion."

Radclyffe Hall, who was called John by her friends, gives a fictionalized version of her own life in *The Well of Loneliness*, depicting her protagonist as a tormented soul in order to pacify the censors, but feels no need to represent Natalie except as she was, only making her twenty years younger so that her love affairs will appear more plausible. Stephen's introduction to Valérie could be an account of the novelist's first encounter with Natalie.

As they drove to her apartment on the Quai Voltaire, Brockett began to extol their hostess, praising her wit, her literary talent. She wrote delicate satires and charming sketches of Greek moeurs—the latter were very outspoken, but then Valérie's life was very outspoken—she was, said Brockett, a kind of pioneer who would probably go down to history. Most of her sketches were written in French, for among other things Valérie was bilingual; she was also quite rich, an American uncle had had the foresight to leave her his fortune; she was also quite young, being just over thirty, and according to Brockett, good-looking. She lived her life in great calmness of spirit, for nothing worried and few things distressed her. She was firmly convinced that in this ugly age one should strive to the top of one's bent after beauty. But Stephen might find her a bit of a free lance, she was libre penseuse when it came to the heart; her love affairs would fill quite three volumes, even after they had been expurgated. Great men had loved her, great writers had written about her, one had died, it was said, because she refused him, but Valérie was not attracted to men—yet as Stephen would see if she went to her parties, she had many devoted friends among the men. In this respect she was almost unique, being what she was, for men did not resent her. But then of course all intelligent people realized that she was a creature apart, as would Stephen at the moment she met her.

Radclyffe Hall lodges Valérie Seymour on the Quai Voltaire partly because that address befits her eighteenth-century temper but chiefly because she wants Natalie's Romantic house in the Rue Jacob for her heroine. Yet despite her classical facade, Valérie Seymour exhibits the same indifference to order as Natalie.

The first thing that struck Stephen about Valérie's flat was its large and rather splendid disorder. There was something blissfully unkempt about it, as though its mistress were too much engrossed in other affairs to control its behaviour. Nothing was quite where it ought to have been, and much was where it ought not to have been, while over the whole lay a faint layer of dust—even over the spacious salon. The odour of somebody's Oriental scent was mingling with the odour of tuberoses in a sixteenth century chalice. On a divan, whose truly regal proportions occupied the best part of a shadowy alcove, lay a box of Fuller's peppermint creams and a lute, but the strings of the lute were broken.

The details here are authentic: Natalie loved chocolates, the lute with broken strings was a familiar part of the decor, and the place looked as if it was never dusted. The description of Natalie is also a photographic likeness:

Valérie came forward with a smile of welcome. She was not beautiful nor was she imposing, but her limbs were very perfectly proportioned, which gave her a fictitious look of tallness. She moved well, with the quiet and unconscious grace that sprang from those perfect proportions. Her face was humorous, placid and worldly; her eyes very kind, very blue, very lustrous. She was dressed all in white, a large white fox skin was clasped round her slender and shapely shoulders. For the rest she had masses of thick fair hair, which was busily ridding itself of its hairpins; one could see at a glance that it hated restraint, like the flat it was in rather splendid disorder.

Natalie and Radclyffe Hall never became close friends. Temperamentally they were too different, to begin with; then they had a falling out when Radclyffe Hall produced an unflattering portrait of Romaine in another novel; and Romaine in turn may have given offense when she painted a merciless portrait of Una Lady Troubridge, who was Radclyffe Hall's great love. Still, they all managed to get along well enough, and the English couple frequently visited the Paris crowd, which included Colette and Lily. Una Troubridge kept up a correspondence with Natalie over a period of forty years and, in *The Life and Death of Radclyffe Hall,* fondly remembered them all as good friends. And Radclyffe Hall, whatever her personal

feelings may have been, did full justice to Natalie's extraordinary
magnetism and empathy.

> Turning her back on the chattering Brockett, she started to talk to
> her guest quite gravely about her work, about books in general, about
> life in general; and as she did so Stephen began to understand better
> the charm that many had found in this woman; a charm that lay less
> in physical attraction than in a great courtesy and understanding, a
> great will to please, a great impulse towards beauty in all its forms—
> yes, therein lay her charm. And as they talked on it dawned upon Ste-
> phen that here was no mere libertine in love's garden, but rather a
> creature born out of her epoch, a pagan chained to an age that was
> Christian, one who would surely say with Pierre Louÿs: 'Le monde
> moderne succombe sous un envahissement de laideur.' And she
> thought that she discerned in those luminous eyes, the pale yet ardent
> light of the fanatic.

Radclyffe Hall also appreciated Natalie's house and indulged in a
bit of wishful thinking by appropriating it as the proper setting for
her fictional self. When Stephen announces her decision to live in
Paris, Valérie recommends a tumbledown house with a fine garden
in the Rue Jacob, immediately calls up the landlord and makes an
appointment for Stephen to see the house the following morning.

> Stephen bought the house in the Rue Jacob, because as she walked
> through the dim, grey archway that led from the street to the cobbled
> courtyard, and saw the deserted house standing before her, she knew
> at once that there she would live. This will happen sometimes, we in-
> stinctively feel in sympathy with certain dwellings.
> The courtyard was sunny and surrounded by walls. On the right of
> this courtyard some iron gates led into the spacious, untidy garden,
> and woefully neglected though this garden had been, the trees that it
> still possessed were fine ones. A marble fountain long since choked
> with weeds, stood in the centre of what had been a lawn. In the far-
> thest corner of the garden some hand had erected a semicircular tem-
> ple, but that had been a long time ago, and now the temple was all
> but ruined.
> The house itself would need endless repairs, but its rooms were of

careful and restful proportions. A fine room, with a window that
opened on the garden, would be Stephen's study; she could write
there in quiet; on the other side of the stone-paved hall was a smaller
but comfortable salle à manger; while past the stone staircase a little
round room in a turret would be Puddle's particular sanctum. Above
there were bedrooms enough to spare; there was also the space for a
couple of bathrooms. The day after Stephen had seen this house, she
had written agreeing to purchase.

The description of that deserted house, with its unweeded garden
and ruined temple, may sound like picturesque scene-painting, but
according to many observers the place was always in a dilapidated
state, inside and out.

Valérie is famous for her parties, but for a long time Stephen
shuns them, as she shuns all homosexual society. When she finally
goes to one, she is disarmed by the casual informality and intrigued
by the people who are there.

> Valérie's rooms were already crowded when Stephen and Mary ar-
> rived at her reception, so crowded that at first they could not see their
> hostess and must stand rather awkwardly near the door—they had not
> been announced; one never was for some reason, when one went to
> Valérie Seymour's.
>
> The erstwhile resentment that she had felt towards Valérie Sey-
> mour was fading completely. So pleasant it was to be made to feel
> welcome by all these clever and interesting people—and clever they
> were there was no denying; in Valérie's salon the percentage of
> brains was generally well above average. For together with those
> who themselves being normal, had long put intellects above bodies,
> were writers, painters, musicians and scholars, men and women
> who, set apart from their birth, had determined to hack out a niche in
> existence.

The salon, as Radclyffe Hall describes it, is more conspicuous for
homosexuality than for talent. Others have described it thus, too,
though in the age of Proust and Gide, homosexuality and talent often went hand in hand. To appease the censors, Radclyffe Hall presents homosexuality as a curse, yet exempts Natalie as one who not

only rises above it but confers a kind of grace on those around her. This is the noblest portrait of Natalie ever written.

> And such people frequented Valérie Seymour's, men and women who must carry God's mark on their foreheads. For Valérie, placid and self-assured, created an atmosphere of courage; every one felt very normal and brave when they gathered together at Valérie Seymour's. There she was, this charming and cultured woman, a kind of lighthouse in a storm-swept ocean. The waves had lashed round her feet in vain; winds had howled; clouds had spued forth their hail and their lightning; torrents had deluged but had not destroyed her. The storms, gathering force, broke and drifted away, leaving behind them the shipwrecked, the drowning. But when they looked up, the poor spluttering victims, why what should they see but Valérie Seymour! Then a few would strike boldly out for the shore, at the sight of this indestructible creature.
>
> She did nothing, and at all times said very little, feeling no urge towards philanthrophy. But this much she gave to her brethren, the freedom of her salon, the protection of her friendship; if it eased them to come to her monthly gatherings they were always welcome provided they were sober. Drink and drugs she abhorred because they were ugly—one drank tea, iced coffee, sirops and orangeade in the celebrated flat on Quai Voltaire.

There are curious verbal echoes of Virginia Woolf in this passage, beginning with the phrase Virginia Woolf uses to present her fictional hostess, Mrs. Dalloway, and running through the imagery and rhythms for several sentences: "There she was, this charming and cultured woman, a kind of lighthouse in a storm-swept ocean. The waves had lashed round her feet in vain; winds had howled; clouds had spued forth their hail and their lightning; torrents had deluged but had not destroyed her." It is hard to know what to make of these echoes of Virginia Woolf. Perhaps they are only subconscious imitation, but possibly Radclyffe Hall was trying to draw some sort of parallel between Natalie and the queen of Bloomsbury. Apparently Natalie was not acquainted with Virginia Woolf or the Bloomsbury group, though she knew a good many English writers and corresponded with Vita Sackville-West, who was the model for

Virginia Woolf's *Orlando*. This androgynous tour de force must have fascinated Natalie, as did another Bloomsbury book, Dorothy Bussy's memoir of her education in lesbianism at Les Ruches, *Olivia*. Natalie knew Dorothy Bussy and once remarked of her brother, Lytton Strachey, "He was a very ugly man; he looked like Jesus Christ." But this does not prove that she knew him, much less Virginia Woolf. All that can be said is that there was some kind of association in the mind of Radclyffe Hall.

During the twenties and thirties, Natalie's circle included a number of talented young American women who were not lovers but literary friends. Of these, Djuna Barnes was recognized as the most talented, not only in Natalie's circle but among all the Americans in Paris, where her drawings and stories enjoyed quite a celebrity. Ford Madox Ford, who as editor of the *Transatlantic Review* was always in search of new talent, "discovered" her and introduced her to Natalie. "Djuna was one of the strongest personalities around Natalie," according to Janet Flanner, "and one of the most devoted, one of the most appreciated." She was one of the few Americans of the younger generation who frequented the salon and the only one to be included in the Académie des Femmes. In presenting this youngest member to her fellow academicians, Natalie translated one of her stories and several poems, praised her sense of humor, which resembled that of Rabelais and Cervantes, and observed that this independent young woman had a capacity for great friendship with two or three chosen spirits. These were qualities Natalie prized, and it is easy to understand why Djuna Barnes was one of the personalities she appreciated most. Natalie seems to have adopted her as a member of her inner circle and a special friend. It was Djuna Barnes who discovered Berthe Cleyrergue, who was to be Natalie's housekeeper and an institution at 20 rue Jacob from 1927 until Natalie's death.

The correspondence between Natalie and Djuna Barnes reflects their mutual interest in writing, beginning with their own. They admired each other's works and made efforts to get them recognized. Natalie wrote a review of Djuna Barnes' first book, entitled *A Book*, and asked her to contribute to the magazine she and Sinclair Lewis proposed to publish, which was to be called "How to Live by Those Who Have." When Djuna Barnes went to America for a visit, she tried to find a publisher for *The One Who Is Legion*. When Faber and Faber published Djuna Barnes' *Nightwood*, Natalie corresponded with T. S. Eliot and thanked him for writing the introduction. They also discussed the work of other writers, both disapproving of Proust's treatment of lesbianism in *Remembrance of Things Past*.

Natalie had had a correspondence with Proust, published in *Aventures de l'esprit*, and had met him once during the last year of his life. The correspondence began when he read *Pensées d'une Amazone* and decided to pursue his research in Sapphic love by conferring with an author of such expertise. He also wanted to see the famous "Temple à l'Amour," as he called it, but it was difficult to arrange a rendezvous because he rose at an hour when the rest of the world went to bed, and his visit had to be postponed repeatedly on account of illness. When he finally came—at midnight—the visit was not a success. Proust was too nervous to broach the topic he wanted to discuss. Natalie, who was probably not in a very good humor so long after her bedtime, was unable to interrupt the flow of his chatter about high society in order to bring it around to the subject of lesbianism. On the whole she was unfavorably impressed by the man and his work. When the first volume of his *Sodome et Gomorrhe* appeared, he assured her that although his Sodomites were horrible, his Gomorrhans would all be charming. Instead Natalie found them unbelievable and remarked dryly that Proust's knowledge of "the love that does not speak its name" was not sufficient to penetrate these Eleusinian mysteries.

Djuna Barnes, on the other hand, was well qualified to deal with such material in her *Ladies Almanack*, which she later summed up as follows:

> Neap-tide to the Proustian chronicle, gleanings from the shores of Mytilene, glimpses of its novitiates, its rising "saints" and "priestesses," and thereon to such aptitude and insouciance that they took to gaming and to swapping that "other" of the mystery, the anomaly that calls the hidden name. That, affronted, eats its shadow.

In January, 1928, Natalie wrote a letter to Richard Aldington in-
quiring about the prospects of publishing a little book whose robust
sense of humor appealed to her. "All ladies fit to figure in such an
almanack should of course be eager to have a copy, and all gentlemen disapproving of them. Then the public might, with a little judi-
cious treatment, include those lingering on the border of such islands and those eager to be ferried across." The phrasing here could
have been borrowed from the book itself, which is written in a highly figurative, whimsically archaic prose style. The subject of *Ladies
Almanack* is roughly the same as that of *The Well of Loneliness*, but
the treatment is totally different, full of rowdy farce and bawdy metaphor. This satiric spoof pokes good-natured fun at some of the bet-
ter-known lesbians of Paris, centering around a heroine named
Evangeline Musset, who is their patron saint. It is easy to imagine
that much of the humor was bandied about in Natalie's circle and
that some of it even originated with her, such as the mock-epic account of Evangeline's birth and upbringing. Her parents had been
expecting a son, so when "she came forth an Inch or so less than
this, she paid no Heed to the Error." Accordingly, she "set out
upon the Road of Destiny," following her own particular inclinations and "composing, as she did so, Madrigals to all sweet and
ramping things."

> Her Father, be it known, spent many a windy Eve pacing his Li-
> brary in the most normal of Night-Shirts, trying to think of ways to
> bring his erring Child back into that Religion and Activity which has
> ever been thought sufficient for a Woman . . . and Evangeline was
> in order of becoming one of those who is spoken to out of Generos-
> ity, which her Father could see, would by no Road, lead her to the
> Altar.
> He had Words with her enough, saying: "Daughter, daughter, I
> perceive in you most fatherly Sentiments. What am I to do?" And
> she answered him High enough, "Thou, good Governor, wast ex-
> pecting a Son when you lay atop of your Choosing, why then be so
> mortal wounded when you perceive that you have your Wish? Am I
> not doing after your very Desire, and is it not the more commend-
> able, seeing that I do it without the Tools for the Trade, and yet noth-
> ing complain?

All that was long ago, when Evangeline was ostracized by society; now she has found her proper place and acquired a new reputation.

> In the days of which I write she had come to be a witty and learned Fifty, and though most short of Stature and nothing handsome, was so much in Demand, and so wide famed for her Genius in bringing up by Hand, and so noted and esteemed for her Slips of the Tongue that it finally brought her into the Hall of Fame, where she stood by a Statue of Venus as calm as you please, or leaned upon a lacrymal Urn with a small Sponge for such as Wept in her own Time and stood in Need of it.

Later, Djuna Barnes makes fun of her heroine's pontifical manner and missionary zeal. It may be no coincidence that Claude Mauriac called Natalie "the pope of Lesbos" and that in *The Well of Loneliness* Valérie Seymour expresses her disgust in a homosexual bar by saying, "I think I preferred it when we were all martyrs!"

> "In my day," said Dame Musset, and at once the look of the Pope, which she carried about with her as a Habit, waned a little, and there was seen to shine forth the Cunning of a Monk in Holy Orders, in some Country too old for Tradition, "in my day I was a Pioneer and a Menace, it was not then as it is now, *chic* and pointless to a degree, but as daring as a Crusade, for where now it leaves a woman talkative, so that we have not a Secret among us, then it left her in Tears and Trepidation. . . . What joy had the missionary," she added, her Eyes narrowing and her long Ears moving with Disappointment, when all the Heathen greet her with Glory Halleluja! before she opens her Mouth, and with an Amen! before she shuts it!

Times have changed, but Dame Musset has no regrets when she remembers the early eighties, when "Girls were as mute as a Sampler, and as importunate as a War, and would have me lay on, charge and retreat the night through."

> "Still," she remarked, sipping a little hot tea, "they were dear Creatures, and they have paced me to a contented and knowing fifty. I am well pleased. Upon my Sword there is no Rust, and upon my

Escutcheon so many Stains that I have, in this manner, created my own Banner and my own Badge. I have learned on the Bodies of all Women, all Customs, and from their Minds have all Nations given up their Secrets. I know that the Orientals are cold to the Waist, and from there flame with a mighty and quick crackling Fire. I have learned that Anglo Saxons thaw slowly but that they thaw from Head to Heel, and so it is with their Minds. The Asiatic is warm and willing, and goes out like a Firecracker; the Northerner is cool and cautious, but burns and burns, until," she said reminiscently, "you see that Candle lit by you in youth, burning about your Bier in Death."

In the end Saint Musset dies at the ripe age of ninety-nine, mourned by forty women and many poems. When her body is burned on a funeral pyre, her tongue remains, and this relic is placed in an urn on the altar of the Temple of Love. *Ladies Almanack* was published anonymously "by a Lady of Fashion," though the author's identity was an open secret. A limited number of copies had the illustrations hand-colored by the author, and Natalie owned one of these, in which she had written marginal notes identifying all the characters.

16
Dolly Wilde

During the 1920s and 1930s Natalie continued to have as many love affairs as ever. The most vivid love of this period was Dolly Wilde, the daughter of Oscar's brother Willie. With her long, pale, rather horsey face, Dolly bore a striking resemblance to her famous uncle, a resemblance which only increased with age, as her features and her figure grew heavier, and which she made no attempt to disguise. "I am more Oscar-like than he was like himself," she said. Once, at a masquerade party at Lily's, she came dressed as her uncle, Janet Flanner reported, "looking both important and earnest." Natalie came to the same party in an equally redundant costume, dressed "as a *femme de lettres.*"

The resemblance to Oscar and his equally brilliant brother was not only physical. Dolly had the same extravagant gifts and failings, the indolence, the personal magnetism and that breathtaking effortless wit. "When she was in a room it became charged with her vital aliveness," Allanah Harper recalled. "Her positive personality dominated any place she was in, dispelling dullness, with a dart of wit, or some only too apt remark about the atmosphere, or the weaker points, the hidden failings of persons present." She also had the same self-destructive tendencies. Her uncle had given up the will to live after he was released from prison, and her father had drunk himself to death before she was born. Dolly did her best to follow her father's example, with drugs as well as drink, almost committed suicide twice and seemed fated to die young. "Half in love with death . . . she felt that she was still the caterpillar waiting to be released from the cocoon into the perfection of the butterfly."

These quotations come from a book of reminiscences that Natalie gathered from the friends who had known and loved Dolly, *In Memory of Dorothy Ierne Wilde.* The best of these is by Bettina Bergery, herself a great wit and storyteller. Here is how she recreates Dolly at dinner with Victor Cunard and the Count and Countess Yorke:

> Her face is exactly Aubrey Beardsley's drawing of Oscar Wilde. The others are talking, she is looking dully at an empty glass as she strips the leaves from a sprig she had taken from the flowers on the table. A tall red-headed boy comes in and recognises Victor, who begins introducing. Dolly's eyes light up as she interrupts: "Darling you do introduce so badly, you don't know how to introduce at all: you just mention names he doesn't know, and that makes conversation so general!" Now she addresses the boy directly: "Victor, you don't need to be told, is the White Knight from Alice in Wonderland, and this," pointing her twig at Yorke—a golden-headed German—"is Siegfried. It's not red wine in his glass, he only drinks blood, dragon's blood, that's why he is smiling at the impertinent things the canaries in the cage over the caissière's desk have been saying about us. He understands them perfectly. She"—the twig now points at Ruth Yorke—"whose features are as taut as a red indian's, who knows what rites she performs when the moon is full. As for me . . . you should have recognised me first and rushed to me—even without my turban, because I am Madame de Staël. If you've forgotten my face you should have remembered my branch"—here she waves her twig—"and my beautiful hand and forearm."

That is not the end of the story, and the witty remarks go on for page after page. Even more than her uncle, Dolly had a natural literary talent which she dissipated in delightful talk. She was a great reader and, according to Janet Flanner, knew most of the English and French writers of her day. Many of them she met at Natalie's salon, which she particularly enjoyed, Bettina Bergery said, "and there she shone her brightest." Only her letters remain as evidence of her literary gift, and some of these appear in the memorial volume, addressed to a thinly disguised "Emily."

These letters show that Dolly and Natalie discussed a good many writers, and one in particular, Virginia Woolf, with whom they identified closely. In 1931, when *The Waves* appeared, Dolly referred to it as "dear Virginia-Dolly-Emily's" but soon withdrew from this trinity, saying, "Alas! I said there is no Virginia-Dolly—only Virginia-Emily. I *am* cousin-germaine—but no nearer." As she wrote this, Dolly was looking forward to meeting this awesome personage: "I am to dine with Virginia one day next week—but I dread the ordeal and she will never know what marginal notes of understanding mark every page of her books in my library." The letter that she wrote describing that encounter contains one of the finest of the many portraits of Virginia Woolf.

> Cambridge on a frosty night. The Dean's room in King's College, fire-light, books, sober colours, elegance and a group of charming people holding conversation. We are waiting for dinner when someone says "Leonard and Virginia are very late." The smooth waters of my mind are ruffled by fear by this unexpected remark, and my heart beats perceptibly quicker. The chief Lama of Thibet will be here any moment—easy manners must give place to decorum, familiar friendship be brought stiffly to attention. Then the door opens and a tall gaunt figure, grey-haired, floats into the room. Her age struck me first, and then her prettiness—shock and delight hand in hand. How explain? There is something of the witch in her—as in Edith Sitwell—with the rather curved back and sharp features. She is dressed in black, old fashioned elderly clothes that make me feel second-rate in my smart clothes—her feet are very long and thin encased in black broché shoes with straps of the Edwardian period. All is faded and grey about her, like her iron grey hair parted in the middle and dragged into a 'bun' at the back. And yet immediately one sees her *prettiness* and a lovely washed away ethereal look making all of us look so gross and sensual. The eyes are deep-sunk and small the nose fine and pointed, a little *too* pointed by curiosity, but the feature that most strikes one is the mouth—a full round mouth, a pretty girl's mouth in that spinster face. It is so young, young like her skin that is smooth and soft. She greets Honey and me without looking at us and

at dinner never once makes us the target of her eyes—there is embarrassment around the table and she only talks to her intimates. She is witty and kindly malicious. Then suddenly I say something that makes her laugh and the curtain of her eye-lids are raised and we talk together, flippantly delightfully. I had once been told one must never mention her books and as we threaded byeways of humour I thought of your letters about her so much. I saw her, too, all the time as such a pretty little girl in a big hat, and Kew Gardens with the governess planting a kiss on the back of her neck—do you remember?—which was the parent of all the kisses in her life.

After dinner they went to the theater to see *Hamlet,* and Dolly had to turn her head away when she saw Virginia Woolf yawning, ''as if I had caught God in a domestic moment of relaxation.''

She has nothing to do with maternal life—is supposed to be a virgin, to have experienced no physical contact even with Orlando. She says she has no need of experience—knows everything without it: and this impression she gives as one meets her. I felt cruelty in her, born of humour—tiredness, great tiredness and her eyes *veiled* with visions rather than brightened by them.

Janet Flanner thought ''there was an unfulfilled literary quality'' about Dolly, and by this she did not mean that Dolly should have written, but that she was ''like a character out of a book,'' perhaps a romantic international novel by Stendhal. Actually, the story of her love for Natalie was rather like such a novel, and the plot has an air of *déjà vu,* with Dolly assuming the part played earlier by Renée Vivien. However, instead of being the doomed passive victim of a Decadent love story, she plays her part like one of Evelyn Waugh's bright young things, terribly sophisticated and, underneath that hard finish, terribly unhappy, but not, at any rate, given to self-pity.

Scraps of Dolly's unhappy love story can be found in the excerpts from the letters Natalie published, commemorating her love affair with this wonderful creature who seemed to her ''half androgyne and half goddess.'' Natalie, who collected everything, never threw away any of the letters she received and left forty thousand of them, all carefully filed by name, when she died. Most love letters make tedious reading, except to the persons involved, and even then, only at the time, as Dolly pointed out.

> I know you think that your past letters will one day be agreeable read-ing—but they won't, darling, they won't! Forgotten sentiment goes rotten—and love letters rarely contain the interest of incident or the pleasure of wit.

But Dolly's letters are wonderfully alive and moving, at least in the small portion that Natalie selected from a large boxful.

The story of their love is not complete or explicit, but there is enough to sketch an outline. Most of the letters were written when Dolly was banished because Romaine had become jealous. In exile she remembered little details from daily life, like Natalie's "cool dusty house," where she had often stayed. When Natalie was away, she stayed there again, all alone in that empty house, reading Renée's melancholy poetry. One letter was written while she was "Sitting in the DARK of the stairs while you take your bath! (Is *this* the 'home-life' I crave for??)" Sometimes they tried to arrange rendezvous despite Romaine, and Dolly anticipated:

> That strange ending of all intimacy at the very moment of rejoining— that suspicious getting-acquainted-again with the beloved—that hor-rible shyness and small talk—that sudden cessation of emotion—the dead level of reality, flat and terrifying. Is that hour a provision of Nature to prevent spontaneous combustion?

Often Romaine came between them, "the herald of unimaginable suffering." But at other times Natalie was gadding about some-where, out of touch, and Dolly worried, "Are you cross, forgetful or faithless? Or all three?" Forgetfulness was worst, when Natalie sent instead of letters "an American business man's telegram." Like so many other women, Dolly discovered the "tender, heart-less, paradoxical One" and must often have wondered, "Where are you, darling? In what bed do you lie, and under what sky? Time stretches between us like a quarrel." Like Renée commenting on Natalie's love of different costumes and guises, she wondered at

Natalie's "inexplicable love of bals masqués," which was part of that ever-changing, ever-elusive self. Echoing Liane, she exclaimed:

> Darling moonbeam I think of you so much. Pale, lunar enchantress—the fatal moon herself shedding magical seasons around me. I am caught in your bright attractions—wheel kindly in your course and spare me.

She also addressed Natalie as "Darling Amazone!" and "greedy Dame Musset!" Natalie *was* greedy, as her friend Jenny Bradley recalled, illustrating this statement with an anecdote about Dolly Wilde. Natalie once made up her mind to break off with Dolly, bought her a plane ticket and sent her off to London. But Natalie was so chagrined at this parting that she started eating a chocolate cake to console herself. Meanwhile, at the airport, Dolly saw no reason to go to London after all and took a taxi back to the Rue Jacob. There she found Natalie weeping and eating, her tears running onto the cake and discoloring the chocolate. This episode may have occurred in 1937, when Dolly addressed her as "greedy Dame Musset." By then Natalie had put on weight and, according to Bettina Bergery, looked like Benjamin Franklin. By then she was sixty, and the love affair with Dolly had gone on for ten years.

There were more melodramatic episodes, like "the Chinese situation" which Dolly reported to Romaine. Now it was Dolly's turn to be jealous, as Natalie became interested in a remarkable Chinese woman. Nadine Hoang was a lawyer who was sent on a political mission to Paris by the Chinese communists in the late 1930s and who later fought in the Chinese Army for four years, wearing a man's uniform. When she ran out of money in Paris, Natalie took her in. This was not pure charity, however, but a typical hardheaded bargain; in exchange for room and board Nadine Hoang was required to work as secretary, chauffeur and general factotum. Berthe, who told the story, had a photograph of Nadine dressed as a man. She was wearing this suit when she met André Germain, who was immediately taken with this pretty young fellow, only to be crestfallen when he discovered that he had been attracted to a woman.

There were more serious episodes. Once, when Natalie went off with an actress, Dolly tried to commit suicide by cutting her wrists. Berthe had the task of nursing and comforting Dolly, staying at her bedside for a week. Ominously, one of Dolly's letters reports that on another occasion she took a whole bottle of sleeping pills *"unconsciously,"* she said, "in my sleep," and barely survived. Some of the published reminiscences mention her addiction to opium and her ostentatious cocaine-sniffing but dismiss this as a foolish fad of the period.

There are those who blame Natalie for Dolly's death as well as Renée's. But although both were deeply afflicted with a love that was only intermittently requited, the circumstances do not suggest that Natalie was to blame for either death. Dolly contracted cancer and, in 1940, went so far as to seek a miraculous cure at Lourdes. She died in London a year later, after the German invasion forced her to part from Natalie for the last time. Natalie's train left first, and Dolly bravely saw her off, leaving Natalie with a poignant memory: "I am still haunted by the twitch in her smile at our parting."

Dolly left by the last boat train for London. She had come to Paris during the first war as a girl still in her teens. Alice Toklas remembered her "almost mythical pristine freshness in 1916—that, alas, became a bit tarnished, though she never completely lost it." Gertrude Stein summed up Dolly's life with the remark, "Well, she certainly hadn't a fair run for her money." But Dolly might not have agreed.

17
Godless Nuns in Gardens Florentine

Writing to Gertrude Stein from Beauvallon in August, 1939, Natalie complained, "Summer is too great a disperser—and I shall look forward to the fall—and to our walks at night dans notre vieux quartier." But a greater disperser was destined to keep them apart, and they were never to resume their walks. The second war marked the end of an era for Natalie and her friends, affecting them more profoundly than the other war and bringing greater changes in their lives. For one thing, they were all older now, in their sixties, and the war meant the beginning of old age for some of them, death for others. When war broke out, they decided not to return to America, feeling that they belonged in Europe. Gertrude and Alice remained at their country home in the French provinces, Natalie and Romaine at their villa in Beauvallon, for the time being. Then, during the winter of the "phoney war," Natalie returned to Paris to collect warm clothing and put away her paintings. Once there, she stayed on, wishing that she and Gertrude could walk the dark streets with Basket II. "Paris is being nice and dim like a village. The people who go about like trivial ghosts are the same," she wrote, mentioning friends and acquaintances.

When the war began in earnest, Dolly announced that everyone should go home to her native country—Dolly, who had run away from home to drive an ambulance during the first war. Natalie's

French friends had joined their families in the provinces. Romaine, who was "a foreigner everywhere," had gone to Italy, where she felt as much at home as anywhere, and bought a villa in the hills above Florence. Natalie was warned by the American embassy that her safety could not be guaranteed if she remained in a country that was at war. But though she had made no secret of being one-quarter Jewish—had in fact boasted of her Jewish blood—she, like Gertrude and Alice, decided to stay. They were a special breed of Americans, the Americans of Europe. Natalie's sister Laura, who always did the right thing, booked passage to return to the United States, and Natalie went with her to the travel agency. Thus, by chance, Natalie was on hand when someone turned in a ticket on the *Rome Express,* and decided on the spur of the moment to join Romaine. Italy, she thought, would be the best place to spend the summer. And thus it happened that she spent the war there, living quietly with Romaine at the Villa Sant'Agnese.

Florence was a kind of neutral ground where the Anglo-American colony had been established for generations and seemed to enjoy a special status, immune to politics and pogroms. In the first chapter of *Traits et portraits,* Natalie describes the civilized life at the Berensons' Villa I Tatti in 1940. There in the hills of Settignano, overlooking Florence, in that little domain of gardens and fountains and Renaissance paintings, they enjoyed the company of gracious friends. It was like the time of Boccaccio, when the Florentines withdrew from the city to escape the plague and whiled away the time in their beautiful villas, telling each other the stories of the *Decameron;* or like Dante's *Vita Nuova,* "the tale of ladies gifted with intelligence in love." Was Natalie referring to any particular lady in this passing remark? Was she being faithful in her fashion, or in Dante's? Romaine's given name happened to be Beatrice, but that was no guarantee of Natalie's single-minded devotion. She mentioned no new love affairs in her memoirs; but then, she published only her literary love affairs, and those very discreetly, and few of them at that. In *Traits et portraits* she mentions Nijinsky's daughter, who danced for them once, and describes her dancing so sensuously that one wonders.

In Florence she renewed her old acquaintance with Bernard Ber-

enson and his wife, Mary, a tall, stately white-haired woman who
looked like King Lear, contrasting with her small, neat husband.
Berenson spent most of the day working in his library, which to
Natalie looked like a chapel, emerging at tea time to embrace the ladies. Berenson, who more than most people lived through his sense
of touch, often held Natalie's hand, renewing the intimate feeling
that had existed between them when they first knew each other, in
1917. Berenson confessed to several people that he had been madly
in love with Natalie and even hinted to Harold Acton that "this
affection had been more than platonic." He told Jenny Bradley that
he had not realized Natalie was a lesbian until she introduced him to
his rival, Romaine Brooks, wearing a top hat. But that was long before they were neighbors outside Florence, and now they were all
old friends. Every day after tea, the Berensons asked Romaine to
read to them a chapter from her memoirs, "No Pleasant Memories," to which she was just putting the finishing touches after all
these years, with no prospect of publication.

Ezra Pound was also in Italy, though not within easy reach, and
Natalie had kept in touch with him, too, over the years, corresponding in a friendly way about their common interests, such as needy
writers and various publishing projects. In 1939 their correspondence had turned to politics; she shared his confidence in Mussolini
but warned Pound to be discreet in his utterances when he visited
the United States that year. During the war she wrote to him fairly
frequently. In 1940 she sent him half a dozen poems she had written
about the war, scornfully indicting British and American policy and
agreeing with Pound's views on the economic causes of the war.
There was also a poem that clearly referred to herself and Romaine
and their life in Florence.

> Here happy exiles find a home at will
> ....
> These godless nuns, in gardens Florentine
> ....
> Worldlings, who dread the world's destructive din
> Take refuge in these silent well planned bowers
> —Where solitude is sadness undefined—

In the Villa Sant'Agnese these happy exiles listened with interest to news of the war and to propaganda on the radio. Natalie may have started Ezra Pound on the road to treason when she gave him a radio and praised Lord Ha-Ha's anti-British broadcasts. Presently Pound also began broadcasting propaganda, and Natalie wrote expressing agreement with his views and his fascist sympathies. Once she suggested that Lily, whose political views had now swung around to the extreme right, might also broadcast over Rome Radio; Lily wanted to visit Natalie in Florence but was unable to get there. The journal that Romaine kept during the war shows that she, too, was in sympathy with fascism and had such a phobia about the Russians that she hoped the Germans would defeat them; Natalie probably shared these views.

Natalie managed to keep in touch with Gertrude and Alice during most of the war, although the censor sometimes kept them from saying much. The letters written at this time are touching expressions of her attachment to old friends, longing for news, worrying about them, feeling cut off. She could not write to Dolly, so she wrote poems instead.

> Your life has hurt me more than all the lives
> That living long with love has gathered round
> My hearth. . . .
> Prisoned in war I can no longer fight
> To save you from yourself. . . .
> We know not who had died nor who survives. . . .

Then she heard that Dolly had died "peacefully" in London and wrote to Gertrude and Alice, who had first met Dolly as a young girl in uniform during the other war, expressing her sense of loss: "Dolly is ever very dear to me and I wish I could go on doing things for her." For all her professed indolence, Natalie was never one to be idle, and she immediately started thinking of things she could do for Dolly, planning the book in her memory, in which she would eventually include the many poems about Dolly that she wrote at this time. She also kept in touch with the faithful Berthe, who had stayed at the Rue Jacob, from whom she heard that the house was being sold. Sadly she reflected, "I have more memories than if I had lived a thousand years . . . and friends like the Duchess hope to save the Temple l'Amitié—which has been mine for 33 years." But somehow things worked out, and the temple was to be hers for another thirty years.

In the darkest days, when it seemed the war would never end, Natalie wrote about Gertrude's *Paris France* and her own books, safely preserved in the Bibliothèque Nationale, to prove what true friends of Europe they were. Then, as the war ended, she looked forward impatiently to returning to Paris. Harold Acton was the first harbinger of peace to appear on their hill above Florence, bringing news of Gertrude and Alice. Natalie was relieved to see him and found his company a refreshing change after too many lady water-colorists, conceited poetesses and writers who had retired to these hills to avoid unpleasant competition. Plainly this was not the kind of company she had enjoyed in her salon, and after five years in Flor-ence her views on the Anglo-American colony had changed. Of course, the war had taxed everybody's nerves. Romaine's journal records their fright at the American bombings as the war ended, but during most of those war years they had been preoccupied mainly with the petty business of day-to-day living, quarreling with ser-vants and worrying about food. The news Harold Acton brought was that Gertrude was having an enormous success with the American soldiers in France: "For them she was one of the living monuments of Paris, and they were attracted to this elderly frump as if she were a glamorous film-star," he wrote in *More Memoirs of an Aesthete* and went on to quote Natalie's reaction in an epithet, "this intellec-tual *vivandière*."

Gertrude had dreamed that Natalie would never return to her home in the Rue Jacob, but the dream proved only temporarily true. After six years the *pavillon* was in a sad state of disrepair, and Berthe greeted Natalie at the train station with the news that rain was falling in her bedroom; so Natalie decided to stay in her sister's apartment across town until repairs could be made. It seemed far from their old neighborhood, as she wrote in her first letter from Paris, at the end of May, 1946.

I long to be your 'voisine' again and resume our night-walks—and be
greeted by Alice, and revisit your lovely home rue Christine in the
meantime; —when shall that be? The newly arrived have very little
to do, except moon about, and like the newly married reacquaint
themselves with things strangely familiar, realized as in a dream. I
have dreamed of getting back to our old quarter so long, that, like a
somnambulist, I shall find my way to your door, and see the doves of
your bedroom flutter, and the easy chairs contain us as before, and
your portrait seating you above us looks down; uniting past and present to whatever future we have yet to live through. . . .

For Gertrude there was hardly any future left. She died suddenly
two months later, and Natalie's next letter was one of condolence.

Ah Alice what can I send you now? No words can match such a loss,
and what consolation can be found amongst Gertrude's things—without so vivifying a presence? Perhaps her works, which you will continue later on, may bring a feeling of accomplishing those duties
which you have always filled to the utmost.

It was characteristic of Natalie that she would immediately start
thinking about what the living could do for the dead. During the war
she had written several times about the death of Dolly in London,
turning from grief to planning the book in her memory. And in 1946
she was planning to edit the poetry of another dear friend, Lucie Delarue-Mardrus, who had died the year before. At the same time she
was also trying to place one of Romaine's paintings in the Tate Gallery in London, and this reminded her that Romaine had always
meant to do a portrait of Gertrude: ". . . what a pity that she never
did Gertrude's portrait, but then the Picasso is and should perhaps
remain unique."

In the same spirit, two weeks after Gertrude Stein's death, as she
contemplated returning to the Rue Jacob, Natalie wrote again to Alice:

. . . and shall we arrange to give in this old place, which Gertrude
liked and felt so at home in, a recital of fragments of her work both

published and unpublished, en souvenir d'elle et de notre amitié? And perhaps if Virgil Thomson is back in time he might play and have sung some of their compositions. Or would such a commemoration be painful—too painful to you just now? Do, I beg of you, direct me to the least of your wishes in this and all things concerning our friendship. . . .

The *pavillon* was not yet fully repaired; Natalie had only a temporary visa and was not at all certain the authorities would allow her to remain in Paris. But she was determined to stay, if she could, "in a place where I've lived for over 35 years and where I could be much more useful than in my native land," for she was already thinking of reopening her salon.

18
The No-Man's-Land of Old Age

When Dolly Wilde left Paris, she told Berthe never to leave Natalie but to stay with her through her last years, when she would be very much alone. During the war Berthe faithfully looked after Natalie's interests, but she also worked as a seamstress to earn her livelihood and was not sure she wanted to go back to being a housekeeper. Natalie and her sister Laura prevailed upon her, however, and under Berthe's supervision the *pavillon* was restored to its former condition and the household set in operation again.

Natalie was past seventy when she settled in again at the Rue Jacob, and the remaining twenty-five years of her life were bound to be less eventful than the past. Her main interest from this point on was her salon, which she now revived, gathering together old friends and welcoming any newcomers. This venerable institution seemed something of an anachronism during the grim postwar years, when Sartre's existentialists gathered around the corner in Remy de Gourmont's old café. To a young writer like Célia Bertin the salon appeared very *démodé*, stuffy and musty and dull, a curiosity surviving from the past. The setting, the people and their manners all belonged in a museum, she thought. But the place had always been like that, and Dolly had used a similar expression, calling it the "Musée de Province," because it looked just like a provincial museum with all those old portraits and busts and memo-

197

rabilia gathering dust. Still, the company had been lively in Dolly's day, while now the old friends were becoming very old and decrepit, until finally, toward the end, a visitor described them as "just a lot of old moles looking for crumbs."

In her seventies Natalie was still vigorous and busied herself in a variety of ways, looking after old friends and frequently using the salon as a means of doing so. After Gertrude's death, for instance, she might have dropped Alice, but instead she looked after her and cultivated her as a special friend who took Gertrude's place. In this, Natalie showed great tact and sympathy, and Alice, who had not attended the salon regularly before, now became a devoted and honored habituée. Similarly Natalie's letters to Sylvia Beach, whose bookstore she had always patronized, now showed that she had drawn nearer to this old friend, expressing solicitude and concern for Sylvia and her lifelong friend Adrienne Monnier as the ills of old age came upon them. She remained loyal to Ezra Pound when he was incarcerated at St. Elizabeth's Hospital, corresponding with him and sending a subscription to the *Figaro*. During these later years she was always sending thoughtful gifts to old friends, coddling them without being patronizing.

Some of the old friends were dead, and Natalie, who had a horror of funeral services, nevertheless had her own way of remembering the dead. Far better to honor their memory, she found, by doing something constructive, like organizing readings from their works or publishing books that kept their achievements alive. Thus, as the salon reopened its doors, she wrote to Bernard Berenson, "I'm busy getting up a recital of poems by Renée Vivien & Lucie Delarue-Mardrus—to be presided over by Paul Boncour." And two years later she established the Prix Renée Vivien for young poets, following the example, ironically enough, of Baroness van Zuylen, who had established such a prize after the first war. In the 1950s Natalie edited and published at her own expense the book about Dolly and the two collections of Lucie's poems, and also wrote her preface to the Yale edition of Gertrude's *As Fine as Melanctha*. At first, when Carl Van Vechten asked her to write the preface, she had misgivings: "For I am far from a practiced and 'easy-going' writer, and can only, therefore, write when inspired—seldom enough, fortunately, for my peace of mind!'' Yet she went on to write two more volumes of memoirs, the last appearing as she turned eighty-seven.

In 1953 she also wrote to Van Vechten that she had a biographer, ''prodding me for such, to me negligible, details, irksome to one like myself who seldom reads and even more seldom writes—so how can I promise to do anything of the sort?'' The biographer was Renée Lang, a Swiss scholar who had met Natalie the year before, when she came to Paris to do research on Rilke, Gide and Valéry. André Germain, who had met these writers in the salon during the twenties, advised her to look up Natalie, describing her as the most intelligent woman he had ever known. Renée Lang was astonished to learn that Remy de Gourmont's *Amazone* was still alive. As a girl of fourteen she had avidly read *Lettres à l'Amazone* and *Aventures de l'esprit,* but she thought of them as belonging to another era and never ceased to regard Natalie as an enchanted creature and 20 rue Jacob as a place outside of time.

Following Germain's suggestion, she wrote to Natalie, who promptly telephoned, asked her to call, invited her to the Fridays and opened her house to her. In her old age Natalie not only looked like Queen Victoria, Renée Lang found that she also ruled like Queen Victoria, very imperiously ordering people around. She installed Renée in a splendid apartment in the house of her friend Marcelle Fauchier-Delavigne, and Renée soon found that her life was being run a little too much for her. She remained in Paris until 1957, often attended the salon and spent two years going through Natalie's papers with the idea of writing a book about the salon. But here again Natalie proved very strong-willed, with her own ideas about how the book should be written, and Renée decided that she could never publish the book she wanted to write while Natalie was still alive.

Natalie introduced Renée to all the old friends who still came to the salon and took her to call on Colette, who was bedridden, and Marie Laurencin. André Rouveyre, who lived nearby, was a frequent visitor. Frère André, as Natalie called him, was one of her oldest and closest friends, going back to the days of Remy de Gourmont. He and Natalie liked to gossip about the women with whom they were having love affairs.

But the old friends were dying. Most of those Natalie wrote about in her memoirs had died before the war, and others had died since: Max Jacob, in a Nazi concentration camp in 1944; Valéry, in 1945; Dr. Mardrus, in 1949; Gide, in 1951. Then, in 1954, both Colette and Lily de Clermont-Tonnerre died. The loss of Lily was the one she felt most keenly in all her life, and for once she broke her rule of never visiting the dead. When she saw her beloved friend lying there, as though she were sleeping peacefully, Natalie broke down and wept, "wracked with sobs unworthy of that calm and noble face."

At least Romaine was still alive, and she was destined to go on living almost as long as Natalie. Romaine became dearer to her than ever. As they grew older, they worried more and more about each other's health, sending anxious messages and bits of advice. On the thirtieth anniversary of her mother's death, Natalie jotted down a note that described their condition exactly:

> Retired into that no-man's land of old age; that age of shawls and chills and increasing ill, where with resignation, if not anticipation, one awaits that unavoidable last visitor.

19
The Last Lover

"Natalie had become the lover and Romaine the courted one," writes Meryle Secrest in her biography of Romaine, surmising that this shift in their relationship occurred after the war, when Natalie wanted to go on living with Romaine and Romaine would not agree to it. "So the pattern of their lives took shape: letters interspersed with frequent visits that Natalie almost always organized since, she said, 'I am never quite happy away from you.' Romaine was Natalie's bright Angel, the only one she loved for keeps." Romaine now lived mostly in Nice, visiting Paris in the late spring and spending summers in Fiesole, outside Florence. Natalie now went to Nice every winter for a prolonged visit. Renée Lang, who was there one winter, gave a charming description of the two old ladies admiring a Maillol nymph in a garden and noted that Romaine was one person Natalie could not dominate. Each was the other's greatest love, and each tried to extend this love beyond the grave by naming the other as beneficiary and planning to be buried in the same tomb.

Then something happened. One day, when Natalie was in Nice, she went out for a walk on the Promenade des Anglais and sat down on a bench opposite the Hôtel Negresco. A woman came along and sat down beside her, and they began talking. There are different versions of what happened, the most reliable of which is probably Renée Lang's, since Natalie had adopted her biographer as a confidante at that time. Natalie, then in her latter seventies, had told Renée that she had retired from love: "I renounced love before it renounced me." In 1953, however, she met Janine Lahovary and was once again "struck by lightning," as the French expression has it. Renée remembers walking with Natalie in her garden, under those untrimmed trees, Natalie asking, "Renée, what shall I do?" And Renée replied, "Why, Natalie, since fortune has smiled on you again, take advantage of your good fortune."

Natalie had been lucky in love all her life, Renée observed, for everyone fell in love with her, and she had had "a thousand liaisons." And here, at the end of her life, she fell in love all over again and had a "complete" love affair. It was Janine who had made the overtures, striking up an acquaintance on that public bench overlooking the Mediterranean. She had fallen in love with the myth of l'Amazone and had been waiting for an opportunity to meet Natalie. She then presented herself to Natalie "body and soul" and "erupted like a volcano."

Janine was in her early fifties, a married woman who had not been conscious of any lesbian tendencies before. The wife of a retired ambassador, she had lived mostly in fashionable society but had begun her life under modest circumstances in Geneva. Renée, who also grew up in Geneva but traveled in intellectual circles, looked down upon Janine as a very ordinary person who had married far above her station. As a pretty girl of seventeen, Janine had been the secretary of a Romanian diplomat who had fallen in love with her. Nicholas Lahovary was a man of wealth and culture who came from an aristocratic family with international connections. Thus, when he married Janine, she became acquainted with the world of Anna de Noailles and Marthe Bibesco, who had been stylish beauties and friends of Proust and had become two of the greatest French women writers of their time, though they were actually Romanian. When the communists took over Romania, the old aristocracy was evicted; since then, the Lahovarys had been living in Switzerland and, like Natalie, going to Nice in the winter. In her fifties Janine was still a handsome, well-groomed woman, not very happily married to a somewhat older husband.

Natalie, who had been so unsentimental in her past love affairs, succumbed completely to love in her old age and fell under this woman's influence. This, at any rate, was the view of a number of her friends who did not take kindly to Janine and regarded her as an interloper. It was certainly Romaine's view, though Janine did her best to establish a friendship with Romaine, inviting her to Switzerland whenever Natalie came for a visit. The Lahovarys lived in the village of Grandson, on the Lake of Neuchâtel, a place that now became part of Natalie's geography as she began spending summers there. Natalie continued to spend winters in Nice, and sometimes Romaine accepted Janine's invitations to Grandson, but she did so with growing reluctance as she became increasingly jealous of Natalie's new love. "It was the old rivalry in which Romaine was competing with another for a faithless Natalie," Meryle Secrest concluded. "Unlike Lily de Clermont-Tonnerre, who had been the epitome of discretion, Janine Lahovary was insinuating herself between them, Romaine believed."

Nicholas Lahovary had the same feeling. He was a gentleman of the old school, Renée Lang said, yet here he was in the embarrassing position of playing host to his wife's lesbian lover. But when he objected to Natalie's visits, she dealt with him as man to man, pointing out that it was best to avoid scandal and to share Janine. Her will was as strong as ever, and the husband was forced to capitulate to the lover. When he died, in 1963, Natalie had Janine to herself.

She lost Romaine, however. Try as she might to convince her Angel that she loved her as much as ever, Natalie could not overcome Romaine's jealous and bitter resentment. In 1968 the day came when Romaine would no longer tolerate this infidelity and decided that her only recourse was to break off entirely. It was the story of Renée Vivien all over again, only this time the lovers were in their nineties. Like Renée, Romaine withdrew into a darkened room and refused to acknowledge Natalie's importunate letters and telephone calls. In her old age she had grown increasingly paranoid and eccentric in her ways. More than ever she needed the affection and comfort that Natalie had provided for so many years. But nothing

204 THE AMAZON OF LETTERS

could change her mind. When Natalie came to Nice the following year, Romaine refused to see her. So ended Natalie's greatest love, and here is how Meryle Secrest narrates that ending:

> On July 9, 1969, she sent a last message. All it said was, "My Angel is, as ever, first in my thoughts and deepest in my heart." Romaine never answered it. She simply marked the envelope in heavy black ink and a large firm hand, "Miss Barney—Paris."

Romaine died in December, 1970, at the age of ninety-six. Natalie, devastated by Romaine's death, lived on for a little more than a year, but as an invalid and not completely lucid. For the last few years Janine had been her nurse, at the end devoting herself exclusively to Natalie, and now it was Berthe's turn to be jealous. Over the years Berthe had become indispensable to Natalie, performing many services above and beyond those of housekeeper and enjoying Natalie's complete confidence. Before Berthe had appeared on the scene, Natalie had had a hard time keeping servants because she was a very demanding mistress as well as a scandal to the servants. Berthe herself had wanted to leave when she found out what kind of house she was in, but she stuck it out, in time becoming the head of the household staff and, what mattered most to her, a friend to Natalie, with whom she was on a democratic footing. After forty-odd years she fancied her role as Natalie's chief companion and resented this usurper who insisted on treating her as a servant. But a serious illness forced Berthe to relinquish her position for a while, and at the same time Natalie's decline made it desirable for her to leave her old house for the modern convenience of a luxury hotel. So she moved across the river again, for the last time, ending her days in the Hôtel Meurice with Janine to keep her company.

Natalie died shortly after midnight on February 2, 1972. Janine's friend Edouard Macavoy came to keep her company through the night. A French artist who specialized in portraits, Macavoy had already done two of Natalie, and now he did another, of Natalie on her deathbed. Her body was taken to the crypt of the American Cathedral, where Renée Vivien had mourned by the body of Violet Shilleto seventy years before. Two days later Natalie was buried near Renée in the little cemetery of Passy. Her friend Paul Boncour had given her a plot there a few years before, for as Bettina Bergery explained, "it's a cemetery that has been full, with no more places since forty years or so." She went on to describe it as "typically 1900—all the old friends are there. . . ." Another friend who went to the funeral remarked, "Natalie wouldn't have come—she never went to a funeral in her life—she said they were barbaric." Berthe went to the funeral, too, of course, and counted the attendance: twenty-three people. As the service ended and they were all about to leave, Berthe suddenly realized that it was Friday and this was the last gathering of Natalie Barney's salon.

PART II

EPILOGUE

Introduction

I only saw Natalie Barney twice, some six months before her death. She was by then a very old lady, too far removed from life to answer the questions I would have asked, but a historic monument nonetheless. During the two years that followed I returned to Paris three times to interview other people, gradually acquiring much of the information that has gone into this book. In the United States, also, I found people who had known Natalie Barney, sometimes in unexpected places and quite by chance. In Milwaukee, for instance, where I happened to spend the fall of 1971, I discovered Professor Renée Lang and, during the course of four long conversations, learned more about Natalie Barney and her circle than from all the books I read.

Originally I wanted to publish a book of interviews and documents, the raw materials of biography rather than the biography itself. Interviews are fascinating in themselves and all the more so when they concern a subject like Natalie Barney, about whom there are so many conflicting opinions. What intrigued me most was the problem of establishing biographical "fact," the whole vexed question of "truth." So instead of trying to decide which of several versions of the same story was the most reliable, I wanted to let each version stand on its own apparent merits alongside the others and let readers decide for themselves. The idea was to preserve repetitions, contradictions and inconsistencies, even in successive interviews with the same person. Even unproductive interviews seemed worth preserving because they always had something to tell. But though the interviews seemed wonderful to me, each one full of little ironies and dramas, they did not seem so to everyone, and at times I had to ask myself if I was only interested in Natalie Barney because of the strange encounters along the way.

The interviews are reported in different styles, ranging from notes to direct quotation. Only a few were tape-recorded, for I have found that interviews are often inhibited by tape recorders. As a rule I did not take notes while interviewing, either, but wrote up the interview immediately afterward in whatever form came naturally. Of course, my summaries are more organized and condensed than the original interviews, which usually rambled for two or three hours; and in some cases several interviews have been combined into one. But whatever the reporting technique, I have done my best to preserve the phrasing and spirit of the interview. In reporting what people said about Natalie Barney I have followed their usage, referring to her variously as Natalie, Miss Barney, Mademoiselle, or whatever. In other words, I have not sought consistency in method when reporting the inconsistencies in point of view, the many different angles and interpretations, the fallible memories, biased opinions and gossip that lie at the heart of this enterprise.

1971

Paris, June 15 and 19

The beginning was pure *Aspern Papers*, this extraordinary survivor from another era, this fabled creature, once a legendary beauty who defied convention, now ancient and shrunken. The sequel was *Aspern Papers*, too, for I never got my hands on the manuscripts; and though never denounced as a publishing scoundrel, I had the distinct feeling at times that my desires were illicit. Oh, not in Natalie Barney's eyes. She wanted nothing more than to have a biographer, cared little about what would be published after her death or, for that matter, about the notoriety she had lived with all her long life.

I had first heard about her some eight years before, when I was writing a book about the Americans in Paris. At that time the magazine *Adam* devoted an issue to Natalie Barney containing selections from her work and commentaries by members of her circle. But what impressed me more was the remark made by Janet Flanner in declining to contribute to *Adam*: "Miss Barney is a perfect example of an enchanting person not to write about." At the time I took this as a warning that the enchanting person wanted to be left in peace, and I have always had scruples about invading the privacy of writers who do not wish to be disturbed. As it turned out, Natalie Barney did not take this view at all. Eight years later, when I finally met her, she kept exclaiming, "Oh, why didn't you come before?" and "Why have you waited so long?"

But first I had to find my way into her presence. Luck was with me at the start in the person of my friend Michel Fabre, a Sorbonne professor who happened to know two of the key people who could introduce me. As soon as I arrived in Paris he took me to meet Berthe. Michel Fabre was writing a biography of Richard Wright and had become acquainted with Berthe during the course of many visits to 20 rue Jacob, where Wright's widow lived. He was also acquainted with François Chapon, the curator of the Bibliothèque Littèraire Jacques Doucet, where Natalie Barney's manuscripts were to be deposited after her death.

The official introduction required a series of diplomatic overtures. First I had to meet Monsieur Chapon, then Mme. Lahovary; then, if I proved presentable and the moment propitious, I might be ushered into Natalie's presence. M. Chapon made very precise arrangements to meet me downstairs at the Hôtel Meurice, cautioning me that I could spend only five minutes with Miss Barney because she was frail and easily tired. Then, at the appointed time, before being ushered in, I met Mme. Lahovary, who was quite literally of the diplomatic world, with all those airs and graces that leave you ill at ease. She only meant to be helpful, but her presence and that of M. Chapon left me feeling rather unfocused during that first encounter. I suspect Natalie Barney felt the same way herself, for she had always preferred talking with one person at a time.

Anyway, there she was, this small, fragile, incredibly aged person, wrapped in a pale-blue dressing gown to match her pale-blue eyes and very fine white hair. She looked like a carefully wrapped doll in that expensive hotel drawing room with its vases of tall expensive flowers—not at all the setting in which she had lived her life—but there was still a spark of animation behind the vague look in her eyes. It was then that she kept repeating, as though aware that her mind was no longer functioning well, "Oh, why didn't you come sooner?" She understood perfectly what my errand was and knew that I had written a book about the Americans in Paris, which, in fact, she asked to see, but the conversation didn't go much beyond that, and this first visit was brief—fifteen or twenty minutes rather than the allotted five.

Afterward, Mme. Lahovary invited M. Chapon and me to dinner in a nearby restaurant, during which she said that Natalie had been looking forward to my visit all day and had been in exceptionally good form. Before parting, she invited me to meet her at the Rue Jacob the next day for a guided tour of the *pavillon*. Knowing that there was some friction between her and Berthe, I didn't mention that Berthe had already taken me on a tour. Besides, I was only too willing to visit the *pavillon* again, in the company of another guide who had spent years there and who could offer another point of view.

The next morning Mme. Lahovary reported Natalie's reaction to my visit. It was a case of love at first sight, she said, and Natalie wanted me to come again. So two days later I returned to the Hôtel Meurice, announced myself at the desk, and proceeded upstairs to Natalie Barney's suite, where I was surprised that Mme. Lahovary did not greet me at the door. After ringing and knocking several times, I finally heard a small, faint voice saying, "Come in." When I opened the door, Natalie Barney was sitting there by herself, reading my book. Evidently she had decided to see me alone and was prepared to talk indefinitely.

This time she was not at all the sacred personage with whom it was a privilege to have an audience but a very frank and forthright old lady with whom I could talk as easily as with the great-aunts of my childhood—except that Natalie's wits were sharper, when they were not rambling. She was not very good at answering questions but quite acute in asking them, particularly when questioning me about my private life. Most of the time she preferred to speak English, but she kept testing my French; then, seeming to forget she'd done so, she would lapse from English into French again. I had the impression that she expressed herself more deftly in French, though she was totally bilingual. Her English had a nineteenth-century flavor about it, reminding me of the way my grandmother spoke.

Natalie Barney didn't say much about the crucial period in her life, about what made her decide to live in Paris and to live the way she did. She only commented several times, "It was very dangerous

then.'' Of her intimates she mentioned only Romaine Brooks, who
had died in Nice the past December. Romaine was her oldest friend,
and she felt her death most keenly.

She repeated over and over several little anecdotes or remarks
about Gertrude Stein, Ezra Pound and George Antheil. Disconcertingly she kept asking me if I knew them, if I'd been in Paris then,
what had happened to them and others, most of them dead. Here
especially her mind wandered, repeating itself like a worn record.

She used to go for walks around the *quartier* every night with
Gertrude Stein and her dog. This must have been after 1937, when
Gertrude moved to the Rue Christine, near the Rue Jacob. They
used to talk about family quarrels, and Gertrude always said: Never
mind, families always quarreled, that was what consanguinity was
all about. Evidently Alice Toklas didn't accompany them on these
walks, for her memories of Miss Toklas were vague ("What's her
name? What's become of her?''), while she clearly remembered
walking the dog and spoke of Gertrude as a good friend. When the
dog died, it didn't seem to bother Gertrude. She simply got a new
one and gave it the same name.

Ezra Pound she remembered in the company of Olga Rudge—his
protegeé, Natalie explained, a violinist. But she could not date this
visit, which could have been the latest one, six years ago. Still, she
remembered playing tennis with Pound, so that must have been in
the early twenties, when he lived in Paris. And Pound brought other
poets to call. She kept trying to recall a remark, with three adjectives in crescendo, something like, "Ezra Pound was arrogant, outrageous and unspeakable.'' But she couldn't get the adjectives
straight. I gathered that her intention was not to criticize Pound,
whom she liked, but to fix him in a phrase.

George Antheil she remembered as a tiny little man with a tiny
little wife; she wondered if they had ever had any children. She also
remembered Virgil Thomson and the man who lived with him,
though she couldn't remember his name. Thornton Wilder continued to come and call on her. Julien Green she did not like, finding
him too straitlaced and puritanical.

Before the conversation ended, Mme. Lahovary returned and

another friend came to call. Natalie Barney was most lucid and even witty in conversation with them as they talked about mutual friends like Germaine Beaumont, Romaine Brooks, Edouard Macavoy, Paul Morand and Marguerite Yourcenar. After two and a half hours she was still going strong, and I had to excuse myself because I was overdue for a dinner invitation, never having expected the interview to last more than half an hour. That was the last I saw of Natalie Barney, for I left Paris two days later, and the following winter she died.

BERTHE CLEYRERGUE   *Paris, June 10 and 17*

Mme. Berthe Cleyrergue, Natalie Barney's *gouvernante* since 1927, proved very approachable and informative from the start. We soon became friends, and I ended up talking with her more than anyone else over the two years I spent gathering material for this book. Berthe was a vigorous woman in her latter sixties and plainly possessed of qualities that fitted her for her life's work: devotion, endurance, industry, discretion and a hearty sense of humor. There is something indestructible about her, a vitality that is her essential quality and that may explain the improbable sense of adventure which drew her to Natalie Barney's household and kept her there. When we knew each other better, she told me the story of her life. She had grown up on a farm in Burgundy but decided that she didn't want to spend her life at hard labor and went to Paris, where she found a job in a store. In 1925 she met Djuna Barnes, whom she remembers fondly, and two years later, when she told Miss Djuna she wanted to see the world, Miss Djuna asked if she would like to go to work for Miss Barney. At that time there was a staff of six or eight at the Rue Jacob, including a majordomo, chauffeur, cook, and maids. Before Berthe came, Miss Barney had been unable to keep servants, and Berthe herself had often thought of leaving. She had to put up with a great deal during all the years she worked there, but what she chiefly recalls is much joking and good fun. She was treated quite democratically, attending the soirees and sitting down at table when Mademoiselle had dinner with her closest friends. Mademoiselle always included Berthe in the conversation, and when no one else was around, often asked Berthe to sit and talk with her for an hour or two.

Berthe is married, but her husband remains off in the background somewhere, while she seems to have devoted far more of herself to Miss Barney. Very respectable and conventional, she made a point that she had never slept in the *pavillon* but always retired to her little low-ceilinged apartment over the carriage entrance at 20 rue Jacob, now a shrine to her memories, with all kinds of souvenirs of Miss Barney and her friends, such as the paintings inscribed to Berthe by Marie Laurencin and Edouard Macavoy. From that vantage point she was able to look out her window at the *pavillon* and keep watch on the comings and goings of visitors, as she does to this day. She must have saved her money like a good Burgundian, for she has at various times given or lent money to friends of Mademoiselle, and she now owns her own apartment—in contrast to Natalie Barney, who always rented the *pavillon* and was now being dispossessed by its new owner, Finance Minister Michel Debré.

Berthe showed me her collection of photographs, hastily passing over several provocative poses of Miss Barney in her prime, arrayed in nothing but the great outdoors. As she went through the photographs, she reminisced about Miss Barney's friends and lovers. There was a photograph of Miss Barney and Miss Djuna (who was a friend, not a lover) taken at the villa in Beauvallon, which was "inaugurated" in 1927, shortly after Berthe began working for Mademoiselle. There were always many visitors at Beauvallon and plenty of parties. Berthe remembered that soon after she went there for the first time, there was a party at Mme. Colette's in nearby Saint-Tropez, where everyone danced all night. Berthe hinted that there was much more she could tell, but she was being discreet.

In discussing Miss Barney's loves, Berthe mentioned so many names I couldn't keep track of them all. There were women of talent and intellect, of wealth or noble birth; actresses, alcoholics and addicts; French, English and American; most of them beautiful, all of them distinguished in some way. Berthe showed me photographs of many of these women and gave me a generous selection of photographs of Miss Barney, most of those that appear in this book. She also produced two horoscopes Miss Barney had ordered, one giving her birthdate as 1876, which Berthe assured me was the correct date. Miss Barney always said she was born in 1877 because she didn't like the number six. She seemed to share Berthe's interest in numbers and dates. Five of her close friends were born on her birthday, October 31, and they used to celebrate together each year: Germaine Beaumont, Marie Laurencin, Lucie Delarue-Mardrus, André Germain and the bookseller Richard Anacréon.

Miss Barney had a strand of Eva Palmer's beautiful long red hair, which Eva Palmer had given her when they were young. For many years Miss Barney kept it in a tortoise-shell case, but eventually she gave it to an old professor who worshiped the memory of Eva Palmer's beauty and begged for the hair. Berthe was thoroughly disgusted with this infatuated old man of seventy-eight, weeping and kissing a young girl's hair.

Berthe also talked about neighbors at 20 rue Jacob. Le Corbusier had lived there for thirty years—until the second war—but he was not a friend of Miss Barney. In fact, they were enemies. Mademoiselle was the first person in the building to have electricity, having paid to have it brought in from the Boulevard Saint-Germain. When Le Corbusier discovered this, he tapped her line and used her electricity, whereupon she filed a lawsuit against him.

The Bernheim family owned the property for a long time, and Miss Barney had differences with them, too. She once ordered a pink marble statue from the Bernheim Gallery, had it transported to Beauvallon at great expense, then refused to pay. The statue may still be in the public square of Beauvallon. Miss Barney's villa was destroyed during the war, looted and vandalized apparently. Berthe hasn't been there since, but is thinking of making a trip with her husband.

Berthe is most illuminating on a guided tour, which leads her to reminisce about the good old days, even those before her time. Miss Barney had been at 20 rue Jacob since October, 1909, and in the summers before the first war she gave grand outdoor *fêtes* for as many as two hundred people, the garden illuminated with candles. In the years following the war there were several big parties, each honoring a particular woman. But chiefly Berthe reminisced about the meetings of the salon, on Friday evenings from five to eight. She reenacted those weekly soirees—the table in the middle loaded with food, Mademoiselle always seated there, in the far corner, while Berthe stood over here, near the entrance, to greet the guests as they arrived. The poets stood in the alcove at the end of the salon when they read from their works, and dancers sometimes performed.

The principal rooms are classical in design, with squares framing circles, and something about each of them suggests that it was designed for some ritual. This is particularly true of the Temple à l'Amitié, in the garden behind the *pavillon*. The interior is now in ruins, the flooring rotted away, but one of the photographs shows that the small circular interior once contained a dinner table and a kind of mantel or altar on one side. Berthe said that before her time, Miss Barney used to give intimate dinners there. During the first war, when Big Bertha was bombarding Paris, Miss Barney and her friends sometimes took refuge in the temple. On the ground floor of the *pavillon* are two large rooms, the farther one with windows at one end that once gave out on a conservatory, long since vanished. This is the salon in which the weekly gatherings were held. Like the temple, this room is square, with a domelike circle in the middle of the ceiling. The circle is framed by four long paintings of shapely nudes representing the four elements by Albert Besnard. Strangely enough, Miss Barney was leaving these nymphs to Berthe. Could this be a practical joke? Certainly Berthe didn't want them, whereas the artist's family was clamoring for them, Berthe said.

Upstairs, over the salon, Natalie Barney's bedroom is another square with a circle in the ceiling. Here, in place of the performer's alcove, there is an Empire couch, larger than life, on which one might undertake strange voyages, and on the floor beside it, an enormous polar bear skin. At the window end is Natalie Barney's bed and her writing desk with shelves of books.

Some of the paintings and furnishings had been removed, and of course, the place had not been lived in for two years. It seemed even mustier and more dilapidated than that. Mademoiselle never spent money on the house and was totally unattached to her possessions. Once, when she was away, burglars broke in and stole some silver candlesticks and antiques. This was an inside job, and the servant involved went to jail; but Berthe suspected outside collusion, too, and went to great lengths, searching all the antique shops, in hopes of finding the culprit. Mademoiselle, when she returned from Nice, was totally unconcerned and saw no need to go to all that fuss.

She was always going off on a sudden impulse, leaving every-thing behind her, leaving the house open without ever a thought of those consequences that haunt the bourgeois mind. Presumably Berthe was remembering their younger days, before the second war, when Mademoiselle was more mobile. In recent years, especially since the death of the duchess de Clermont-Tonnerre, in 1954, the salon and Mademoiselle's spirits had been much diminished. And Mademoiselle was prostrated with grief at the death of Romaine Brooks the previous December.

1972

By the time I returned to Paris the following year, many changes had taken place. After Natalie Barney's death Mme. Lahovary had remained at the Hôtel Meurice for several months, seriously ill most of the time, and had finally returned to her house in Switzerland. Berthe, of course, remained in her apartment at 20 rue Jacob and continued as caretaker, kept busy by a variety of tasks connected with settling the estate. Natalie Barney's will had been read and a number of expectations dashed. Apart from a few small bequests, all of her fortune went to her sister, at whose death it would go to a family trust fund to be distributed to respectable charities like the Red Cross. Her papers had been sorted out and transported to the Bibliothèque Doucet for cataloguing. Her furniture and personal effects were still in her unoccupied house, awaiting shipment to various museums. Michel Debré, the government minister who owns the *pavillon,* had been impatiently awaiting her death so that he could take possession and modernize the premises. Only the satirical weekly *Canard Enchainé* had kept him from doing so during her lifetime and had preserved the Temple à l'Amitié as a historical monument.

In all, I had three long, friendly visits with Berthe, each lasting

four or five hours. On my second visit Berthe served me a sumptuous six-course dinner, convincing me that her gastronomy should
have its place in this book. For what could be more appropriate than
to immortalize the cuisine that had nourished Natalie Barney for so
many years? The main course was one of Miss Barney's favorites,
Poulet Maryland, and I was interested to learn that she was quite a
gourmet and, contrary to common report, fond of good wine, like
the delicate Burgundy that Berthe served with the dinner. It was
Miss Barney's taste that had made a cook of Berthe, who had never
cooked before.

Twice when I arrived, Berthe had another visitor, a fellow resi-
dent of 20 rue Jacob whom she introduced as Monsieur Philippe,
explaining that his last name was Polish and unpronounceable. This
gentleman took a lively interest in Natalie Barney, knew everything
about her and understood quite a few things better than Berthe, being a lawyer by training and a witty worldling to boot. Thus he
could explain such recent developments as all the protracted proce-
dures in settling the estate, all the unnecessary expense and exces-
sive fuss over a lot of worthless furniture. The Smithsonian would
spend more in shipping costs than the furniture was worth, he said,
and the châteaux of France, to which some pieces were left, had
reservations about accepting them. The Musée Carnavalet had selected a few dresses.

Miss Barney turned out to be much richer than Berthe had suspected, but she left only modest sums to a few friends. Berthe indicated that she had received one thousand dollars, which was as
much as anyone got. And she couldn't help remembering Miss Barney's promise that after her death Berthe would never have to worry
about money. Fortunately, Berthe and her husband had savings and
pensions, but what a sorry conclusion to her forty-five years with
Miss Barney! That was certainly not the way Mademoiselle would
have wanted things done.

The villainness was Mme. Lahovary, who had exercised an unho-
ly influence on Miss Barney at the end. This "adventuress" had
been attracted by the glamour of Miss Barney's reputation and had
designs on her wealth. She was a person of lowly origins who had
remained "common," even though she had been an ambassador's

wife; Miss Barney used to laugh at her social gaffes. Berthe gave Mme. Lahovary credit for having faithfully tended Miss Barney during the last eighteen months of her life, when Berthe herself was ill, but otherwise she had not a good word to say for her.

Since Miss Barney's death Mme. Lahovary had fallen out with everyone, Berthe said, as a consequence of her disappointment over failing to inherit everything. At first she had taken a rather high hand, but then it turned out that her powers as literary executrix were limited, and she was by no means free to do as she pleased. The manuscripts had all gone to the Bibliothèque Doucet, beyond her control. And the books were of no particular value, M. Philippe explained, with the exception of two which had belonged to the duchesse de Clermont-Tonnerre.

All the letters to Miss Barney had been sorted out the previous April, the scandalous letters burned and the others taken to the library. But who decided which were scandalous and which had redeeming literary significance? And if Berthe is right in saying that there were forty thousand letters, who could have read them all? The task of sorting took three people three cold weeks, Berthe helping and feeding them and keeping them warm while they worked in that unheated house. She was a great help in identifying handwriting, and, of course, she had known many of the persons involved.

Berthe had already sorted out some of the letters with Miss Barney before her death, chiefly love letters from Eva Palmer, Liane de Pougy, Renée Vivien and others, dating from 1892–1910; some had even come from male suitors, about whom Berthe had joked, saying that now Mademoiselle had nothing left to conceal. There were letters from nonliterary conquests, too, usually erotic and pornographic but not interesting, M. Philippe said, with the exception of salty letters from Colette, which he had particularly relished, the earthiness always lightened by the wit. He quoted one: "Willy kisses your hands. I all the rest." The love letters showed that Miss Barney was cruel in her love affairs. When Renée Vivien spent evenings with Baroness van Zuylen, Miss Barney used to wait outside in her carriage, all night, if necessary, and then coldly reject her. Berthe reckoned that Miss Barney had had affairs with about forty women. Her affair with Colette was very brief, Berthe was certain. All this, of course, is hearsay, but Miss Barney often talked with Berthe about her past.

JANINE LAHOVARY   *Grandson, Switzerland,*
                                   September 17–18

I would certainly not have gone all the way to Switzerland to see Mme. Lahovary if Edouard Macavoy had not urged me to do so, for my previous meetings with her had been relatively unproductive. However, at that time she was playing the role of *grande dame,* graciously condescending, and now, bereaved and lonely, she seemed more like her true self. Not that she solicited sympathy—there was still much of the *grand dame* about her—but she was prepared to talk more openly and anxious to discuss her duties as literary executrix, which she took very seriously.

I scarcely recognized her when she came to her door, she had shrunk and aged so. Since Natalie's death, she said, she had gone through a succession of illnesses, and now the doctors had given her only a year or eighteen months to live.

Mme. Lahovary showed me around her lovely eighteenth-century house overlooking the Lake of Neuchâtel, the finest house in Grandson, with perfect lines in mellow ocher stone and elegant furnishings to match. She showed me the room where Natalie always stayed and then Romaine's room, the two flanking her own room. All told, Natalie had spent years in this house, she said. The pictures included a portrait of Natalie by Macavoy, several paintings by Marie Laurencin, and a portrait of Anna de Noailles by Romaine Brooks.

Mme. Lahovary never explained how she and Natalie became intimate, although she commented frequently on how close they were and how much Natalie meant to her.

"Natalie was a visionary and a seer," she said. Comparing her to Rimbaud, Mme. Lahovary cited several instances of Natalie's uncanny intuition and clairvoyance. For instance, upon meeting a beautiful English girl of eighteen who was engaged to an English duke, she predicted that this girl was destined for trouble. Sure enough, one night when the duke escorted her home, the girl went out again, with some young people who were taking drugs and ended up in an automobile accident.

This is a cautionary tale such as Natalie might have heard in her Jamesian youth. The moral of the story is clearly that a pretty girl who avoided scandal might end up marrying a duke. And one remembers Albert Barney's deathbed wish that his wayward daughter might yet marry an English nobleman. Though incongruous with the life of "the wild girl from Cincinnati," the story demonstrates that she retained something of her father's snobbery and sense of propriety to the end.

Mme. Lahovary recalled what Natalie had said about her parents. Natalie's mother was remarkably talented and vivacious, her father dull and uninteresting. Mrs. Barney was inclined to be flirtatious, which made him jealous. Perhaps as a consequence, or because he could think of nothing better to do, he used to spend his evenings at his club, drinking. His end was sad, for he died all alone in the Grand Hôtel de Monte Carlo.

Mme. Lahovary's doctors were mistaken when they gave her a year or more to live. She died five months after I saw her, a little more than a year after her beloved Natalie.

JEAN CHALON   *Paris, September 22*

Berthe had often spoken of Jean Chalon as a loyal friend, always considerate and kindhearted. She remembered the first time he came to visit, when Mademoiselle asked Berthe how she liked this young fellow and whether she should invite him again. Jean Chalon is a journalist for the *Figaro Littéraire* and a novelist. He might be described as the third man in Natalie Barney's life, the successor to Remy de Gourmont and André Rouveyre, for she appears to have talked as openly with this young man of her old age as she did with the aging Gourmont in her youth, though perhaps not so intimately as she talked with Rouveyre during the half century that they were the closest of friends. Chalon appeared on the scene less than a year after the death of Rouveyre and no doubt helped to fill the void left by that death.

It is easy to see why she immediately took to this likable young man. Chalon hails from the south of France and is a typical Proven-çal, both in appearance and manner: dark, with bright beady eyes, disarmingly open and friendly, ebullient and ingratiating. Quite un-derstandably, he has cultivated friendships that provide excellent copy for his literary journalism and fiction, and, in the process, has collected the treasures and trophies with which his tiny study is crammed; but both his friendships and collections have been a labor of love. He seems to specialize in old ladies, for he made friends with Louise de Vilmorin and her patroness, Florence Gould, as well as Natalie Barney. When I first met him, he was writing a book about Louise de Vilmorin, *Une Jeune Femme de soixante ans*. Mrs. Gould had sent him a case of champagne, as she does every year on the anniversary of Louise de Vilmorin's death. We drank a bottle of Piper Heidsieck as he reminisced:

"I first met Natalie in the fall of 1963. When I read *Traits et por-traits*, I called the publishers and with great embarrassment asked if the author was still alive. They assured me that she was indeed, though not in Paris at the moment, but due to return in a few months, and I could see her then. You know, she felt rather neglect-ed toward the end of her life. She didn't want fame, but she didn't want to be forgotten either.

"As soon as she came back to Paris I went to call. We got along famously right from the start; she asked me to come again the fol-lowing week, and soon I was having lunch with her, tête-à-tête, ev-ery Wednesday. Those lunches were uproarious—as Berthe will tell you—one long explosion of laughter from start to finish. Natalie would say anything that came into her head. She could ask you all kinds of questions of the most personal nature without being the least bit offensive. She was always *une grande dame*.

"Her French was faultless and distinguished, much better than my own. She spoke perfect eighteenth-century French. I picked up her style of expression from associating with her, just as I did with Louise de Vilmorin. Natalie's speech was so swift and concentrated that you had to speak the same way in order to keep up. Some of her writing has the same quality, her *pensées* particularly. I am not at all sure that they can be translated into English.

"So for almost ten years I spent hours with her every Wednesday whenever she was in Paris. You can imagine what an education that was for a young man fresh from the provinces, what an introduction to the whole world she had known!

"She was an old lady when I met her, but her mind was as quick and sharp as it had ever been. She remembered everything that had happened before 1940 and told me about it in great detail without any reticence. One day she'd talk about Renée Vivien, another about Colette, another about the duchesse de Clermont-Tonnerre."

Jean Chalon has kept a notebook of these conversations, which is what he would publish rather than a biography. But he doesn't want to publish anything yet, not while Lahovary is still alive, because he fears she would give him trouble. Natalie used to make fun of Lahovary to him, even to her face, saying she'd leave her nothing but work to do.

He had thought about the biographer's problems, especially the problem of explaining what happened in the years between her childhood and her friendship with Remy de Gourmont that transformed Natalie into *l'Amazone.* Her journal would be a revelation, if only one could see that and other documents at the Bibliothèque Doucet—if indeed they were there.

Then, too, the biographer must beware the wrath of the Clermont-Tonnerres, who are very powerful and who won't allow publication of a book that tells about the duchess' liaison with Natalie. When I pointed out that this was common knowledge, having appeared in all kinds of books, Chalon replied, "Ah, but the Clermont-Tonnerres don't know that!"

Natalie once showed him a list she had written of her *liaisons et demi-liaisons,* placing Colette in the latter category. That love affair didn't amount to much because Willy was jealous and wouldn't allow Colette to be alone with Natalie.

Jean Chalon showed me a stack of letters he had received from Natalie and said he would like to get his own back because they contain all kinds of indiscretions, but he didn't know where they were. He also showed me a few early photos and most of Natalie's books with amusing dedications. He has a copy of her first book, *Quelques Portraits-Sonnets de femmes* with Natalie's notes for editorial revision; her annotated copy of Djuna Barnes' *Ladies Almanack* identifying all the characters; presentation copies of Liane de Pougy's *Idylle saphique*; Renée Vivien's *Une Femme m'apparut*; Gourmont's *Lettres à l'Amazone*; and no doubt other treasures. In parting he gave me a copy of his own novel, *Les Couples involontaires*, which includes the first article he wrote on Natalie Barney.

1973

BERTHE CLEYRERGUE   *Paris, July 18–26*

By the time I saw Berthe again, Natalie Barney's estate had been settled and most of possessions distributed in different directions. This and Berthe's latest operation were the chief topics of conversation at first, but Berthe also reminisced about the past, as she had done on previous occasions. Monsieur Philippe came in during my second visit. He, too, had followed developments with great interest and was able to add further details and amusing anecdotes, many having to do with Michel Debré's recent legal offensives and the residents' countermoves. There was evidence of a good deal of work going on about the premises, but the *pavillon* remained deserted and looked like a haunted house.

Berthe was quite outspoken in criticizing not only Mme. Lahovary but also "those Americans," the lawyers who settled the estate for the Barney trust fund. They had sold everything at auction—furniture, memorabilia, inscribed books, everything—totally indifferent to sentimental or historical value, determined only to convert everything into cash. They even required friends of Miss Barney to pay seventy percent of the estimated value for objects she had promised them. Thus Berthe had to buy several little pieces of furniture that Mademoiselle had given her.

André Germain's tombstone was auctioned off along with every-

228

thing else. This effigy, carved by José de Charmoy before the first war, had been in the Temple à l'Amitié for many years and remained there when Germain died. Berthe had alerted his niece and nephew, but neither had responded, and the tombstone was auctioned off for twenty francs.

Eight or ten people received one thousand dollars in Miss Barney's will, but with the devaluation of the dollar that year, those who didn't collect right away lost money. Mme. Lahovary was left an annuity of fifteen thousand dollars a year but didn't live to collect anything. Berthe got a small pension in addition to her thousand dollars.

Berthe reminisced fondly but unspecifically about good friends of Mademoiselle like Colette, la duchesse de Clermont-Tonnerre, Lucie Delarue-Mardrus, and André Rouveyre, all of whom came frequently to visit. She also exclaimed over some of the scenes that had taken place in the house but, again, not very specifically, because she hadn't witnessed most of them. She had looked after Dolly Wilde when Dolly tried to commit suicide and had known many cases of hysterics over the years.

M. Philippe added his own impressions. He, of course, had witnessed nothing, but he had heard many stories and deduced much more. The house, he remarked, looked as though it had been struck by lightning. All the doors looked as if they'd been beaten in, and there were plenty of other scars about the place. There must have been some fierce storms inside, some scenes he would have liked to watch, of women fighting over one another like furies. This reminded Berthe of one occasion when several women spent the night there, evidently in battle royal, for the next morning a huge urn had been broken. Mademoiselle acted as though nothing untoward had happened, except that by some accident the urn had cracked. Berthe took the occasion to remind me that she had never spent a night over there, nodding her head out the window in the direction of the *pavillon*.

M. Philippe described the pornographic photographs which had been burned, alas, along with the scandalous love letters. There were a great many of them, taken in the Forest of Fountainebleau, he judged by the background. Wonderful period pieces they were, very much in vogue now, Pre-Raphaelite pornography, nudes with lilies draped revealingly in strategic locations. Evidently the nude photograph of Natalie Barney is the sole survivor of this collection.

The last time I came to call, Berthe, with her usual concern for dates, pointed out that this was the Feast of Sainte Nathalie. She poured me a good stiff scotch, her favorite drink, and passed around little cakes like those she had served at the salon.

JEAN CHALON   *Paris, July 12–21*

On my final visit to Paris I saw Jean Chalon several times and had a good time comparing notes with him, for he was not only a warm friend and admirer of Natalie but a real authority, having made a thorough study of her life. He invited me to read some of the rare books in his collection and showed me more of his treasures: a photograph of Liane de Pougy with an inscription to Natalie dated 1901, a lovely photograph of the duchesse de Clermont-Tonnerre signed "Lily 1904," a pastel portrait of Renée Vivien by Mrs. Barney, a picture postcard of Colette and Willy on which Colette had written to Natalie arranging a rendezvous. He also has a tapestry that Liane de Pougy had given Natalie, a bronze bust of Natalie done by Laura, and a self-portrait of Mrs. Barney.

Chalon was wearing Colette's watch, and he has other souvenirs currently on display at the Colette centennial exhibit in the Bibliothèque Nationale. With these collections his small apartment is like a museum or a shrine, improbably located in the working-class district of Clichy. And he seems the proper curator of all these relics, which he appreciates and cherishes more than anyone else.

Once again he stated how much Natalie's friendship had meant to him. "Natalie changed my life," he began. "You can imagine what an experience it was for me, as a young man of thirty, to know such a woman in her nineties.

"When I first moved into this apartment Natalie wanted to come on a tour of inspection. Imagine her in this neighborhood! And yet she acted as though she was perfectly at home. The first thing she asked to see was the bed. She felt it and was reassured: 'Well, at least it's comfortable.'

"Natalie's ideas were extraordinarily advanced for her time. Some of the things she wrote in her early books of *pensées* are only being understood now. Her dress was ageless and anticipated contemporary styles; she had all kinds of costumes (now in the Musée des Costumes) that are just like hippie dress. To the end she remained amazingly youthful in her outlook. There was something timeless about Natalie, as though time didn't exist for her. Once, toward the end of her life, when Picasso came up in the conversation, she remembered who he was: 'Picasso, oh yes, that's Gertrude's protégé.'

"Natalie was always the one who was loved, never the one who loved. Note that people came to her; she never went to them."

Chalon read passages from the love letters of Renée Vivien which proved to him that Natalie had abandoned Renée and not the reverse. When I mentioned that several people had said Colette and Natalie were not very close in later years, he read me a number of letters from Colette to Natalie from early, middle and late years, all demonstrating Colette's warm affection for Natalie throughout her life.

He gave a vivid account of the auction of Natalie's possessions. There, in the front row, sat five of her friends: himself, Berthe, Germaine Beaumont, François Chapon, and Philippe Jullian. The first item to be auctioned off was the kitchen stove. "Oh, my stove!" Berthe cried out. Next came a lamp which Natalie had promised to Germaine Beaumont, and she in turn exclaimed, "Oh, my lamp!" When Jean Chalon recognized some of his own books that he had given to Natalie, an outspoken friend pointed this out to the auctioneer, who grudgingly gave up one of them. Chalon tried to bid for a lamp that Berthe wanted, until the bidding went far higher than his limit. Some of the furniture and paintings proved to be far more valuable than anyone had suspected, such as the paintings of the four nymphs by Albert Besnard that had been on the ceiling of the salon and the portrait of Remy de Gourmont by the Polish painter no one had ever heard of. The more famous portrait of Gourmont, by Henry de Groux, went to Philippe Jullian for a mere two thousand francs. Of course, the antique dealers knew the market value of everything and had the advantage in the bidding. But considering the magnitude of Natalie's estate, the auction did not bring in much; it just about covered expenses involved in settling the estate.

The last item to be auctioned off was Natalie's bed. Jean Chalon

showed me a photograph he had taken of the bed being hauled off
unceremoniously on top of a truck, along with a lot of other junk.

FRANÇOIS CHAPON   *Paris, July 20–27*

After the death of Janine Lahovary, François Chapon was
appointed to succeed her as literary executor. He was the logical
choice because he knew all about Natalie Barney and her circle,
both as a literary scholar and as a habitué of the salon during its last
twelve years; and besides, as curator of the Bibliothèque Doucet, he
had most of her papers under his control. But this dual role of caretaker and executor placed him in the awkward position of wanting to
help a biographer while at the same time protecting the rights of the
heirs of those whose letters and manuscripts are in the collection.
For that reason the library requires the permission of the heirs before
allowing anyone to see manuscripts. Of course, he could authorize
me to see Natalie Barney's manuscripts, but even there he had to exercise discretion.

M. Chapon talked ruefully about the settling of the Barney estate.
All those books which should have gone to the library were sold for
just a little more than his budget could afford, usually because they
were lumped in lots with other items which the antique dealers
wanted. What a pity Miss Barney hadn't willed them to the library!
At least the portrait of Remy de Gourmont would eventually come
here; Philippe Jullian had promised that he would leave it to the
Doucet collection.

Chapon regretted all the disorder of these last years, during which
so many things had disappeared that were destined for the library.
He talked sadly about Janine Lahovary, though he was unwilling to
criticize her. "Janine is an enigma to me," he said.

The manuscripts in the Barney collection would be catalogued after the summer vacation. It was regrettable that I could not come
back then. Meanwhile, he told me to return the following Monday;
and he would show me a few items he could permit me to see.

On Monday he took me to the Barney Corner, as he jokingly
called it, a small room containing manuscripts and memorabilia.
Natalie Barney's writing desk was there, and above it the Lévy-
Dhurmer portrait of her as a girl, all in green and rather elfin. Also

in this room were the busts of Milosz by Vogt, of Rouveyre by Lily de Clermont-Tonnerre, and of Natalie Barney by her sister Laura ("very bad," remarked M. Chapon), two trunks full of family correspondence, and the black armoire in which Natalie filed away the letters she received. Most prominent on its shelves were shoe boxes labeled ROMAINE BROOKS, DUCHESSE DE CLERMONT-TONNERRE, ANNA WICKHAM, and a large orange box, the largest of all, labeled DOLLY WILDE. Did I know this poet, Anna Wickham? The English Verlaine, Miss Barney called her.

In the bottom drawer of the armoire were envelopes containing letters from several dozen different people, mostly writers. M. Chapon went through all of these, occasionally reading a felicitous passage or letter from Anatole France, Valery Larbaud, Sacha Guitry, or letting me hold letters from Pierre Louÿs, Rilke, T. S. Eliot, and a postcard from Joyce. There were quite a few letters from Pound, most of them dating from the postwar years, when he was in St. Elizabeth's Hospital, for Miss Barney had sympathized with him a great deal over his incarceration there. Chapon was present on the occasion of Pound's final visit to the Rue Jacob, in 1965. That was a very strange gathering in his honor, for Pound spoke not a word. Stranger still, when Pound was interviewed on French television, he kept his vow of silence, and Miss Barney had to do all the talking.

M. Chapon showed me a strand of Miss Barney's long blond hair, preserved in a tortoise-shell case (the same reliquary in which Eva Palmer's hair had been kept?) and allowed me to read two manuscripts: a collection of love poems written about 1910–1915 and the journal she kept during her European tour in 1894–1895. However, he had tied a ribbon around the second half of the journal and asked me not to read that portion because it was really too scandalous. Which was a pity, he said, for it was very amusing and lively, dating from the period before her writing fell under the influence of professors and academicians.

CHERYL HUGHES   *Paris, July 20–30*

At the Bibliothèque Doucet, M. Chapon told me about an American student who had been doing research on Natalie Barney and who wanted to meet me. I was to see her when I returned the follow-

ing Monday; but, as it happened, we met at Jean Chalon's flat in the
meantime, and subsequently we had a series of long conversations,
exchanging information, discussing our findings and speculating
about the enigmas that remained. Cheryl Hughes is a young gradu-
ate student in political science at Stanford University who became
interested in Natalie Barney last year and for a time dropped everything else. She even thought of changing her field and writing a the-
sis on Natalie Barney. Despite a limited knowledge of French, she
spent last summer in the Bibliothèque Nationale, reading everything
she could find about Natalie Barney and her circle. She has returned
to Paris this summer to continue her investigations with a diligence
and determination I can only admire, not having the patience myself
to cope with the cumbersome and antiquated machinery of the Bibliothèque Nationale. She now plans to write an article on Natalie Barney for the *Amazon Quarterly.*

Cheryl first learned about Natalie Barney when she read Djuna
Barnes' *Ladies Almanack,* a book she finds very funny, full of excellent gay humor. She loves all of Djuna Barnes' writings and has
read *Nightwood* half a dozen times. She commented on *Ladies Almanack* at some length, pointing out that it gives a very complete
portrait of the predominantly American lesbian circle of the 1920s.
The group centered around Natalie Barney, a veritable patron saint
and missionary of lesbianism, as the book jokingly portrays her.

But Cheryl was more interested in what happened to Natalie
thirty years before that, and she had discovered some interesting
material at the Bibliothèque Nationale. Salomon Reinach is supposed to have deposited Renée's manuscripts there, with the stipula-
tion that they were not to be seen until the year 2000. The library
claims that it doesn't have these papers, but it does have a collection
of books about Renée and her friends, with margins heavily annotated by Reinach. From these notes it would appear that the love affair
between Renée and Natalie began in 1899 and broke off in 1901.

Cheryl Hughes is convinced that Renée was Natalie's "first serious, complete, romantic, sexual love." It was Renée's paganism
that originally attracted Natalie, and their views were very similar
when they first met. But the death of Violet Shilleto altered Renée
beyond recognition and drove her to the Christian death that was en-

tirely contrary to her earlier Hellenism. Natalie herself changed over the years, but in a different way, beginning very romantically and ending up rather cynical about love.

Cheryl Hughes is convinced that Liane de Pougy was straight, but is also convinced that she had an affair with Natalie. *Idylle saphique* narrates a typical encounter between a straight woman and a lesbian. Annhine repeatedly leads Flossie on, only to put her off at the last moment. Of course, Liane de Pougy could have been teasing the reading public, too, with all those long-drawn-out scenes of amorous foreplay that lead to nothing.

Natalie's ideas were incredibly advanced for her time. All by herself in her early twenties, she arrived at positions which are being advanced by the gay liberation movement and the women's movement in the 1970s. Cheryl Hughes pointed out, for example, the comments Flossie makes on *Hamlet* in *Idylle saphique*; and in "Le Malentendu," an essay in *Pensées d'une Amazone,* Natalie compiles quotations from a wide array of sources to support her own statement justifying homosexuality, ranging from Socrates to Walt Whitman and Oscar Wilde.

And yet . . . and yet . . . at the end of our last conversation Cheryl said she kept changing her mind about Natalie. She thought that her treatment of Renée was cruel—*if* some accounts were to be believed—and that Natalie was in certain respects sexist. In characterizing herself as "friend to men and lover to women," Natalie sounded quite masculine, regarding men as equals and women as inferiors. This sort of thing left Cheryl Hughes wondering if she would have liked Natalie after all.

PART III

OTHER
POINTS OF VIEW

What follows is only a small sampling of the many interviews I had with people who had known Natalie Barney at various stages of her life, from childhood to old age. I have selected these interviews because each presents her from a particularly revealing point of view which is not represented in my biography. These interviews have previously appeared in somewhat different form in "A Natalie Barney Garland," published by The Paris Review *in the spring of 1975. Eyre de Lanux has completely rewritten her interview so that it is entirely her own work and I can claim no credit for it. The Truman Capote interview was the work of* The Paris Review *and came as a complete surprise to me when it appeared in print.*

Eyre de Lanux

Elizabeth Eyre was only eighteen and newly married to Pierre de Lanux when she moved into a third-floor apartment at 20 rue Jacob.
From that vantage point she watched with fascination the comings
and goings of a striking group of people on Friday afternoons. She
did not know who their hostess was until one day they happened to
meet at a reception. Eyre de Lanux was too timid to address such a
personality, but Natalie Barney recognized her neighbor and invited
her to the next Friday gathering. Mme. de Lanux soon found herself
attending the salon regularly and continued to go all through the
1920s and into the 1930s. Her unpublished memoir provides a
glimpse of the salon and its hostess in their heyday.

La Maison des Amis des Livres is the welcoming name of
Adrienne Monnier's bookshop and lending library, on the Rue de
l'Odéon. It was here, at a meeting of chosen friends, not many, as
the room could not contain many, that James Joyce read for the first
time an extract from *Ulysses*. I do not remember if Joyce himself
read, or Sylvia Beach. It was on this memorable occasion that I met
Miss Barney.

"I believe we are neighbors?" she said, and to her "Fridays" I
was thereupon invited. The "hazardous Fridays" as Paul Valéry
called them.

The Rue Jacob, now one of the most sumptuous and precious streets of Paris, was then in its eighteenth-century patina of dust. Number twenty had a heavy double door which at night was only opened by ringing the bell and awaking an always deaf or grumbling concierge. Leaning out of the window of my studio on the third floor, I had often seen and often marvelled at the procession of beautiful women and distinguished men which traversed the stone courtyard leading to the pavilion and ivy green garden. Elegant women, many and distinguished men; some might be heavy and pompous, others frail, and seeming to glide as if drawn by a magnet. Berthe, Miss Barney's maid for all those years, knew the name and position of every guest to whom the door opened on Fridays from four o'clock. Why do I remember Fridays as gray-green and dim, as if there had always been a light rain? Was it always that half-season? I cannot remember sun or any bright light, nor can I remember any loud or discordant sound. Muted.

In the salon to the right of the entrance I saw no details. Was I blind? The walls were surely covered with a wine faded damask, and if there were paintings on the walls they were not lit but discreet, needing introduction. Passing through this aquarium was the dining room, one wall of which led on to the garden, the green half-light of which came into the room, reflecting from the glasses and silver tea urn as from under-water. A very large oval table—I suppose the cloth was lace—at one end the tea, the cups, and at the other, glass pitchers of fruit cup. I remember the triangular sandwiches and the harlequin-colored litle cakes . . . and Miss Barney robed (one cannot say dressed) in white, a white not too cruel for the ancient walls, her hair hanging loose like cornsilk, the clear eyes of ice.

Chairs encircled the walls. I was regularly introduced first to Dr. Seignobos, the very old and learned historian, not at all interested in a young American, yet on each visit he was presented to me. Then Dr. Mardrus, the great Orientalist, the translator of *The Thousand and One Nights*. I was introduced as having translated some Egyptian poems. "From the demotic or the hieratic?" Dr. Mardrus asked with sudden interest. As I had only translated from the literal French of Maspero into literal English, the disillusion was complete.

Gertrude Stein was the permanent occupant of right wall center. With her stout tweeds, her sensible shoes, she seemed like a game warden scrutinizing the exotic birds. Miss Barney led me to her time and again, but she gave no sign.

Romaine Brooks, the painter of D'Annunzio, of Cocteau, etc., was a frequent visitor and a lifelong friend, as was the brilliant descendant of Henry IV, Elisabeth de Gramont, la duchesse de Clermont-Tonnerre. Colette was often there—"no serenity as cruel as yours, Amazon."

I found myself or rather lost myself like an invisible fish in exotic waters. The famous and beautiful women sat in file against the wall, lacking indulgence, in which quality the French have frequently been found lacking. Perhaps a certain ferocity lay underneath their exoticism. Gentlemen of all sizes and categories included writers, actors, diplomats—how did she tame such natural antagonists, these lions of their species? Sacha Guitry, Valéry, Rappoport, Philip Berthelot, Edmond Jaloux—the list is infinite—and wanderers from England and Italy, Harold Acton, Bernard Berenson, Prince Ghika, later on, Zadkine, Foujita. Who are the others? Their names are well-known. I remember Gide and Cocteau, rare guests, Eugene Jolas, the publisher of *Transition,* and the formidable Ezra Pound. One afternoon someone was standing alone in the shadow. Someone who could not see. It was James Joyce.

I was there when little George Antheil played his new composition for string quartet and also when the "divine" Isadora danced. One night in the summer—was it 1923?—the garden was illuminated, and 20 rue Jacob was alive with magic. A masked ball. I do not remember if the fête was for Paul Poiret or designed by him. What did Natalie wear? Perhaps one of her many masks.

Later, on returning from America, I found the "Fridays" had changed. Guests were walking in the garden or standing in the salon, "foreigners" were included, cocktails were served. It was the epoch of T. S. Eliot, Hemingway, Janet Flanner, Djuna Barnes, Glenway Wescott, Dolly Wilde, Lady Rothermere and Raymond Duncan in his hand-spun tunic.

Sometimes Natalie would seem to forget her "Fridays," and the faithful Berthe would murmur to her, "Mademoiselle, there are twenty people waiting for you in the salon.'' Then she would *flow* into the room, her pale golden hair flowing to her shoulders, her ice-blue eyes illuming the waiting effigies; and as though she had always been there, her flowing never interrupted a conversation but cntered it as light enters. I was completely aware of this remarkable approach to people, as though she were swimming, or had always been swimming along with them.

I have witnessed both her angers and her cruelties. Concerning her cooks, she said, ''I prefer them a little blind and deaf. It doesn't matter, so long as they can see enough to put in the salt.'' Or about her chauffeurs, ''The tubercular ones are the best. They are gentle and necessarily more careful.'' At that time she had a kind of electric hansom cab, and she carried a riding crop with which she would tap Joseph on the shoulder should he drive too fast.

Natalie was quite fearless and would walk from Passy to the Rue Jacob at night, wearing her cape and a little felt hat. She had a collection of these littlc hats, in all shades of gray. I asked if she wasn't ever accosted.

''Yes'' she said, ''last night.''

And what did you do? I asked.

''I said to that young man, 'Sir you are hardly polite.' ''

New York, August 3, 1973

Virgil Thomson

In May, 1927, Natalie Barney wrote to Gertrude Stein, inviting her and her friends to join in a meeting of the salon to be held in her honor. The program included readings from Gertrude Stein's work and songs by Virgil Thomson, who had set several of her short pieces to music. He and Gertrude had met during the previous year and were already close friends. He had met Natalie Barney about the same time, when his friend and fellow composer George Antheil had premiered several works at the salon. I had talked with Antheil's widow in Los Angeles, but her recollections were rather hazy, so I went to New York to see Virgil Thomson, knowing that I could count on his total recall and precision. Thomson was always welcome at Natalie Barney's Fridays, but he said that he "was not thick with her" and did not attend frequently, because the salon was literary rather than musical. Still, he was interested in Natalie Barney as a phenomenon, he had heard much about her through Gertrude Stein and Alice Toklas, and he remembered everything with great clarity and wit.

VIRGIL THOMSON: Natalie had really very little interest in music. Letters was her affair. She wasn't interested in painting very much either. The only musicians who ever made any kind of manifestation at her house, in my experience, were George Antheil and myself, and that in a very modest way.

244

On one occasion, and through what influence I do not know, a string quartet of George Antheil's was played at Natalie's house. My small manifestation had to do with Gertrude Stein, because I had set some texts of Gertrude's to music and I could sing them. Natalie didn't have pianos downstairs, but there was a small one up in her bedroom, or *petit salon,* up there, and so at the end of the five o'clock tea party we all went upstairs and did those.

Also, a Frenchwoman friend of mine, Mme. Langlois, had translated some of Gertrude's things into French, and those were read on that occasion, I think by the actress Marguerite Moreno.

I don't know of any other musical performances, but there may have been some. Natalie was attached to Germaine Lubin, who was a singer from the Paris Opera.

GEORGE WICKES: Mrs. Antheil told me that Olga Rudge performed there. Was that in the string quartet?

THOMSON: No, more likely she performed a violin sonata of George's or some other violin work. Now, George's support was always literary rather than musical. He was a great friend of Sylvia Beach, Ezra Pound, James Joyce—the Rue de l'Odéon crowd—and it may have been through there that Natalie was induced to pay for a string quartet playing. Natalie was not one to spend money on music. On letters perhaps, and certainly on lesbian ladies who were in need.

WICKES: Was there any connection between Sylvia Beach and Natalie Barney?

THOMSON: Nothing, except that Sylvia Beach was a center of literary frequentations, and whatever Natalie may have thought of Sylvia, she probably got books there, and anyway, that was the center where Joyce and Pound hung out. I don't even remember whether Natalie's mentioned in Sylvia's memoirs.

WICKES: Yes, she is, but rather briefly.

THOMSON: Now, Sylvia's private life is absolutely unknown to me. She was close friends with Adrienne Monnier and shared an apartment with her for years, but I never knew or heard of anybody who knew about any letting down of hair which would indicate that they were doing lesbian practices. In any case, if they did, it was completely secret. They didn't join any club.

WICKES: Yes, but I wonder if there was any kind of personal relationship, because, after all, not every one of Natalie Barney's relationships was lesbian.

THOMSON: Oh, no, of course not. You see, the salon had many aspects. It was that of an American lady of means with literary interests, and so it was predominantly a literary salon. But by the middle twenties, when I knew it, she already was centering it around her Académie des Femmes. But, of course, she also had men writers as well as women. I think Rilke used to be around there, and certainly all those French types—academicians and so forth. I used to see old Siegnobos there, who was a historian, and the Reinach brothers were all around.

The French associates in this "Academy"—it was an informal affair—were women who wrote and, to my knowledge, were lesbians, such as Mme. Fabre-Luce, who was married to a rich man and who was a sister to André Germain, of the family that owned the Crédit Lyonnais. And there was the duchesse de Clermont-Tonnerre, who wrote books of memoirs like Natalie and who was an old friend of mine and of Gertrude's—she was a jolly, entertaining woman. Then there was my next-door neighbor at 17 quai Voltaire, Lucie Delarue-Mardrus, who was the divorced wife of a famous Oriental language scholar, Dr. Jesus-Christ Mardrus, who had translated *The Arabian Nights* and, I believe, the Bible. She spoke Arab because in the early days of their marriage they'd been in North Africa a good deal together.

WICKES: Were there any Americans?

THOMSON: Well, Natalie had her American writer friends, and she would have a Friday in which the Academy honored some woman writer. One week it would be Gertrude Stein, another week Djuna Barnes, another week somebody else.

Djuna was kind of a charity of Natalie's, and I think Natalie gave her money. I don't think Djuna ever lived there. Gwen Le Gallienne did live there for quite a while. Natalie, of course, knew everybody. Natalie was perfectly respectable.

WICKES: Did Edith Wharton ever come?

THOMSON: Never heard of it. But Edith Wharton lived a nonliterary, highly social life centered around her lover, Walter Berry. And Edith Wharton was very social-position-conscious. She was no Ohio politician's daughter, you know. She was straight Newport, old New York, and all that, and she kept that up.

WICKES: Did Gertrude Stein go to the salon much?

THOMSON: Oh, from time to time. If Natalie was throwing a ceremony for Gertrude, with works being read and honors being made, naturally, yes. Or if this were being done for somebody who was a close friend of Gertrude's, then she would. Or if Natalie sent her a little *pneumatique* saying so-and-so's coming on Friday, somebody she'd like to meet, some visiting English or Italian. I don't know how often she would go just casually or accidentally.

WICKES: Was there rivalry between them?

THOMSON: I can't conceive that there was any because they weren't doing the same thing. Gertrude didn't have a salon, didn't have regular days. Gertrude was at home most afternoons at half past four or five o'clock, and sometimes close friends would drop in of an evening. And then Gertrude would throw a bit of a literary party from time to time, but that was all by invitation.

Gertrude and Natalie had a falling out at one point which was all about an indiscretion of Gertrude's. I got to talking to Gertrude and Alice one evening about Natalie, and I said, "Well, here she is a world-famous lesbian practitioner, but who does she do it with, and where does she get 'em?" Alice said—Alice was always thinking the worst—"I think from the toilets of the Louvre Department Store." Well, Gertrude wasn't entirely convinced by that, but it had suddenly been brought to her attention that for all her talk with Natalie, who was always representing the lesbian point of view, Gertrude didn't know really who Natalie slept with (unless there was a big love affair going on, which wasn't always) or what kind of people: whether it was always literary ladies or actresses or whether she had some kind of rough trade.

Gwen was staying in Natalie's house, and Gertrude out for a walk encounters Gwen on the sidewalk in front of the Café des

Deux Magots and, with a *colossal* indiscretion, starts questioning Gwen about her hostess' habits, and this is right in front of the terrace of the Deux Magots, where hundreds of people were listening—not hundreds, but quite a number. Well, Gwen had sense enough not to tell her anything, but she did go home and tell Natalie what Gertrude had done, and Natalie was sore as hell.

Whether she ever mentioned the matter to Gertrude, I don't know, but she bided her time and got her revenge some time later. This story was told me by Esther Murphy, Gerald Murphy's sister, who had married John Strachey and later married Chester Arthur, but who was a practicing girl herself and a great friend of Natalie's. There was a big lunch party with twelve people or so, and Lesbia was being discussed and people identified, and when Gertrude and Alice were brought up, Natalie said, "Oh, nothing like that there at all. It's entirely innocent." That was her revenge, you see, to have made a fool of Gertrude in front of the lesbians and in such a way as to put Gertrude into the position of a complete innocent for having inquired into her life. There were several months when Natalie and Gertrude didn't speak or write.

WICKES: This suggests that they were usually in pretty frequent touch.

THOMSON: Oh, yes, she'd come to Gertrude's house, and Gertrude would come to hers, and they'd write little *pneumatiques* all the time. Besides which, they were exchanging literary people. If the Sitwells came over and were around Gertrude's, she'd probably take them to Natalie's or have Natalie in or furnish them to Natalie for some soiree. If you've got Edith Sitwell on your hands, you don't want to see her every day. You get somebody else to see her, which amuses her, too, you get her around, distribute her.

WICKES: Now, what happened at the Fridays? What was the routine?

THOMSON: Well, it was the French style. There was tea at an enormous dinner table with lots of food. The French are terribly greedy at the end of the afternoon. It's a thing they don't have in their own lives, so that when they go to a party they all want to eat like mad. And there would be sandwiches and huge cakes and all sorts of things like that. And they would continue sitting at the tea table unless there were too many people, in which case they would move off into the parlor or sometimes into the garden in the summertime. It all depended on how many were there. Like any skillful hostess, Natalie always saw to it that some were there, and sometimes would run up a much larger number if some star like Radclyffe Hall or maybe Rilke or someone like that would be around.

WICKES: Now I'm curious about her literary patronage. I know that she gave something to the *Transatlantic Review.*

THOMSON: Well, that would be Ford. Ford was very good at these general literary occasions, salon style, because he was an amiable fellow and could talk about anything and had nice manners.

There's a piece about Natalie in the Hemingway memoirs.

WICKES: The Hemingway memoirs is not a source I go to for information.

THOMSON: Well, any snooting of lesbians on his part is pure tommyrot because he was very thick with Gertrude . . . and according to many persons in love with Gertrude . . . and I think she with him. That's why Alice had to get rid of him.

WICKES: Hemingway writes about the Temple à l'Amitié and Ezra Pound's scheme to get, as he puts it, Eliot out of the bank. Do you know anything about this?

THOMSON: No. I know what he says, and it sounds perfectly reasonable. It was the kind of thing that Ezra would do, trying to get up a subscription so that this very successful poet, already in his thirties, could be got out of that bank job.

WICKES: But I haven't come across any other records of this scheme to subsidize Eliot. It's the kind of thing Pound would propose, but I'm curious about Natalie Barney's role in such a venture as this.

THOMSON: Well, it would all depend on whether she felt like giving any money, and that would depend on what was in it for her. Natalie was not a woman of facile generosity. She spent money graciously, she kept a very luxurious table, she had not only the

Fridays but people were always going there to dinner and to lunch. She led an active generous social life. And people went there and stayed with her. And she helped to get their works published—she may even have paid a bit of money. But she was not an easy touch. No, no, no.

New York, June 7, 1972

Bettina Bergery

Née Elizabeth Shaw Jones, Mme. Bergery was one of three pretty
and gifted American sisters who came to Paris in the early thirties.
She stayed on in France, working for Mme. Schiaparelli, the fashion
designer, and eventually married Gaston Bergery, then a promising
young deputy and later ambassador to Russia and Turkey during the
war. She was nineteen when she first met Natalie Barney and was so
fascinated by her salon that she remained a constant friend and frequent caller until the end of Natalie's life. Of all Natalie Barney's
friends, Mme. Bergery is probably the best qualified to write her biography, for she is a keen observer with a remarkable memory and
wit. Her contribution to the volume of reminiscences *In Memory of
Dorothy Ierne Wilde* is by far the most vivid and it is verbatim. So I
was not surprised when Mme. Bergery proved to be the most talented
and entertaining storyteller I interviewed. She spoke glowingly of
Natalie as a wonderful presence, always gracious and amusing, with
extraordinary sparkle and gaiety.

"Though she looked like a Mother Superior or an abbess presiding with great dignity, she laughed like a schoolgirl. Because of her
stately bearing she seemed tall. Actually she wasn't.

"In her earlier years we know she was beautiful. At ninety, she
still had beautiful manners, very blue eyes and a nice skin. Natalie

251

had extraordinary eyes, very sparkling, with stars in them; the irises had a delicate marking like the little round petals of pompom dahlias. This is a rare phenomenon that sometimes occurs in blue eyes. Mme. René Clair has it and so had Maréchal Pétain. I know of no one else with eyes like that.

"By 1930 Natalie was less slender and began to look like Benjamin Franklin. The first one of her Fridays I went to, Natalie seemed an elegant version of the Wizard of Oz and Romaine Brooks looked like Tweedledum or Tweedledee. I remember lunching with Natalie and Romaine and a long-eyed skeleton in an old old dress made by Leon Bakst, a scarecrow left over from the Ballet Russe who turned out to be Ida Rubinstein: all three congratulating themselves and each other on having reached the summits of their chosen careers. Natalie sometimes wore a long velvet dress which was made for her by Mme. Vionnet, with astrological signs all over it. I believe it ended up in the Musée du Costume.

"Natalie, Romaine and the duchesse de Clermont-Tonnerre were not grotesques like Gertrude Stein and Alice Toklas, or in a lesser way like Colette—who was a squat, neckless woman with toes like bunches of muddy carrots and a forehead like a Greek temple, concealed by a shrubbery of frizzled hair—though the old cat eyes were piercing.

"Natalie was very feminine. She did not approve of mannishly dressed women and found them ridiculous. Even in her most Sapphic moods she was always very ladyish, in white Vionnet tea gowns—she only patronized the best Paris couture houses. Once when we visited Raymond Duncan's Academy together, she wore a gray suit with a gray toque, like any correct American lady of good society.

"Unless there was a poetry reading or a concert or some special occasion, there were never more than twenty people in her salon. After all, there was not room for great numbers, since everyone sat around a large mahogany table with a lace tablecloth and everyone had tea and ate. Of course, people came and went, and only the intimate members of the circle stayed longer than half an hour. Dolly Wilde called these 'the Knights of Natalie's Round Table.' In warm weather the doors to the garden were open and tables were set up outside. Once Dolly remarked, 'Oh, Natalie, you forgot to put the hermaphrodites in the bushes.' Dolly had a very Firbankish sense of humor.

"In the thirties, in addition to a sprinkling of senior politicians and members of the Académie Française, lady poetesses and American writers like Janet Flanner—who was one of the Knights—there were lots of English visitors of distinction. Harold Acton, Victor and Nancy Cunard, Georgia and Sacheverell Sitwell are the ones I remember best. When Nancy brought her Negro friend, Henry Crowder, he and Natalie were quite comfortable with each other. Henry's mother was a respectable laundress back in Washington, so Natalie understood him better than Nancy, who was always taking up causes.

"Sometimes there were recitals upstairs, in Natalie's room, where there was a grand piano and a crystal harp, which accompanied the overly operatic singers. But the real tendency of the salon was literary. The flowers were always 'the Lilies and Languors of Virtue, the Roses and Raptures of Love.' There were little cucumber sandwiches like damp handkerchiefs in memory of those served by Oscar Wilde and other poetic and delicious delicacies with semiclassical references that one of the faithful usually quoted between munchings.

"In addition to Berthe's marvelous cooking, Natalie supplied a feast of reason and a flow of wit. When I wondered why she always seemed to agree with each of her guests' opposing opinions, she laughed and quoted Dr. Johnson: 'An agreeable man is one who agrees with me.' When asked, 'What are your real opinions?' she answered, 'I have none. I gave them up long ago. An opinion is a limit to understanding. There are two and sometimes two hundred sides to every question. Why limit yourself?'

"She didn't read much at this late period, though she must have read a great deal at one time, but there were piles of the latest books from all the writers she knew, and she would quote appropriate phrases from them to the authors, though she had probably only glanced through their new work just before their arrival.

"People in a position to know said that she spoke the best eighteenth-century French, better than any of her learned French contemporaries.

"Natalie understood and appreciated good food, but she didn't like alcohol or even wine, which she preferred sweet. She did not smoke cigarettes or ever approve of opium, which was fashionably exotic in the Paris thirties.

"I never quite understood the motive behind Natalie's love of conquest. I believe her passions were mostly cerebral and that her strongest desire was to dominate—in a velvet-glove way.

"Natalie didn't like funerals, but she was one of the few people to attend the services for Robert de Montesquiou. She was a materialist and saw no reason to make a fuss when someone died. 'Funerals? Why trail in tears after a worn-out dress the owner has no more use for?'

"Natalie's own funeral was on a Friday, the day of her weekly receptions. 'Mademoiselle's last Friday,' sobbed Berthe. 'I don't feel Natalie's presence at all,' said Mme. Lahovary. But Natalie wouldn't have come!

"Her tomb is next to the grave of Renée Vivien—to whom Natalie once sent herself in her nightgown, with her long golden hair undone, concealed in a box of enormous lilies."

Paris, September 14 and 23, 1972

Truman Capote

In July, 1948, Alice Toklas noted, "The other day at Natalie Barney's Mrs. Bradley was full of the new young Parisian hero—Truman Capote—Gallimard is launching his novel with immense publicity and as Mrs. Bradley is his agent she has every interest to make the most of the sensation he is causing." Truman Capote went to Natalie Barney's salon off and on for almost ten years. His afternoon in the deserted studio with Miss Barney made enough of an impression to be adopted as a device to introduce a character in his novel-in-progress, *Answered Prayers*. What follows here is a summary of Truman Capote's conversation with George Plimpton and Fayette Hickox, of *The Paris Review*.

"I met Natalie Barney in 1947 through Jenny Bradley, who was the number one literary agent in France for American and English writers . . . a formidably handsome woman with a great sense of style and distinction. She introduced me to Natalie Barney and Romaine Brooks and Alice Toklas and Mercedes d'Acosta, who was Greta Garbo's friend and who created a great stir with her when she brought her to Natalie Barney's. They thought of Garbo as the *ne plus ultra* of what they were all about.

"Natalie Barney was a small chirpy woman who dressed very conventionally. She loved the color gray. She had a gray car and a

255

chauffeur dressed entirely in gray. She wore smart little gray suits. To look at her, and until you got into conversation with her, she seemed like a very refined lady from Shaker Heights. But of course she wasn't that at all.

"She had a party every week. I can't recall what day of the week, but it was arranged so it didn't conflict with Marie Louise Bousquet, who was the Paris editor of *Harper's Bazaar* and had her salons on Thursday. I don't think the two ladies were particularly friendly.

"At Miss Barney's everyone met in a room with a huge domed ceiling of stained glass. The decor was totally turn-of-the-century, with a slightly Turkish quality about it—a kind of cross between a chapel and a bordello. There was always a big buffet on the side with the most marvelous things—I mean the most delicious kinds of strawberry and raspberry tarts in the dead of winter; and always champagne. Tea and champagne. The guests stood, or sat on all sorts of couches and hassocks. Sometimes she had rather curious, unexpected people—Marguerite Caetani, the publisher of *Botteghe Oscure*, Peggy Guggenheim, Djuna Barnes (they always spoke of her as the 'red-headed bohemian'). . . . But it was always very proper . . . talk about this concert or that concert, or so-and-so's paintings, or 'Alice has a fabulous new recipe for eggs.' The only shocking thing I ever remember was when Carl Van Vechten came for tea and peed on the sofa by mistake. Everybody said, 'Oh-oh, wait a minute . . .' and then they turned and down the line Esther Murphy, with the same problem, had lost control of *her* bladder and was peeing on *her* sofa.

"Miss Barney's circle was not limited to lesbians . . . though certainly all the more presentable dykes in town were on hand. She had *tout Paris*. Many of them were friends of Proust who had been characters in *Remembrance of Things Past*—like the duchesse de Clermont-Tonnerre. Miss Barney would say to me very specifically that she wanted me to meet somebody because that person was so-and-so in Proust. She was trying to give me some sense of her particular time—which was typical of her generosity. She was certainly interested in celebrities—that was one of her hang-ups—but on the other hand she was not at all exploitative. She was one of those people who is always trying to bring other people together.

"One day Miss Barney came by—I was living in the Hôtel Pont Royal—to take me to luncheon, after which she wanted to show me something very unusual and extraordinary which very few people had ever seen. She didn't tell me what it was. So we went to a curious little neighborhood place near the Arc de Triomphe—not the sort of restaurant you would associate with Miss Barney—and afterwards she had the gray chauffeur park the gray car somewhere—and we started out walking. We walked for the longest time and finally we came to an ordinary *pension* (at least from the outside) and inside we went up in the cat-smelling, creaky elevator. Out on the landing she rustled around in her bag and came up with this huge mysterious key. She put it in the door and she looked like a burglar at a safe-cracking. She said, 'Now you stand out here because it's all in darkness inside and I have to go in and open the curtains a bit.' So I waited and waited until it seemed like fifteen minutes had gone by when she came back out on her stubby-heeled gray silk shoes and she led me in as if we were going into Ali Baba's cave. We walked into an enormous room! I mean *really* enormous—like a sort of super-loft. The whole room was well kept but it had the quality of total desertion—as if no one had been there for years. In the middle of the room was an easel with a half-finished painting on it, and beside it a table covered with tubes of paint, but all of them rather dry and desiccated-looking. Around the room the walls were covered with paintings shrouded with cloth, each of them with a little pull-cord next to the frame so you could pull it and the cloth would fold back and you could see the picture. I remember it was about four o'clock in the afternoon, a Paris winter afternoon, with that strange, gray pearly light.

"And Miss Barney said, 'This is the studio of my beloved friend, Romaine Brooks,' and I'm quoting that just exactly—'. . . my beloved friend, Romaine Brooks,' and we began moving around the room and she would pull the cords and the cloth would slide back from these paintings and there they were: Lady Una Troubridge with a monocle in her eye; Radclyffe Hall in a marvelous hunting outfit with a terrific hunting hat. It was the all-time ultimate gallery of all the famous dykes from 1880 to 1935 or thereabouts. The paintings were wonderful, they really were . . . with terrific qual-

ity and style, and we looked at them, one after the other, and Miss
Barney described who they were, many of them people I'd never
heard of before . . . Renée Vivien, Violet Trefusis . . . and of
course Miss Barney herself in a wonderful outfit with a pair of
gloves here and a whip in the foreground . . . that's what made the
whole thing so eerie.

"Because it had so little to do with the Miss Barney I was standing with, this cozy little Agatha Christie–Miss Marple lady . . .
and it was not that she was thirty years younger in the picture but
that on the canvas she was this wild thing wearing a cravat, with her
hand on her hip like *this*, and a *whip* over there . . . and I said,
'Miss Barney' (I never called her anything but 'Miss Barney' because . . . well, I was about twenty-five years old and anyone
who was older than me I called 'Sir' or 'Ma'am' and with her it was
just automatic) . . . I said, 'Miss Barney, my goodness, really, is
that really *you*?'

" 'Yes,' said she, this chirpy pigeonlike little lady who had so
little relation to this dominating woman with a whip.

"On the studio walls were one or two portraits of men—one of
Robert de Montesquiou in which he was wearing a black morning
coat with a black cravat and a white rose in his lapel, and then the
other was a fabulous painting of Reynaldo Hahn. He was a pianist, a
great *personage* of the 1880s and '90s who was a tremendous friend
of Proust. The painting shows him playing the piano with a piece of
sheet music in front of him which stretches up off the piano into the
sky, a great ribbon which is held at the far end by a band of angels. I
know it sounds like the corniest thing in the world, but it was sensa-
tional.

"There must have been a portrait of Remy de Gourmont. He was
the ugliest man in Paris; he suffered from lupus. He was madly in
love with Natalie Barney and wrote his *Letters to an Amazon* to her,
though if I've ever met a woman who was not an Amazon, it was
Natalie Barney. I always had the suspicion that she carried on with
him to get even with Romaine Brooks for running off with Lady
Una Troubridge. What a wonderful portrait *that* was—showing her
in a marvelous riding habit, all in black and white, with a beautiful
cravat, and this monocle in her eye. . . .

"Miss Barney was very frank about what we were looking at. She would explain the relationship between this person and that as we walked around the studio—and it was like an international daisy chain. 'Now *she* (don't you think she's rather attractive?) ran off with Romaine, which just broke my heart . . . for two years I couldn't get out of bed . . . I mean I had to put up with *that*, the two of them living in Fiesole, with me in Paris crying my heart out until the relationship finally broke up and she began writing me all these passionate love letters' . . . that sort of thing . . . all from this chirpy woman, rather plump. . . .

"I don't know what has happened to that room. Someone could write such a fantastic novella—just about that afternoon, and this rather usual-looking woman, and the pictures coming one after the other, and what they meant to her, and what the relationships of the various people were and what had happened to them. . . ."

New York, January, 1975

Janet Flanner

Janet Flanner had said, "Miss Barney is a perfect example of an enchanting person not to write about." But whatever her reservations, Miss Flanner was perfectly willing to talk about her for several hours, though she protested that her acquaintance with Natalie Barney was limited. Janet Flanner has been observing the Paris scene since 1921 and writing about it for *The New Yorker,* under the pseudonym Genêt, since 1925. She appears under another pseudonym in Djuna Barnes' *Ladies Almanack*, which sympathetically caricatures Natalie Barney and her friends.

GEORGE WICKES: You mention Natalie Barney several times in *Paris Was Yesterday.* There is a reference to the time that Mata Hari rode in nude on horseback.

JANET FLANNER: That was certainly one of the big events. And I also mentioned the cucumber sandwiches one always had at Natalie's. Her teas were sumptuous. She was an extraordinary person, Natalie. . . . I simply don't think she was an acute literary critic. . . . Her association with the old victim of lupus—what was his name?

WICKES: Remy de Gourmont.

FLANNER: Yes. Well, that was not a very valid qualification for her literary reputation, was it?

260

WICKES: How do you mean that?

FLANNER: I mean that what she said about him furnished no proof of her comprehension of what was going on in literary society. It depended upon her chance meeting with this wretched man who had become a monster in a way, Remy de Gourmont. I've always thought that was an unfair advantage that fate and chance took of Natalie, to place him in her path.

She had an enormous recognition from the French because she spoke such beautiful French. She spoke French as she spoke English, which was at that time almost unnecessary. She knew a lot of elderly representatives of French society and learned academic society. I should think she was not at all a learned woman herself. I don't even know where she had her education. She must have received an enormous education from the women she frequented.

It was very difficult to corral Natalie so that she cut a path among the things in which one was interested or supposed that she was interested. I never felt that I knew her at all well, really. I rarely saw her alone. I used to breeze in and breeze out. I never knew Natalie's friends, except insofar as they were my friends in any case, like Eyre de Lanux. I should think that she was intimate with Colette more than with any other recorder of events. Colette must have been more satisfactory than almost anyone else in her life. Then there were the younger women, whom it would not be fair to name, since they were people with whom Natalie merely fell in love. This gives a very limited scope, because if you weren't in love with her—which I certainly was not, since I brought up the topic—you didn't know as much about her, and you couldn't appreciate her as much either.

WICKES: Well, there was Renée Vivien earlier.

FLANNER: The way she spoke of Renée Vivien was one of the most shocking things in the world. "Oh," she said, "what a bore! Oh, such a tiresome young woman! Her love was almost as tiresome as everything else about her." She had been out all night, Natalie had, Lord knows where. She kept two sets of horses with a little brougham and a coachman; she must have kept two coachmen, too, and I should think two or possibly four horses. So when she'd be out gadding about, talking, exercising her talents and her charms, it might very well be on toward dawn before she would head back toward her home in the Rue Jacob.

Once Natalie had been out all night and thought about Renée Vivien on the way back home: "Oh, she's been so ill, I'd better stop and say good morning to her." And she found a florist shop open—it must have been spring—and she brought an enormous bouquet of *white* violets. You know how they appear in the florist shops in Paris in the springtime—not the purple but the white. And she bought a large bouquet of white violets and stopped by Renée Vivien's address. And the butler eventually answered the bell, with a clean napkin wound around his neck because he obviously hadn't had time to put his shirt on yet and bowed (he knew her well), *"Bonjour, mademoiselle."* And she said, "How is she this morning?" offering these white violets. And he said, "Oh, what tact Mademoiselle has. She has just this minute died, and they're *white* violets. *Quel chance pour vous, Mademoiselle, ça tombe si bien."*

WICKES: What an amazing story!

FLANNER: Yes, and no one has ever used it. Now, that she told me, so I know it is *véridique.* And that is how she discovered that Renée Vivien had died. She is buried in that odd little walled cemetery up there on the Place Maréchal Foch, I think it is, that looks straight across to the Tour Eiffel. And one day we happened to be driving by in her car, going someplace in the afternoon, and she looked at the cemetery, and that's when she said, "What a bore! What a bore . . . and so faithful!" Then she told me about the violets and said, "You see, love doesn't make people any more interesting. It makes them more endearing possibly, or perhaps more tiresome, too," she said, always going along in her absolutely detached voice. She was a commentator, and she would laugh. She would announce this fact, like that, then give this little crow of laughter as she participated in history, and it was really a terminal point. Then she'd either go on to something else or she wouldn't. You might have to supply the next observation.

WICKES: Wasn't the duchesse de Clermont-Tonnerre also an important figure in her life?

FLANNER: I think she was fonder of Colette than of any other woman in French society, but she was almost equally devoted and appreciative of Mme. de Clermont-Tonnerre, whom I also knew—excellent woman, so reliable, so correct, always so accurate, Mme. de Cleromnt-Tonnerre. There are references to her in one of my *Paris Journals* which I had gleaned from Natalie. She was the only great lady of the few that I knew—because I did not frequent French society—who remembered their childhood. I think I say that she had been brought up in a period in which the young male members of the family were always dukes. And when she wrote her memoirs, she wrote about life as it actually had been, with not a sigh of regret. She thought the whole thing had been rather preposterous. She accepted the new regime and the new realities with extraordinary comprehension because she was a woman of fantastic social vitality. So she moved from epoch to epoch, and when she was in her sixties and writing her memoirs, *Aux Temps des équipages,* it might just as well have been a Daimler she was writing about as horses, because she recognized the movement of transportation.

WICKES: You spoke earlier of Natalie Barney keeping horses and a brougham. When did she make the transition to motor cars?

FLANNER: I have no idea. She kept an elderly car which never had had a horse in connection with it but still rather smelled like a stable. It was an old-fashioned kind of car, and it had an equine smell.

WICKES: What about Romaine Brooks? Wasn't that another lifelong attachment?

FLANNER: Oh, yes, I expect she was the one that Natalie loved the most. Her life had its astral influences, and Romaine was certainly one of the stars. I saw Romaine every time she came to Paris. She used to come in June, and she always took a room just two doors down from mine in the Hôtel Continental, a very modest little room in back, looking over what I loved the most of all, the Tuileries Gardens. We never communicated with each other, except a note saying, "Now when are we lunching?" Then we would meet downstairs in the Continental, and she'd come down with her fresh stock tied—she wore a gentleman's stock. She was

a handsome woman and an excellent painter. Those portraits she
did were very observant, though they were already *démodé*. Romaine, I'm sure, never paid any attention to Picasso except to
say, "Oh yes, I daresay." Romaine and Clermont-Tonnerre were
the most remarkable women around Natalie as far as I knew, but
this would be a very limited slice of Natalie's life that I knew
about, because I liked these two women, I enjoyed their company, I enjoyed their recollections, I enjoyed what they used out of
life.

Now what can I tell you about Natalie? What interests you
most?

WICKES: Well, I'm interested in the salon, principally, and particularly in the period between the wars, when it was supposedly
flourishing. I want to know who went there and what the ritual
was.

FLANNER: Cucumber sandwiches. Berthe was part of the ritual.

WICKES: Yes, Berthe enacted the ritual for me in the salon last summer.

FLANNER: I always had a little hugger-mugger with Berthe at the
front door. I used to exchange gossip before I went in, picking up
notes: who was in, who was dying.

Did you meet Mme. Janine Lahovary? Splendid woman. She
was a great figure toward the end of Natalie Barney. Her sons
took it very hard. They said, "We wouldn't mind Mother having
a lover, so many mothers have lovers. But Mother's lovers are
women, and we find it very difficult to deal with the scoffing of
our schoolboy companions."

I don't really see that you can use anything much that I've collected, because there is no question about it, Natalie lived as an
oddment because of her sexual tastes.

WICKES: What about the Académie des Femmes?

FLANNER: Never heard of it. I'm a very spotty recollector. Tell me
what it was.

WICKES: She writes about it in one of her books of memoirs. And
yesterday I saw Virgil Thomson, and he talked about it.

FLANNER: Oh well, Virgil of course knows about everything. There
isn't a sex that was ever invented that Virgil wouldn't be able to

follow its manipulations and circles. In that way he really is a mathematician.

WICKES: Well, perhaps I could ask you about individuals then. Djuna Barnes, for instance.

FLANNER: I knew her very well indeed. Djuna of course is here in New York.

WICKES: Yes, but she won't see me.

FLANNER: No, she's too ill. She was very devoted to Natalie. Deplored the life she led. But a good many people would say that about Djuna's life, as far as that's concerned. Djuna was one of the strongest personalities around Natalie and one of the most devoted, one of the most appreciative. She went to the tea parties—when were they, Fridays?

WICKES: Yes, Fridays.

FLANNER: That's what I thought, vaguely. Well, it's toward the end of the week. Gives the ladies something to talk about and drive over to see each other about over the weekend. The food was delicious. Berthe was an extremely good cook. She was the only person around Natalie who had a husband. I'll see her when I go back to Paris. Her first question is always and invariably, *"Et Mademoiselle Djuna, que fait-elle maintenant? Ah, quelle femme!"* Berthe was so loyal she practically took on Natalie's tastes.

WICKES: She told me that it was through Djuna Barnes that she started working for Natalie Barney.

FLANNER: I didn't know that. Well, I think Djuna and I were more fond of Berthe and certainly knew her better than anyone else. I didn't frequent Natalie's house to that extent, but Berthe always included me as one of the pillars. I think Djuna and I had a more pillarlike figure in Berthe's recollections than anyone else. You've seen the little dining room there?

WICKES: Yes, but it's in a very dilapidated state now.

FLANNER: My dear fellow, it looked dilapidated even then. Not *so* dilapidated, but it was certainly not fresh. I took some English woman in there once, and she was curious about those paintings of the nymphs hanging from the ceiling, and she said, "Is it permitted for me to bend my head back and look at the ceiling? What is it going to be?'' And I said, ''Oh, it's quite decent, quite correct. Fear nothing.'' Everything was so *démodé*. Dolly Wilde declared that Natalie's house was so frowsty and so damp that if you turned up the chairs you would find oysters growing under them. No one ever sat in the drawing room—that's where Dolly said the oysters grew under the chairs. They didn't in the little dining room. That was a rather lively place; it looked straight out into the garden. We all clustered around the teapot in the little dining room. I was never upstairs in my life. Toward the end Natalie broke out—I think at Mme. Lahovary's insistence—in pale-blue silk sheets. Well, I thought that was a luxury! Now what is the name of the man who owns her house?

WICKES: Michel Debré.

FLANNER: Michel Debré, who has a porcine face. The most important thing is, what is going to happen to her house? I have no idea.

WICKES: I believe Michel Debré was just waiting for her to die before renovating, obliterating, who knows what.

FLANNER: Renovating and obliterating, I should think, would be the same thing.

WICKES: To get back to the salon. What happened at the tea parties?

FLANNER: Introductions, conversation, tea, excellent cucumber sandwiches, divine little cakes Berthe baked, and then the result: a new rendezvous among ladies who had taken a fancy to each other or wished to see each other again. Purely social.

WICKES: Was there never any music?

FLANNER: Oh, no, I don't think Natalie knew one tune from another.

WICKES: She told me that she was musical, that she'd played the violin as a girl.

FLANNER: Oh, I think there's a terrible early photograph that proves that. There's a series of photographs of her early youth that are really quite painful. She's acting like a dryad and she peeks from behind tree trunks in the Bois. You know how bad taste was at that time.

I feel sorry for you.

WICKES: You mean for undertaking this subject?

FLANNER: Yes, because I've never entered into anything without knowing which way I was headed. And on this, you see, I'm not competent. I know these two or three anecdotes, which in each case I think are invaluable. That one about the white violets is precious. I can just see that butler with the clean napkin swathed around his probably scrawny neck: *"Oh Mademoiselle, comme ça tombe bien. Elle vient de mourir. Vous êtes juste à l'instant."* Natalie was enchanted with that. There was a sense of the apropos in Natalie which was rather alarming. The woman had been a bore for her, and there she arrived, accidentally apropos. That's the way Natalie liked to be apropos. She could never have contrived it. I've always wondered with whom she'd spent the night—if it was someone frightfully important.

WICKES: There are those who blame her for the death of Renée Vivien.

FLANNER: Well, yes, she was perishing of unrequited love, and also she led so debauched a life in the waste of her affections and in the strain on her gastric system of living on sweets and champagne. No one ever knew who the rich woman lover was who supported her.

Her power over Renée was a thing which impressed the ladies. She would receive these impetuous messages brought by a coachman with another groom waiting outside: "Come at once." And wherever she was and whatever the ladies were all doing, she left at once and followed the very imperious demand to turn up wherever it was.

WICKES: Hemingway mentions Natalie Barney in *A Moveable Feast* in connection with Pound's project to get Eliot out of the bank. Do you know anything about this?

FLANNER: I don't know. I shouldn't think Natalie had been given to any elaborate charitable enterprises. Natalie was not one for good works. She was one for bad works if they interested her. There was a reverse medal in the family; that was her sister, Mrs. Dreyfus—a very dull woman.

WICKES: Natalie Barney knew Ezra Pound well. She used to play tennis with him. That's hard to imagine, isn't it?

FLANNER: I can imagine that costume: flat-heeled white shoes with the toes turning up, and her hair all aswathe in the breeze. Her hair must have been extraordinary when she was young, this long web of blond hair.

The only woman who had at that time extraordinary style sartorially was Mata Hari. *There* was a woman who was equal to any event. Natalie was the one who supplied me with the information on what she wore the day she was shot. She traced down the young lieutenant or captain who had given the signal to fire, the one who said she stood so still it made him tremble. So one has an accurate story instead of that tawdry imagined sable coat over nude flesh invented by someone who wrote for the most scurrilous kind of literary weekly.

WICKES: Was Natalie Barney involved with Mata Hari?

FLANNER: Only insofar as she came to her tea party. Mata Hari wanted to ride in on an elephant. But Natalie said, "No, you'll get in the way of Berthe. There are cookies and tea, and we can't have an elephant stamping around in my garden. Nonsense!" I don't think it was at her house that Mata Hari gave that warrior's dance from whatever remote country she had picked it up in and noticed that one of the ladies' feet looked very large and guessed that it was a husband who had sneaked in—obviously a man of intemperate desires. She was ready to run him right through on the spot with a harpoon.

Natalie was a woman who was never captive. All the rest of them were—to each other or in one way or another. She was an essentially independent American woman from Cincinnati. She was remarkable at the last. She lay on a little straight sofa in the drawing room. This was shortly before her death, toward the end of any public appearance that she ever permitted or ever enjoyed. She laughed the same as ever. There was a curious hard American stoical quality about her.

She was wonderful as she lay there, on that narrow, uncomfortable sofa. And there she lay, already in state, laughing, never loudly. She never laughed loudly, never in her life. Nothing was ever that funny to Natalie.

New York, June 8, 1972

Acknowledgments

In the course of collecting materials and writing this book I have been assisted and encouraged by many people. This book is dedicated to them with my gratitude and with the hope that they will read it with pleasure.

I am most grateful to Berthe Cleyrergue for her warmhearted hospitality and generosity in providing photographs and other materials, as well as a fund of reminiscence, during many long and pleasant conversations. My very special thanks to her.

I owe a similar debt to Jean Chalon, who also provided photographs and kindly allowed me access to his collection of rare books and manuscripts. His book on Natalie Barney, *Portrait d'une séductrice*, appeared in print just as I was finishing mine, too late to be of use except to corroborate certain details.

For their assistance and for permission to see manuscript materials I am grateful to François Chapon, of the Fonds Littéraire Jacques Doucet; Donald McClelland, of the Smithsonian Institution; Donald Gallup, of the Yale University Library; Myron Gilmore, of I Tatti; Valerie Eliot; and the Princeton University Library.

For the privilege of interviewing, and for interviews that were invariably fascinating and informative, in more ways than they may have realized, I am indebted to Boski Antheil, Germaine Beaumont, Bettina Bergery, Célia Bertin, Princess Marthe Lahovary Bibesco,

Jenny Bradley, Morrill Cody, the late Laura Dreyfus-Barney, Janet Flanner, Jessie Fremont, Grace Frick, Marcel Jouhandeau, the late Janine Lahovary, Dr. Marthe Lamy, Renée Lang, Eyre de Lanux, Edouard Macavoy, Louis N. Moulton, Virgil Thomson, Gareth Windsor, and Marguerite Yourcenar.

To Herbert Lottman, Robert Potter, Richard Sieburth, and Esther Wagner I owe special thanks for their help and encouragement. And to the many others who have aided and abetted me in a variety of ways, ranging from research to the process of bringing this book into existence, I give thanks: Sue Baxter, Michel Fabre, Miron Grindea, Barbara Hamlin, Thomas Hines, William E. Huntington, Myrna Lassiter, André Le Vot, George Plimpton, Molly McKaughan, Jerome Reich, Gayle Rubin, Ernest Samuels and the late Thornton Wilder.

For grants which permitted me to travel or sustained life during periods of research and writing, I am grateful to the American Council of Learned Societies, the American Philosophical Society, the National Endowment for the Arts, the University of Oregon, and the Center for Twentieth Century Studies at the University of Wisconsin—Milwaukee.

To the following I am grateful for permission to quote or reproduce materials which they control: François Chapon, for quotations from unpublished writings of Natalie Barney; the late Frank Hallman and Richard Schaubeck, for passages from Romaine Brooks' manuscript, "No Pleasant Memories"; the Ezra Pound Archive, the Gertrude Stein Archive, and the Carl Van Vechten Archive, Collection of American Literature, Beinecke Rare Book and Manuscript Library, Yale University; Farrar, Straus & Giroux, Inc., for passages translated by Helen Beauderu in *Earthly Paradise: An Autobiography of Colette*, edited by Robert Phelps (1966); and for excerpts from Colette, *The Pure and the Impure*, translated by Herma Briffault (1967); Editions Sun, for excerpts from André Germain, *La Bourgeoisie qui brûle* (1951); Miron Grindea, for a quotation from the Natalie Barney issue of *Adam International Review* (1962); Alfred A. Knopf, for a letter by Natalie Barney published in *The Flowers of Friendship: Letters Written to Gertrude Stein*, edited by Donald C. Gallup (1953); Yale University Press, for passages from Natalie Barney's foreword to *As Fine as Melanctha*, by Gertrude Stein (1945); Mr. Rache Lovat Dickson and the Estate of the late Radclyffe Hall, for passages from *The Well of Loneliness* (Covici-Friede, 1928); Djuna Barnes, for passages from *Ladies Almanack* (Harper and Row, 1972); The National Collection of Fine Arts, Smithsonian Institution, for photographs of paintings by Alice Pike Barney and Romaine Brooks; Mille. Adeline Cacan, Musée du Petit Palais, for permission to reproduce portraits of Natalie Barney and the Duchess de Clermont-Tonnerre by Romaine Brooks; Meryle Beveridge, and Doubleday and Company, for photographs of Natalie Barney and Romaine Brooks; Jean Chalon, for interviews and photographs; *The Paris Review* and Bettina Bergery, Janet Flanner, Eyre de Lanux, and Virgil Thomson, for interviews originally published in *The Paris Review*, and to Truman Capote, for an interview by George Plimpton and Fayette Hickox, published with permission of *The Paris Review*, from issue #61, Spring 1975, copyright © The Paris Review, Inc.

Bibliography

WORKS BY NATALIE BARNEY *(Listed chronologically; published in Paris and signed Natalie Clifford Barney unless otherwise indicated)*

CLIFFORD (Barney), NATALIE. *Quelques Portraits-Sonnets de femmes.* Ollendorf, 1900.

TRYPHÉ. *Cinq Petits Dialogues grecs.* La Plume, 1901.

[ANON.] *The Woman Who Lives with Me.* [Privately published, probably 1904.]

Actes et entr'actes. Sansot, 1910.

[ANON.] *Je me souviens.* Sansot, 1910.

Éparpillements. Sansot, 1910.

Poems & poémes: autres alliances. Paris: Emile Paul, and New York: Doran, 1920.

Pensées d'une Amazone. Emile Paul, 1920.

Aventures de l'esprit. Emile Paul, 1929.

The One Who Is Legion, or A. D.'s After-Life. London: Eric Partridge, 1930.

Nouvelles Pensées de l'Amazone. Mercure de France, 1939.

In Memory of Dorothy Ierne Wilde. Edited with an introduction by Natalie Clifford Barney. Dijon: Darantière, 1951.

Foreword to Gertrude Stein's *As Fine as Melanctha.* New Haven:
Yale University Press, 1954.
Souvenirs indiscrets. Flammarion, 1960.
BARNEY NATALIE. *Traits et portraits.* Mercure de France, 1963.
Selected Writings. Edited with an introduction by Miron Grindea.
London: Adam Books, 1963. [A reprint of the special issue of
Adam International Review (1962) containing writings by and
about Natalie Barney.]

OTHER SOURCES

ACTON, HAROLD. *More Memoirs of an Aesthete.* London: Methu-
en, 1970.
ALDINGTON, RICHARD. *Life for Life's Sake: A Book of Rem-
iniscences.* New York: Viking, 1942.
ANDERSON, ELIZABETH AND GERALD R. KELLY. *Miss Elizabeth:
A Memoir.* Boston: Little, Brown, 1969.
ANTHEIL, GEORGE. *Bad Boy of Music.* Garden City: Doubleday,
1945.
BARNES, DJUNA. *Ladies Almanack.* New York: Harper & Row,
1972.
BEACH, SYLVIA. *Shakespeare and Company.* New York: Har-
court, Brace, 1959.
BREESKIN, ADELYN D. *Romaine Brooks, "Thief of Souls."* Wash-
ington, D.C.: Smithsonian Institution Press, 1971.
BURNE, GLENN S. *Remy de Gourmont: His Ideas and Influence in
England and America.* Carbondale: Southern Illinois University
Press, 1963.
[BUSSY, DOROTHY STRACHEY.] *Olivia.* London: Hogarth Press,
1949.
CHALON, JEAN. *Les Couples involontaires.* Paris: Flammarion,
1966.
———. "Natalie Barney." *Connaissance des Arts* (November,
1965), pp. 82–87.
———. *Portrait d'une séductrice.* Paris: Stock, 1976.
CHAMPION, PIERRE. *Mon Vieux Quartier.* Paris: Grasset, 1932.

COLETTE. *Claudine s'en va.* Paris: Ollendorf, 1903.

————. *Mes Apprentissages.* Paris: Ferenczi, 1936.

————. *Le Pur et l'impur.* Paris: Ferenczi, 1941.

————. *Trois . . . Six . . . Neuf.* Paris: Correa, 1944.

————. *Earthly Paradise: An Autobiography, Drawn from Her Lifetime Writings.* Robert Phelps, ed.; Herma Briffault, Derek Coltman, et al, trans. New York: Farrar, Straus & Giroux, 1966.

COOPER, CLARISSA BURNHAM. *Women Poets of the Twentieth Century in France: A Critical Bibliography.* New York: King's Crown Press, 1943.

CROFT-COOKE, RUPERT. *Bosie: Lord Alfred Douglas, His Friends and Enemies.* New York: Bobbs-Merrill, 1963.

CROSBY, CARESSE. *The Passionate Years.* New York: Dial Press, 1953.

CROSLAND, MARGARET. *Colette: The Difficulty of Loving.* Indianapolis and New York: Bobbs-Merrill, 1973.

DAMON, GENE AND LEE STUART. *The Lesbian in Literature: A Bibliography.* San Francisco: The Daughters of Bilitis, 1967.

DELARUE-MARDRUS, LUCIE. *L'Ange et les Pervers.* Paris: Ferenczi, 1930.

————. *Mes Mémoires.* Paris: Gallimard, 1938.

————. *Nos Secrètes Amours.* Paris: Les Isles, 1951.

ELLMANN, RICHARD. *James Joyce.* New York: Oxford University Press, 1959.

FORD, FORD MADOX. *It Was the Nightingale.* Philadelphia and London: Lippincott, 1933.

FOSTER, JEANNETTE. *Sex Variant Women in Literature.* London: Frederick Muller, 1958.

GALLUP, DONALD, ed. *The Flowers of Friendship: Letters Written to Gertrude Stein.* New York: Knopf, 1953.

GERMAIN, ANDRÉ. *Les Clés de Proust.* Paris: Sun [1953].

————. *La Bourgeoisie qui brûle: propos d'un témoin (1890–1940).* Paris: Sun [1951].

————. *Renée Vivien.* Paris: Crès, 1917.

GIDE, ANDRÉ. *Journal, 1889–1933.* Paris: Pléiade, 1951.

DE GOURMONT, REMY. *Lettres à l'Amazone.* Paris: Crès, 1914.

————. *Lettres intimes à l'Amazone.* Paris: La Centaine, 1926.

_____. *Letters to the Amazon.* Translated with an introduction by Richard Aldington. London: Chatto and Windus, 1931.

DE GRAMONT, E. [Duchesse de Clermont-Tonnerre]. *Mémoires* (4 volumes). Paris, Grasset, 1928–1935.

HALL, DELIGHT. *Catalogue of the Alice Pike Barney Memorial Lending Collection.* Washington, D.C.: Smithsonian, 1965.

HALL, RADCLYFFE. *The Well of Loneliness.* New York: Covici-Friede, 1928.

HALL, RICHARD. *Stanley: An Adventurer Explored.* Boston: Houghton Mifflin, 1975.

HEMINGWAY, ERNEST. *A Moveable Feast.* New York: Scribner's, 1964.

HOLLIDAY, JOSEPH E. "Notes on Samuel N. Pike and his Opera House." *The Cincinnati Historical Society Bulletin* (July, 1967), pp. 165–183.

HUDDLESTON, SISLEY. *Paris Salons, Cafés, Studios.* Philadelphia: Lippincott, 1928.

HYDE, H. MONTGOMERY. *Oscar Wilde.* New York: Farrar, Straus & Giroux, 1975.

JALOUX, EDMOND. *Le Saisons littéraires, 1904–1914.* Paris: Plon, 1950.

JOSEPHSON, MATTHEW. *Life Among the Surrealists.* New York: Holt, Rinehart and Winston, 1962.

JOYCE, JAMES. *Letters.* Vol. 3. Richard Ellmann, ed. New York: Viking, 1957.

JULLIAN, PHILIPPE. *D'Annunzio.* Stephen Hardman, trans. New York: Viking, 1973.

_____. "Fresh Remembrance of Oscar Wilde." *Vogue* (November, 1969), pp. 176–179, 229–234.

_____. *Prince of Aesthetes: Count Robert de Montesquiou, 1855–1921.* John Haylock and Francis King, trans. New York: Viking, 1968.

KLAICH, DOLORES. *Woman Plus Woman: Attitudes Towards Lesbianism.* New York: Simon and Schuster, 1974.

LÉAUTAUD, PAUL. *Journal littéraire* (19 volumes). Paris: Mercure de France, 1954–1966.

LOTTMAN, HERBERT R. "In Search of Miss Barney." *New York*

Times Book Review (September 28, 1969), pp. 2, 46–47.

LOUŸS, PIERRE. *Aphrodite*. Paris: Mercure de France, 1896.

———. *Les Chansons de Bilitis*. Paris: Librairie de l'art indépendant, 1895.

LUHAN, MABEL DODGE. *Intimate Memories*. Vol. 2. New York: Harcourt, Brace, 1935.

MARTIN DU GARD, MAURICE. *Les Mémorables*. Paris: Flammarion, 1957.

MARTIN-MAMY, EUGENE. *Les Nouveaux Païens*. Paris: Sansot, 1914.

MILLAY, EDNA ST. VINCENT. *Letters*. Allan Ross Macdougall, ed. New York: Harper, 1952.

MIZENER, ARTHUR. *The Saddest Story: A Biography of Ford Madox Ford*. New York and Cleveland: World, 1971.

MORAND, PAUL. *Journal d'un attaché d'ambassade, 1916–1917*. Paris: Stock, 1948.

PAINTER, GEORGE D. *Proust* (2 volumes). Boston: Little, Brown, 1959, 1965.

PATMORE, DEREK. *Private History: An Autobiography*. London: Jonathan Cape, 1960.

POUGY, LIANE DE. *Idylle saphique*. Paris: La Plume, 1901.

POUND, EZRA. *The Cantos*. London: Faber & Faber, 1964.

PUTNAM, SAMUEL. *Paris Was Our Mistress: Memoirs of a Lost and Found Generation*. New York: Viking, 1947.

ROGERS, W. G. *Ladies Bountiful*. New York: Harcourt, Brace and World, 1968.

ROSE, FRANCIS. *Saying Life: The Memoirs of Sir Francis Rose*. London: Cassell, 1961.

ROUVEYRE, ANDRÉ. *Deux Series complètes des illustrations composés pour Lettres intimes à l'Amazone*. (n.p., 1926).

———. *Souvenirs de mon commerce*. Paris: Crès, 1921.

———. *Visages des contemporains: Portraits dessinés d'après le vif (1908–1913)*. Paris: Mercure de France, 1913.

SECREST, MERYLE. *Between Me and Life: A Biography of Romaine Brooks*. New York: Doubleday, 1974.

SKINNER, CORNELIA OTIS. *Elegant Wits and Grand Horizontals*. Boston: Houghton Mifflin, 1962.

STEIN, GERTRUDE. *The Autobiography of Alice B. Toklas*. New York: Harcourt, Brace, 1933.

STOCK, NOEL. *The Life of Ezra Pound*. New York: Pantheon, 1970.

THOMAS, HUGH. *John Strachey*. New York: Harper & Row, 1973.

THOMSON, VIRGIL. *Virgil Thomson*. New York: Knopf, 1966.

TOKLAS, ALICE B. *The Alice B. Toklas Cookbook*. New York: Harper, 1954.

_____. *Staying on Alone: Letters of Alice B. Toklas*. Edward Burns, ed. New York: Liveright, 1973.

_____. *What Is Remembered*. New York: Holt, Rinehart and Winston, 1963.

SANSOT, EDOUARD. *Souvenirs sur Renée Vivien*. Nice: Modern Studio, 1924.

TROUBRIDGE, UNA VINCENZO, LADY. *The Life and Death of Radclyffe Hall*. London: Hammond, Hammond, 1961.

VALÉRY, PAUL. *Oeuvres*. Vol. 1. Paris: Gallimard, 1957.

VAN VECHTEN, CARL. *Fragments from an Unwritten Autobiography* (2 volumes). New Haven: Yale University Library, 1955.

VIVIEN, RENÉE. *Poésies complétes* (2 volumes). Paris: Alphonse Lemerre, 1934.

_____. *Une Femme m'apparut*. Paris: Alphonse Lemerre, 1904.

WEINTRAUB, STANLEY. *Whistler: A Biography*. New York: Weybright and Talley, 1974.

WICKES, GEORGE, ed. "A Natalie Barney Garland." *The Paris Review*. (Spring, 1975), pp. 86–134.

WILLIAMS, WILLIAM CARLOS. *Autobiography*. New York: Random House, 1951.

Index

Académie des Femmes, 99, 153, 167, 178, 246
Académie Française, 153, 163, 164
Acosta, Mercedes d', 255
Actes et entr'actes (Barney), 68, 69, 94, 95, 112–13, 155
Acton, Harold, 192, 242, 253
Adam (magazine), 211
Aiglon, L' (Rostand), 46
Aldington, Richard, 10, 130, 162, 180
A l'Heure des mains jointes (Vivien), 72
Amazon Quarterly, 234
Americans Abroad (Sardou), 36, 88
Anacréon, Richard, 217
Anderson, Sherwood, 165, 168
Ange et les Pervers, L' (Delarue-Maldrus), 83–87
Anglesey, Lady "Aunt Minnie," 145, 146
Answered Prayers (Capote), 255
Antheil, George, 152, 164, 214, 242, 244, 245
Aphrodite (Louÿs), 49, 51
Apollinaire, Guillaume, 125
"Apology" (Barney), 143
Arabian Nights, 78, 83
Arman de Caillavet, Mme., 105, 107–8, 163

As Fine as Melanctha (Stein), Barney's preface to, 168–69, 198–99
Atthis, 58, 59
Aulard, François, 110
Aurel, Mme., 127, 166, 167
Aux Temps des équipages (Barney),263
Aventures de l'esprit (Barney), 10–11, 17, 48, 49, 50, 51, 82, 108–9, 128, 161, 167, 179, 199

Bakst, Leon, 252
Ballet mécanique (Antheil), 164
Balzac, Honoré de, 150
Barbusse, Henri, 141
Barnes, Djuna, 166, 167, 171, 178–82, 215, 226, 234, 242, 246, 256, 260, 265; her literary portrayal of Natalie Barney, 180–82
Barney, Albert Clifford (father), 16, 20–21, 22, 23, 29, 32, 35, 41, 42, 47, 64, 80–81, 152, 224
Barney, Alice Pike (mother), 11, 15, 21, 22–24, 26, 34, 35, 37, 44, 46–47, 88–89, 93, 105–6, 224, 230
Barney, Eliam Eliakim (paternal grandfather), 18–19
Barney, Com. Joshua, 17, 18
Barney, Laura (sister), 21, 23, 25, 28,

55, 68, 89, 141, 152, 167, 191, 197, 230, 233. *See also* Dreyfus, Mme. Hippolyte
Barney, Natalie Clifford: and Djuna Barnes, 178–79, 180–82; Bernard Berenson's letters to, 153–58; Bettina Bergery on, 251–54; birth, 7, 21; and Romaine Brooks, 144–51, 200, 201, 203–4, 258; Brooks on, 144–45, 146; Truman Capote on, 255–59; Jean Chalon on, 224–27, 230–32; childhood, 7–8, 15–16, 21–22, 25–30; and Lily de Clermont-Tonnerre, 139–41, 142, 143, 147, 148, 149; Berthe Cleyrergue on, 215–19, 220–23, 228–30; and Colette, 97–99; and Olive Custance, 58–61; death and funeral, 7, 68, 204–5, 220, 254; as debutante, 35–36; and Lucie Delarue-Mardrus, 82–87; education, 8, 25–26, 27–29, 31, 33; and T.S. Eliot, 161–63, 249; European tour as student, 31–33; Elizabeth Eyre de Lanux on, 240–43; and father, 20–21, 41, 42, 81; and father's death, 64; feminism of, 26, 115–16; Janet Flanner on, 260–68;fortune of, 20, 23; French language, knowledge of, 27, 47; friendships with men, 9–10, 41–42, 43–44, 108–9, 153–54; genealogy, 16–21; André Germain on, 131–38; and Remy de Gourmont, 119–29, 130–31, 136–38; Radclyffe Hall's portrayal of, 172–77; horoscope, 100–2, 217; house at 20 rue Jacob, 100, 102–4, 175–76, 217–18, 228–29, 265–66; Cheryl Hughes on, 233–35; interview with, 211–15; and Janine Lahovary, 202–3; Janine Lahovary on, 223–24; lesbianism of, 8–9, 27–28, 29, 30–31, 40–41, 171–78, 179–82, 234–35, 247–48; literary studies, 43, 45; and Pierre Louÿs, 49–51; love affairs, 8–9, 222–23, 226, 231; manuscripts and letters, 220, 222, 226–27, 231, 232–33; and the Mardrus', 78–82; and mother, 24; nicknames, 25, 39, 126–27, 128; old age, 198–204; 211–15; and Eva Palmer, 30–31, 96–97; and Paris, 34–35, 44–45; *pensées*, 113–18, 127, 145, 153, 158, 159–60, 225; plays, 94–95; poetry, 43, 45–47, 48, 50, 65, 68, 140, 141, 143, 145, 150, 155–56, 159, 160; portraits of, 26–27, 46, 151, 204, 232–33, 258; possessions auctioned at death, 228–29, 230–32; and Liane de Pougy, 37–41, 42, 48–51; and Ezra Pound, 158–61, 164–65, 192, 193, 198, 214; and Proust, 179; salon, 99, 102, 103, 104–11, 117, 131, 141–42, 149, 152, 153, 161, 164, 165–67, 168, 170, 171, 172, 176–77, 178, 197–98, 199, 241–43; 245–47, 248–50, 252–53, 256, 264, 265–66; Sapphic circle formed, 58–60; and Gertrude Stein, 165–6, 167–70, 194–96, 247–48; and Stein's death, 195–96; theatricals, 88–95, 97, 98; Virgil Thomson on, 244–50; and Paul Valéry, 161–63, 249; and Renée Vivien, 48, 54, 55–60, 61–64, 65–67, 69–76; and Vivien's death, 65, 67–68, 118, 131, 262, Vivien's portrayal of, 57, 58–59, 69–76; and Dolly Wilde, 183–89, 193; Oscar Wilde's influence on, 11–12, 113–14; will and estate settlement, 220, 221–22, 228–30, 232; and World War I, 139–44; World War II spent in Italy, 191–94, 195; writing, 7, 10–12, 22, 48–52, 94–95, 112–18, 127, 129, 150, 153, 158, 159–60, 170, 198–99, 225
Barney Studio House, 22, 24
Bassiano, Princess di. *See* Caetani, Marguerite
Beach, Sylvia, 171–72, 198, 240, 245
Beaumont, Germaine, 215, 217, 231
"Bel Esprit," 161–62, 163
Berenson, Bernard, 43, 110, 142, 153–58, 191–92, 198, 242

Berenson, Mary, 192
Bergery, Bettina, 188, 205; on Natalie
  Barney, 251–54; on Dolly Wilde,
  184
Bernhardt, Sarah, 40, 46, 58
Berry, Walter, 247
Berthelot, Philippe, 43, 109, 111, 155,
  242
Bertin, Célia, 197
Besnard, Albert, 218, 231
Bibesco, Princess Marthe, 106, 202
Bibliothèque Doucet, 220, 222, 232–33
Bibliothèque Nationale, 234
Bilitis, 49
Boccaccio, 191
Boncour, Paul, 111, 198, 205
Book, A (Barnes), 178
Botteghe Oscure, 256
Bousquet, Marie Louise, 256
Bradley, Jenny, 188, 192, 255
Bromfield, Louis, 165
Brooks, Romaine, 9, 62, 87, 144–51,
  164, 166, 167, 168, 174, 187, 188,
  190, 192, 193, 195, 200, 214, 215,
  219, 223, 233, 242, 252, 255,
  263–64; portraits by, 151, 257–59
Brun, Charles, 45, 48, 63, 66, 108
Bussy, Dorothy Strachey, 28, 178

Caetani, Marguerite, Princess di
  Bassiano, 163, 256
Calvé, Emma, 63–64, 91
Cambon, Jules, 43, 45, 106
Canard Enchainé, 220
Cancel, Oswald, 32, 41
Cantos (Pound), 164–65
Capote, Truman, on Natalie Barney,
  255–59
Carolus-Duran, 11, 22, 26–27, 46
Cattaui, Georges, 110
Chalon, Jean, 234; on Natalie Barney,
  224–27, 230–32
Champion, Edouard, 111, 121, 142
Chansons de Bilitis, Les (Louÿs), 49,
  50, 51, 142
Chapon, François, 212, 213, 231; on
  Natalie Barney, 232–33
Charmoy, José de, 111, 142, 144, 229

Chassaigne, Anne-Marie, 37. *See also*
  Pougy, Liane de
Chesterton, Gilbert K., 22
Cinq Petits Dialogues grecs (Barney),
  51, 73, 89–90
Clair, Mme. René, 252
Claudel, Paul, 108–9
Claudine s'en va (Colette), 98
Clermont-Tonnerre, Lily Duchesse de
  (Elisabeth de Gramont), 9, 107–8,
  139–41, 142, 143, 147, 148, 149,
  151, 164, 166, 167, 168, 174, 183,
  193, 200, 203, 219, 226, 229, 230,
  233, 242, 246, 252, 256, 262–63,
  264
Cleyrergue, Berthe, 100, 178, 189,
  193, 194, 197, 204, 205, 213, 241,
  264, 265; on Natalie Barney,
  215–19, 220–23, 228–30
Cocteau, Jean, 10, 109, 149, 151, 163,
  164, 242
Cody, Morrill, 165
Colette, Sidonie Gabrielle, 9, 10, 39,
  56, 66, 91–94, 95, 97–99, 109, 133,
  149, 152, 155, 165–66, 167, 174,
  199, 200, 216, 222, 226, 229, 230,
  231, 242, 252, 261, 262; her literary
  portrayal of Natalie Barney, 98; on
  theatricals, 90–93; on Renée Vivien,
  53–54
Couples involontaires, Les (Chalon),
  227
Courrière, Berthe de, 120
Crowder, Henry, 253
Cunard, Nancy, 253
Cunard, Victor, 184, 253
Curzon, Lord, 30
Custance, Olive, 58–59, 60, 73

D'Annunzio, Gabriele, 10, 109, 110,
  146, 149, 151
Dante Alighieri, 191
Daughters of Bilitis, 49
Debré, Michel, 216, 220, 228, 266
Decameron (Boccaccio), 191
Decadence/Decadents, 42, 69
Delarue-Mardrus, Lucie, 9, 71, 73, 78,
  79–81, 82, 83–87, 89, 108, 132,

140, 141, 147, 166, 167, 195, 198,
217, 246; her literary portrayal of
Natalie Barney, 82–87
Delavigne, Marcelle Fauchier-. *See*
Fauchier-Delavigne, Marcelle
Deslandes, Baroness, 133, 134
Dial, The, 159, 160, 161, 162
Dialogue au soleil couchànt (Louÿs),
90–91, 98
Doucet, Jacques, 212
Douglas, Lord Alfred "Freddy," 11,
42, 60–61, 64, 72, 146
Dreyfus, Mme. Hippolyte, 141, 267.
See also Barney, Laura
Du Deffand, Marquise, 119
Duncan, Isadora, 96, 110, 242
Duncan, Raymond, 95, 242
"D'Une Amazone américaine"
(Barney), 141
Duran, Carolus-. *See* Carolus-Duran

École à crinaline, L' (ballet), 88
Egyptian Vaudeville, An, 88
Eliot, Thomas Stearns, 10, 120, 153,
161–62, 179, 233, 242, 249, 267
Ely, Miss, 31–32
Emerson, Ralph Waldo, 113
Éparpillements (Barney), 113–18, 121
Équivoque (Barney), 94–95, 98
Este, Louisa (great-aunt), 17–18
Études et préludes (Vivien), 48
"Evening with M. Teste, An"
(Valéry), 160
Eyre de Lanux, Elizabeth, 151, 261; on
Natalie Barney, 240–43

Fabre, Michel, 212
Fargue, Leon-Paul, 163
Fauchier-Delavigne, Marcelle, 199
Femme m'apparut, Une (Vivien),
69–73, 227
Figaro Littéraire, 224
Fitzgerald, F. Scott, 10, 165
Fitzgerald, Zelda, 165
Flanner, Janet, 165, 178, 183, 184,
186, 211, 242, 253; on Natalie
Barney, 260–68
Ford, Ford Madox, 160–61, 166, 168,
178, 249

Foujita, Tsugouharu, 242
France, Anatole, 10, 105, 107–8, 109,
142, 163, 164, 233
Franklin, Benjamin, 18

Garbo, Greta, 255
Gauthier-Villars, Henry "Willy," 97,
98, 226, 230
Genêt. *See* Flanner, Janet
Germain, André, 8–9, 68, 73, 93, 111,
142, 188, 199, 217, 228–29, 246; his
literary portrayal of Natalie Barney,
131–38; on Remy de Gourmont,
136–38; on theatricals, 93–94
Ghika, Prince, 242
Ghika, Princesse, 37. *See also* Pougy,
Liane de
Gide, André, 10, 12, 108, 109, 160,
163, 199, 242
God's Heroes (Laura Barney), 89
Gould, Florence, 225
Gourmont, Remy de, 7, 9, 10, 43, 48,
106, 109, 119–29, 130–31, 134,
140, 153, 154, 156, 158–59, 162,
163, 171, 197, 199, 224, 226, 227,
231, 232, 258, 260–61; André
Germain on, 131, 136–38; his
literary portrayal of Natalie Barney,
122–24, 125–56, 130–31
Gramont, Elisabeth de, 107–8. *See also*
Clermont-Tonnerre, Lily Duchesse de
Grasset, Bernard, 111
Green, Julien, 214
Gregh, Fernand, 105
Groux, Henry de, 231
Guggenheim, Peggy, 256
Guîtry, Sacha, 98, 233, 242
Gwynn, Mary, 61–62

Hahn, Reynaldo, 258
Hall, Radclyffe, 171, 172 ff., 178, 249,
257; her literary portrayal of Natalie
Barney, 172–77
"Harlequin à l'Académie" (Barney),
164
Harper, Allanah, 183
Harper's Bazaar, 256
Hemingway, Ernest, 10, 165, 242,
249, 267

Index 283

Hemmick, Christian, 23
Henner, Jean-Jacques, 22
Hickox, Fayette, 255
Hoang, Nadine, 188
Howland, Leonora, 31, 32, 33
"How to Live by Those Who Have,"
179
Hughes, Cheryl, on Natalie Barney,
233–35
Huxley, Aldous, 130

Idylle saphique (Pougy), 39–41, 42,
47, 48, 73, 98, 227, 235
"I Have a Rendezvous with Death"
(Seeger), 142
In Memory of Dorothy Ierne Wilde
(Barney), 184, 251
International Council of Women, 141
Irving, Sir Henry, 97

Jacob, Max, 109, 111, 200
Jaloux, Edmond, 111, 242
Jeanneret, Charles Edouard. See Le
Corbusier
Je me souviens (Barney), 65, 68, 73,
112
Jeune Femme de soixante ans, Une
(Chalon), 225
"Jeune Parque, La" (Valéry), 142–43,
152
Jolas, Eugene, 242
Jones, Elizabeth Shaw, 251. See also
Bergery, Bettina
Jouvenel, Henry de, 99
Joyce, James, 10, 109–10, 233, 240,
242, 245
Jullian, Philippe, 11, 231, 232

Khayyám, Omar, 143

Ladies Almanack (Barnes), 171,
179–82, 226, 234, 260
Lafayette, General, 17
Lahovary, Janine, 202–3, 204, 212,
213, 214, 220, 221–22, 226, 228,
229, 232, 254, 264, 266; on Natalie
Barney, 223–24
Lahovary, Nicholas, 202, 203
Landowska, Wanda, 125

Lang, Renée, 199, 201, 203, 209
Langlois, Mme., 167, 245
Lanux, Elizabeth Eyre de. See Eyre de
Lanux, Elizabeth
Lanux, Pierre de, 240
Larbaud, Valery, 163, 233
La Rochefoucauld, François Duc de,
113
Laurencin, Marie, 110, 199, 216, 217,
223
Lauzun, Duke de, 125
League of Nations, 141
Le Corbusier, 217
Lecouvreur, Adrienne, 132
Lee, Carol, 31
Le Galliene, Gwen, 246, 247–48
Leiter, Victoria, 30
Lenéru, Marie, 166
Lepman, Frau, 32
Letters to the Amazon (Gourmont),
130, 162
Lettres à l'Amazone (Gourmont), 7,
122, 126–27, 128, 130–31, 159,
199, 227, 258
Lettres à une Connue (Barney), 48–49
Lettres intimes à l'Amazone
(Gourmont), 122–25, 129
Lévy-Dhurmer, 232
Lewis, Sinclair, 161, 165, 178
Life and Death of Radclyffe Hall, The
(Troubridge), 174
Lind, Jenny, 19
Livingstone, David, 21
Louÿs, Pierre, 47, 49–51, 89, 90, 91,
95, 98, 108, 109, 142, 163, 175, 233
Loy, Mina, 166, 167
Lubin, Germaine, 245
Luce, Fabre-. See Fabre-Luce

Macavoy, Edouard, 204, 214, 216, 233
Maeterlinck, Maurice, 126
Making of Americans, The (Stein), 167
"Malentendu, Le" (Barney), 235
Mardrus, Dr. Joseph-Charles-
Victor, 78–79, 81–82, 83, 107,
108, 110, 111, 133, 140, 163, 200,
241, 246
Mardrus, Lucie Delarue-. See
Delarue-Mardrus, Lucie

Marie Antoinette, 18
Mary Magdalene of Repentance, Sister,
    37. *See also* Pougy, Liane de
Mata Hari, 91–93, 260, 268
Mata Hari (Alice Pike Barney), 93, 98
Maugham, W. Somerset, 149
Mauriac, Claude, 181
Maximes (La Rochefoucauld), 113, 117
Mercure de France, Le, 120, 121, 126,
    131, 159, 163
"Mes Morts" (Barney), 143
Milhaud, Darius, 109, 142
Millay, Edna St. Vincent, 165
Miller, Judge, 17
Miller, Mrs., 17
Milosz, Oscar Venceslas, 110, 111, 233
Miomandre, Francis de, 111
Monnier, Adrienne, 163, 198, 245
Montesquiou, Count Robert de, 79,
    106–7, 254, 258
Morand, Paul, 142, 164, 215
Moreno, Marguerite, 94, 98, 245
Morrow, William, 35, 41
Moveable Feast, A (Hemingway), 267
Muhlfeld, Mme., 133
Murphy, Esther, 248, 256
Murphy, Gerald, 248

Napoleon III, 38
"Near Enemy, The" (Barney), 143
New Yorker, The, 260
New York *Herald,* 141
Nightwood (Barnes), 179, 234
Noailles, Anna de, 70, 106, 202, 223
"No Pleasant Memories" (Brooks),
    144–45, 192
Nos Secrètes Amours
    (Delarue-Mardrus), 82–83
Nouvelle Revue française, 163

Ohanian, Armen, 142
Olivia (Bussy), 28
*One Who Is Legion, or A.D.'s
    After-Life, The* (Barney), 150, 179
Opals (Custance), 73
Orlando (Woolf), 178

Painter, George, 105
Palmer, Courtlandt, 96

Palmer, Evaline "Eva," 20, 30–31,
    41, 61, 64, 65, 71, 72, 78, 81, 82,
    90, 91, 95–97, 217, 222, 233; Lucie
    Delarue-Mardrus on, 80. *See also*
    Sikelianos, Eva Palmer
Paris France (Stein), 194
"Parisian Roof Garden in 1918, A"
    (Barney), 143
Paris Journals (Flanner), 263
"Paris Letters" (Pound), 159–60
Paris Review, The, 239
Pavlova, Anna, 88
Pensées d'une Amazone (Barney), 141,
    162, 171, 179, 235; Pound on,
    159–60, 165
Pétain, Maréchal, 252
Petri, Herr Konzertmeister, 33
Picasso, Pablo, 195, 231
Pike, Samuel Nathan (maternal
    grandfather), 19–20, 88, 105
Plimpton, George, 255
Poiret, Paul, 99, 166, 242
Polignac, Prince Edmond de, 107
Polignac, Princess Edmond de, 145,
    146
Pougy, Liane de, 8, 37–41, 42, 46, 48,
    54, 56, 69, 81, 98, 121, 131, 140,
    147, 188, 222, 227, 230, 235; her
    literary portrayal of Natalie Barney,
    39–41, 48–51
Pound, Ezra, 10, 120, 130, 153,
    158–61, 162, 164–65, 192, 193,
    198, 214, 233, 242, 245, 249,
    267–68
Prix Renée Vivien, 198
Proust, Marcel, 10, 93, 105, 106, 109,
    155, 176, 179, 202, 256, 258
Pur et l'impur, Le (Colette), 53–54, 76
Putnam, General, 17

Quelques Portraits-Sonnets de femmes
    (Barney), 45, 226

Rachilde, 166, 167
Rappoport, Charles, 110, 242
Regnier, Henri de, 105
Reinach, Salomon, 8, 43, 71–72, 108,
    111, 142, 153, 154, 158, 162, 234,
    246

Remembrance of Things Past (Proust), 105, 256
"Repercussion" (Barney), 160
Rilke, Rainer Maria, 10, 109, 110, 111, 199, 233, 246, 249
Riversdale, Paule, 63. *See also* Vivien, Renée; Zuylen de Nievelt, Baroness Hélène
Rives, Amelié, 46
Rodin, Auguste, 109
Roggers, Henriette, 98
Rösell, Herr Kappelmeister, 33
Rostand, Edmond, 46
Rothermere, Lady, 162, 242
Rouveyre, André, 8, 43, 111, 121–22, 126, 127, 128, 163, 199–200, 224, 229, 233
Rubenstein, Ida, 146, 151, 252
Rudge, Olga, 214, 245

Sackville-West, Vita, 177–78
Samuels, Ernest, 154
Sapho désesperée (Delarue-Mardrus), 83
Sappho, 48, 49, 51–52, 57, 58–59, 66, 73, 90, 94–95, 96
Sardou, Victorien, 36, 88
Sartoris, Cecile, 159
Sartre, Jean-Paul, 197
Schmitt, Florent, 109
Schwob, Marcel, 108
Secrest, Meryle, 147, 148, 201, 203, 204
Seeger, Alan, 142
Seignobos, Dr. Charles, 110, 111, 241, 246
Séraphita (Balzac), 150
Shakespeare and Company (Beach), 171–72
Shaw, George Bernard, 22
Shilleto, Mary, 55, 62, 63
Shilleto, Violet, 55, 56, 60, 61, 62, 68, 71, 72, 73, 89, 90, 204, 234
Sikelianos, Angelos, 96
Sikelianos, Eva Palmer, 9, 96. *See also* Palmer, Evaline "Eva"
Sikelianos, Penelope Duncan, 95, 96
Singer, Winnaretha, 107
Sitwell, Edith, 168, 185, 248

Sitwell, Georgia, 253
Sitwell, Sacheverell, 253
Sodome et Gomorrhe (Proust), 179
"Sonnet to My Lady with the Jaundice, A" (Barney), 140
Souvenirs de mon commerce (Rouveyre), 121–22
Souvenirs indiscrets (Barney), 11, 26, 28, 37, 38–39, 42, 48, 56, 63, 66, 76, 78, 97, 121, 123, 128–29, 240
Stanley, Henry M., 21
Stein, Gertrude, 9, 10, 109, 110, 153, 165–66, 167–70, 189, 190, 191, 193, 194–95, 195–96, 198, 214, 231, 242, 243, 245, 246, 247–48, 249, 252; Natalie Barney on, 168–70
Strachey, Dorothy. *See* Bussy, Dorothy Strachey
Strachey, John, 248
Strachey, Lytton, 28, 178
Symbolist movement, 119–20, 126

Tagore, Rabindranath, 109
Tarn, Pauline M., 46, 47. *See also* Vivien, Renée
Temple à l'Amitié, 167, 218, 220, 229
Thomson, Virgil, 167, 214, 264–65; on Natalie Barney, 244–50
Toklas, Alice B., 168, 189, 190, 191, 193, 195–96, 198, 214, 244, 247, 248, 249, 252, 255
Tombeau de Renée Vivien, Le (Barney), 68, 118
Ton de Paris, Le (Lauzun), 125
Traits et portraits (Barney), 191, 225
Transatlantic Review, 160–61, 178, 249
Transition, 242
Trefusis, Violet, 258
Troubetzkoy, Princess, 46
Troubridge, Una Lady, 151, 174, 257, 258

Ulysses (Joyce), 240

Vagabonde, La (Colette), 99, 152, 165–66
Valéry, Paul, 10, 108, 109, 111, 135, 142–43, 152, 153, 155, 160, 161, 162–63, 163–64, 199, 200, 240, 242

Vallette, Marguerite. *See* Rachilde
Van Vechten, Carl, 168, 198, 199, 256
Villars, Henry Gautier-. *See*
  Gautier-Villars, Henry "Willy"
Villon (Pound), 164
Vilmorin, Louise de, 225
Vionnet, Mme., 252
Vita Nuova (Dante), 191
Vivien, Renée, 8–9, 47, 48, 49–50,
  53–58, 59–60, 61–68, 69–77, 78,
  79, 80, 82, 83, 84, 87, 89, 93–94,
  96, 106, 118, 121, 123, 131, 144,
  145, 146, 147, 166, 167, 186, 187,
  198, 203, 204, 222, 226, 227, 230,
  231, 234, 254, 258, 261–62, 267;
  Romaine Brooks on, 62; Colette on,
  53, 76–77; Lucie Delarue-Mardrus
  on, 79; her literary portrayal of
  Natalie Barney, 57, 58–59, 69–76.
  See also Tarn, Pauline M.

Walpole, Horace, 119
Waste Land, The (Eliot), 161
Waugh, Evelyn, 186
Wauthier, Magdeleine, 142
"Weeping Venus, The" (Barney), 150

Well of Loneliness, The (Hall), 171,
  172–74, 175–77, 181
Wescott, Glenway, 165, 242
Wharton, Edith, 159, 246–47
What Is Remembered (Toklas), 168
Whistler, James A., 22, 34
Wickham, Anna, 167, 233
Wilde, Dorothy Ierne "Dolly," 11,
  168, 183–89, 190, 193, 197, 198,
  229, 233, 242, 252–53, 266
Wilde, Oscar, 11–12, 42, 111, 113–14
Wilde, Willie, 183
Wilder, Thornton, 168, 214
Woman Who Lives with Me, The
  (Barney), 112; Bernard Berenson on,
  157–58
Woolf, Leonard, 185
Woolf, Virginia, 177–78; Dolly Wilde
  on, 185–86

Yorke, Count, 184
Yorke, Countess, 184
Yourcenar, Marguerite, 215

Zuylen de Nievelt, Baroness Hélène
  von, 63, 67, 77, 84, 87, 145, 198, 222

690